SLIM

TO

NONE

SLIM
TO

A JOURNEY THROUGH
THE WASTELAND OF
ANOREXIA TREATMENT

NONE

jennifer hendricks

McGraw·Hill

New York   Chicago   San Francisco   Lisbon   London   Madrid   Mexico City
Milan   New Delhi   San Juan   Seoul   Singapore   Sydney   Toronto

Library of Congress Cataloging-in-Publication Data

Hendricks, Jennifer.
    Slim to none : a journey through the wasteland of anorexia treatment / by Jennifer
Hendricks ; edited and narrated by Gordon Hendricks.
        p.   cm.
    ISBN 0-07-141069-4 (hardcover) — ISBN 0-07-143371-6 (paperback)
    1. Hendricks, Jennifer—Mental health.   2. Anorexia nervosa—Patients—United
States—Diaries.   3. Anorexia nervosa—Patients—United States—Biography.
I. Hendricks, Gordon.   II. Title.

    RC552.A5 H454   2003
    616.85′262′0092—dc21   2002035050

1 2 3 4 5 6 7 8 9 0   AGM/AGM   2 1 0 9 8 7 6 5 4 3

ISBN 0-07-141069-4 (hardcover)
ISBN 0-07-143371-6 (paperback)

McGraw-Hill books are available at special quantity discounts to use as premiums and sales
promotions, or for use in corporate training programs. For more information, please write to
the Director of Special Sales, Professional Publishing, McGraw-Hill, Two Penn Plaza, New York,
NY 10121-2298. Or contact your local bookstore.

This book is printed on acid-free paper.

For all who know the pain of a child lost.

For those with anorexia-damaged minds and bodies—

for those who strive to repair them.

May your searches be successful.

Contents

PART TWO—SEARCHING FOR A CURE

PART THREE—SEARCHING FOR RELEASE

Foreword

*E*ating disorders have the highest mortality rate of any mental illness. Long an unrecognized epidemic, serious eating disorders afflict seven million women and one million men in the United States. They affect young and old, rich and poor, and all ethnic groups. Eighty-six percent of sufferers report onset of their illness by age twenty. Only 50 percent report being cured, while a significant number struggle with their disease for many years or a lifetime.

Jennifer Hendricks's diary, which comprises the following pages, chronicles her life-destroying encounter with anorexia nervosa.

Jenny's father, Gordon Hendricks, spent the better part of a decade preparing this extraordinary book to continue the protracted war in which his daughter died. His basic premises are that treatment is often ineffective and that knowledgeable treatment centers were unavailable during his daughter's illness in the 1980s. There is now a growing number of health professionals who treat eating disorders, but unfortunately many still lack adequate training to provide proper diagnosis and treatment.

Anorexia nervosa, bulimia nervosa, and related illnesses are confusing and complex. There are many theories regarding their cause, among them early trauma, low self-esteem, sexual abuse, body image distortion, impact of the media, striving to be perfect, family dysfunction, and inability to cope. There can be serious physical consequences, including heart failure, kidney failure, osteoporosis, gastrointestinal problems, and death. Researchers increasingly claim that these illnesses have a genetic component and are biologically driven.

People still die when treatment has not been engaged soon enough, maintained long enough, or is ineffective. These conditions may exist because the ill refuse to engage in treatment, insurance companies refuse appropriate access, or parents are manipulated out of supporting treatment. Treatment is expensive, and families or individuals may not know how to fight for treatment, nor have the strength or money to overcome the obstacles encountered.

The despair in this book is pervasive, but Jenny would not want her story to lead anyone away from hope. In fact, large numbers of people with eating disorders report full recovery, according to a study done by the National Association of Anorexia Nervosa and Associated Disorders (ANAD). By reading Jenny's words, we can see how anorexia is a lethal obsession, and it's this education and awareness that can help to understand and overcome this disease and others associated with it. What's most valuable is that Jenny touches upon many themes to which any person suffering from an eating disorder can relate. We see Jenny's struggle for power over herself, her yearning for simpler times and the chance to experience a normal teenage life, and her reaction to her many therapists who were unable to figure out the mystery that was Jenny's plague.

Through it all we see a family struggling to cope on Jenny's behalf—for eating disorders are devastating to families, too. *Slim to None* shows how these illnesses can widen the gulf between parents and other family members. Part of the drama in Jenny's story is the terrible uncertainty of haunting and unresolved childhood memories called up through psychoanalysis.

It is true that many afflicted people live unrewarding lives, constantly battling their eating disorder. They never find the strength to direct their talents or intellect positively because they fear letting go of the behaviors. Parental involvement and early recognition of the disorder may be helpful. Families should be aware that advances in understanding the treatment process have been made since this story took place.

Individuals and families must be encouraged to always work toward a positive outcome, however difficult this may seem. Families facing these illnesses should let the sufferers among them know how much they want them to get help and suggest avenues of help. They should use any leverage they have to persuade participation in recovery. People reading this book need to know there is hope.

Eating disorders are still major illnesses in our nation but receive totally inadequate funding, understanding, and support. In *Slim to None*, Jenny and her father have presented the strongest case possible for immediate, ongoing action. The best possible response to this tragedy is working together in demanding research, training of professionals, education, loving support systems, advocacy, and prevention.

In *Slim to None*, Jennifer Hendricks and her father have made a heroic statement, for which we are grateful.

CHRISTOPHER ATHAS
Vice President
National Association of
Anorexia Nervosa and
Associated Disorders (ANAD)

Narrator's Preface

*I*n *Slim to None*, my daughter speaks to you from her journals. Selected from Jenny's 707 pages of neatly penned script, her journal entries are presented as she wrote them (with gentle editing). To complete the chronology of her journey, I created a few entries covering significant events and circumstances that Jenny did not journalize. Narrated scenes and dialogue are real-life events based, when Jenny is present, on her journals—using mostly her own words—or what she told me, and, when I am present, on my own notes and recollections. To fully dimension her story, I created a few scenes where neither Jenny nor I am present. They are based on known events or events reasonably inferred from known circumstances. Although most names and some locations are changed, all persons and places are real. My intention is for you to experience Jenny's long journey just as she did.

Jenny's first anorexic symptoms appeared at age fourteen. Six years later her doctor pronounced her terminal and resigned. She died at age twenty-five. In her last five years she enjoyed fewer than forty days free from hospital confinement.

During ten years of treatment, Jenny's case involved twenty-three principal doctors (psychiatrists, psychologists, and M.D.s) and over a hundred other doctors, social workers, and nurses.

Under pressure from a powerful, confrontational therapist to reveal the cause of her anorexia, Jenny developed hazy recollections, which grew into nightmarish flashbacks, of sexual molestation or abuse by an older friend, a horse trainer, a horseshoer, and a stepuncle.

A wannabe Christian savior tried to exorcise her. Acting on a doctor's orders, two nurses victimized her. Late in her illness, on a doctor's advice, her mother shunned her.

Jenny's physical growth stopped at slightly over 5 feet. Osteoporosis shrunk her an inch. During most of her illness she weighed less than 80 pounds. Frequently her weight dropped into the 50s and 60s and stayed there for extended periods. At death she weighed 45 pounds. Side effects of Jenny's eating disorder included electrolyte (generally potassium and sodium) deficiencies, renal failure, pervasive depression, sight and hearing loss, hair loss, and gum disease.

Jenny's health care costs exceeded $1 million, most of it paid by insurance. Insurance companies denied coverage twice. Social Security declared her disabled two years before she died. She completed but one year of college, held no job longer than four months, never sustained a romantic relationship, became virtually estranged from her siblings, and after age nineteen developed few friendships outside a hospital environment.

This is her story.

ACKNOWLEDGMENTS

As with her treatment journey, the journey of Jenny's story to publication was long and difficult—but with a better ending. Along the way, many assisted. Michele Pezzuti at Contemporary Books provided a shared vision and personal commitment that made this book possible. A writer could not have a better advocate. Others believed in the book's importance and offered generous assistance: Harriet Freiberger, Michael Moore, Doris Booth (founder of AuthorLink), Elisabeth Weed, Meredith Phelan, and Rena Copperman. With her compassion for others, enthusiasm for life and new adventure, sensitive companionship, humor, friendship, love, and understanding, Bonnie McGee helped me find the important balance in life.

G.H.

PROLOGUE
No Time Left for Me

I should've died in the nursing home where I was supposed to, when Dr. Steiner said I would . . . four months ago. I was in a safe place called Resthaven where I could hear meadowlarks sing after a spring rain, like at home when I was little. I could've died peacefully with my family around me.

But I didn't.

Mom tried so hard to orchestrate a perfect death . . . to make up for such an imperfect life. She even slept in the vacant room next to mine so I wouldn't be alone. After all those years of feeling abandoned, I liked thinking of her there, close and wanting to comfort me in case I cried out in the night. She called my brothers and sisters home to say good-bye: Brian from college in Boulder, Janis from San Antonio, Nancy from Portland, and David all the way from Australia. For a while Mom didn't look so old and tired . . . and she quit blaming me for getting sick.

I disappointed everyone again, including myself. I guess I wasn't ready to die. I thought I was. Nancy and Janis were ready for my death. I could tell. For the first time they felt needed in a way they could respond to. They forgave me and were really nice. We smiled a lot and talked easily together . . . about comfortable things, our childhood, and their busy lives. They touched and hugged me, even rubbed my arms and legs to keep me warm. They said, "We won't leave you, Jenny." But they did, after I ran away. They had to, of course. They could be with me and comfort me in death, but not in life. They rejoined happiness and left me to resume misery . . . my choice.

My brothers were ready, although they never understood why I was so sick. How could they understand what my doctors couldn't? When David and Brian came into my room they said, "Hi, Jenny," and then hesitated, as if afraid to add, "How are you feeling?" I'm glad they never asked me that . . . what a stupid question to ask someone who's dying. They sat silently in chairs on either side of my bed and looked uncomfortable, like mute sentinels assigned to unfamiliar stations. Each reached out and gave one of my hands a squeeze. That gave me a secure, protected feeling, but they didn't know what to talk about, and I didn't know what to say. I wanted to tell them how much I'd missed them, how good it felt just to see and touch them, but the right words wouldn't come out. They looked like they wanted to cry but couldn't. So we zombied out and watched television together. TV numbed us, saved us from the boredom and mental pain of waiting. Now I wish Brian had brought his guitar. It's been so long since I've heard him play.

Dad was ready. Even he finally gave up. I knew when he stopped smiling and telling me, "Keep trying, Jenny, there's still time left for you." He quit coming to see me on his way home from work every day. He became more distant as the rest of my family moved closer, a reversal of my sick years. "I can't bear to watch you waste away to nothing," he said. He still cared but didn't know how to show it except by doing something, and there wasn't anything more for him to do. He realized he couldn't help me live anymore but didn't know how to help me die. He said once that I had taught him when to listen and how to cry. I'm glad I did something for him.

April 11, my twenty-fifth birthday, was some kind of turning point. It should've been a good day. I'd been doing okay in the nursing home, eating regularly on my own, working some, exercising like crazy—90 miles on the stationary bike some days, starting a new support group, reading the newspaper, and arranging to take piano lessons. I even finished three new card drawings and sent them off to Hallmark. Mom and I were fighting about my driving, though. She was terrified I'd get spacey, have an accident, and hurt someone. I couldn't convince her I knew when I was too sick to drive.

But we didn't fight on my birthday. She and Dad came to have lunch with me. Resthaven's kitchen crew baked a chocolate cake with pink candles and fixed us fancy chicken salad sandwiches the way I like them, on toasted wheat bread with the crusts sliced off and cut in quarters, with cottage cheese and a fresh pear. After lunch I opened cards and a present from Mom and Dad, two old Carpenter tapes I had asked for, tapes we always played in the car on family vacations. The wrapping paper had jumping horses on it, which triggered memories of happier times. Mom and I cried happy tears as we reminisced about my last horse shows. I got up from the table, hugged them both, and said, "Thanks, Mom and Dad, thanks for the good years." Then I felt other eyes on us. We were surrounded by all those old people in Resthaven's dining room. They sat there silently and stared at us, looking like they were dozing with their eyes open. Dad got that wicked look in his eye and popped one of my balloons. "That'll wake 'em up," he laughed.

Although I didn't have any bad urges after lunch, that night after I played my birthday tapes I started feeling sad about Karen Carpenter and went to the kitchen, binged on leftover birthday cake, returned to my room feeling guilty, and threw it all up. I'm not sure why I did that. Maybe I'd been suppressing my feelings of despair about so many wasted years. When I'm exhausted, like now, I know I obsess about how this illness stole my adolescence and is still robbing me . . . of a college education and a normal life. Or maybe the abuse flashbacks got worse then. I don't remember. I guess I don't care. After all these years, I can really say it: *I don't care anymore.* Screw the experts and their insistence on discovering *why.* Why means nothing to me . . . nothing. I'm through searching for reasons for the way I feel, searching for cures. It's too tiresome and useless. All those roads lead nowhere. Now it's only release I seek.

After my birthday, bulimia took over worse than ever. I couldn't control it, and I kept overeating and barfing almost every day until the end

of April when I decided to stop eating. Totally. Not eating, the ultimate control. But whose? Mine? The illness's? At Resthaven no one
made me eat, and I've never been strong enough to overcome my
destructive urges alone. I know now that I'm also not strong enough
to beat anorexia with others helping me. Although I stopped eating,
maybe I really didn't want to die then . . . at least not like now. Maybe
I just accepted the inevitable and quit fighting to live.

After I stopped eating, I didn't laugh very much . . . only twice. Once
when Diane brought *A Fish Called Wanda* and we watched it on my
portable TV. I could still see then, and we both got a little crazy laughing at the guy who stuttered so bad. The second time was with my family. Some lady called and wanted money. "We need help for children
who have terminal illnesses," she said. "Well," I said, "I'm seriously dying
myself." Then David took the phone. "Bugger off," he said, "you've no
right to call here." We all had a big laugh over that one.

By then I had only a few friends left. They all thought it was so weird,
a young woman living with old people in a nursing home. They didn't
understand that living or dying was finally my responsibility and a choice
hospitals always denied me. Mostly my friends were tired of seeing me
sick all the time and stayed away. "She looks like a death mask," I
overheard someone whisper.

Some couldn't accept what was happening. They urged me to keep
trying. "Please eat, Jenny," they pleaded. Or, they insisted, "There must
be a hospital program for you somewhere."

But they didn't understand, even when I explained why I couldn't try
any longer. "Mental hospitals and their doctors are afraid of me," I told my
friends. "I'm a big risk because they don't know what to do. They can't
help me and they make me feel worse, like a prisoner. They take away my
rights, my privacy, make me feel like I'm unworthy and not a real person, like I don't have a life or a future outside my illness. All they're interested in is forcing food into me. 'Eat or be punished,' they all say. They
bury my thoughts in anorexia but ignore my feelings about eating. They

don't know how to treat bad feelings. I'm through with them. No one is going to lock me up, tie me down, watch me pee, put tubes into me, or force me to eat greasy bacon and runny scrambled eggs . . . not ever again."

Diane couldn't cope. "You can't give up now, Jen," she said. "You've fought this too long . . . over ten years."

"Please, Diane, don't make it harder for me," I said.

"But it's not right. Nobody's doing anything."

"You don't understand, Diane. We all agreed. Everyone. To let my illness run its course."

"But . . . they're all sitting around like a bunch of mindless ghouls, letting you starve yourself to death."

"That's what I want, to end the torment. And this is the only way the system will let me do it with dignity. I don't want anyone trying to save me this time."

"I don't think you know what you want. You're too sick. You should not be here. If you were in a hospital, they wouldn't let you do this."

"That's why I won't go to a hospital."

"I've . . . I've got to do something."

"Please, Diane, don't. Don't do anything."

"God, Jen. I can't let them do this. It's like . . . like a mercy killing. It's not right. Your parents, Dr. Steiner, the administrator here. What they're doing is immoral, illegal even. They all could be arrested. They should be. I've got to call someone."

"Diane, do you still love me?"

"Yes."

"Then please don't call anyone."

"I . . . I don't know." She covered her head with her arms, face down on the bed beside me, and sobbed. "It's so wrong . . . so goddam wrong."

She never called anyone. And she never spoke to me again.

It took three weeks for my body to shut down. When I was close to the end, I couldn't see very well and could talk only in hoarse whispers because my mouth was so dry. I slept most of the time. But I didn't feel sick. I felt at peace, finally emptied of all the mind and body filth. No more terrifying flashbacks. No more disgust with my body, with me. Nothing hurt. I wasn't even hungry. And I didn't have to worry about how guilty I feel when I eat and throw up and, even worse, how anguished I feel when I eat and don't throw up.

I overheard Mom, Nancy, and Janis talking with Dr. Steiner outside my room when they thought I was asleep.

"Does she feel any pain?" Mom asked.

"No. The drugs control that," Dr. Steiner said.

"But . . . but, she's going blind," Nancy said, her voice breaking and sounding scared.

"Unfortunately, it's a side effect from morphine."

"And she's so . . . so wasted," Nancy whispered, as if someone wrenched the words from her. "So fragile . . . like a living mummy. No flesh. Bones all protruding. Skin over them stretched tight . . . and translucent like old parchment."

Mom said, "She was too weak to weigh today, but yesterday she was down to—"

"Don't, Mom," Nancy interrupted. "I don't want to know."

"I can't believe they're weighing her," Janis said.

"They're not. It's Jenny. She wants to know. She records her weight every day."

"Measuring her decline," Nancy said. "It's bizarre."

"There may be some medical value to the information, and—"

"Sure," Janis interrupted this time. "Medical value. And we can have a contest, see who guesses her death weight."

"That's not funny, Janis."

"No it's not, Mom. It's not even close. It's goddam tragic."

Janis started to sob and I wondered if I should say something. I was getting angry with them for talking about me as if I wasn't nearby, even if they thought I was asleep.

Then Mom asked Dr. Steiner, "How much time does she have?"

"Not much. Her electrolytes dropped off the chart three days ago, and she quit sucking on crushed ice yesterday. Her kidneys failed this morning. That's the first sign. She could lapse into a coma anytime."

Mom said, "I'll call Father Potter, ask him to give her last rites."

"Tell him to hurry," Dr. Steiner said.

I wasn't asleep when Father Potter came, either. I really startled him when I opened my eyes after his last "Amen" and looked through the dark cloud between us. For a moment I saw that judgmental look in his eyes. I didn't say anything, just stared up at him. He was all white and black and blurry, with sunken, unblinking eyes glaring at me, condemning me . . . more devil than priest. He scared me.

Then that hospice priest came. Mom must have called him, too. Behind the cloud I saw kind eyes, gentleness. He took my hand and asked, "How do you feel about death?"

I was able to talk a little. "Scared," I croaked.

"Most are."

"And guilty." Father Potter had rekindled my guilt.

"Guilty?"

"Because I'm starving myself to death?" I was having trouble thinking.

"Maybe. Why are you starving yourself to death?"

"Because I'm so tired of trying to live."

"Are you sure?"

"Sometimes I'm not."

"Accepting death is difficult. But it needn't be feared when it's God's will."

"But . . . but what if it's not . . . not God's will, just mine?"

"Do you believe your illness may not be terminal, that you can control it? Even now?"

"Sometimes. I just don't know."

He paused a long time. His eyes pierced the cloud just like Father Potter's, and I could see impatience in them. "You need to decide now, Jennifer," he finally said. "Die or get well, but quit torturing yourself and your family." He started my agony cycle—save me/leave me alone/save me—all over again. He pushed me back to living without grace, without hope.

They say it was a miracle, that I was able to rally somehow, get out of bed the morning after the priests came, and stagger down the street to Dunkin' Donuts. I don't remember, but they say I couldn't talk, so I scratched out a note asking a clerk to call 911. I wish I hadn't.

David was the one most upset with me when I ran away from Resthaven. "Don't keep doing this to your family," he scolded me, as I lay rehydrating on a gurney in the emergency room. Then Metro General admitted me for a five-day medical rehab. Only five days to make the transition from death's door to independent living. Independent living . . . HAH! I was terrified of being on my own again after so much time in institutions. Except for Dr. Steiner, nobody really believed I could take care of myself. I moved back into an apartment and went through the motions. Tried to work, tried to renew contacts with others, tried to get involved with a support group, tried to eat right; but I was still bingeing and purging all the time, still overexercising, still exhausted, still sick beyond cure. In and out of hospitals three more times. Nobody could figure out what to do with me. One psychiatrist even said I was stable. Idiot.

I couldn't function in my apartment anymore. Too lonely. Too malnourished. Too depressed. Too suicidal. The day after Mom and Dad got back from visiting Janis for her birthday, I went home, even though they'd told me I couldn't come home again. But I didn't have any other place to go. Nobody was home, and I tried to relax by myself. But I couldn't. Couldn't stand the pain. I gulped down all the Tylenol I could find, but I didn't think I'd found enough, so I lay down on my old bed and started cutting my wrists with a razor blade. When Dad came home early from work, I hid my arms under the sheets. He didn't seem angry that I'd come home. He talked to me for a minute before he went outside, but he didn't come over and hug me. And his eyes avoided mine.

He didn't want to see my suffering, nor did he want me to see his. Right after, Mom came home from church, saw some blood, and called 911. Before the ambulance came, I heard them arguing about something in the driveway through my open window.

Maybe I didn't really want to die then either, so I hurt myself where someone would find me. I don't know anymore. I'm so confused. Fucking doctors. They fixed me up again and sent me here to Glenbrook, my twelfth psych hospital admission.

When Dr. Weintraub resigned four years ago, she said I would die, that I was untreatable. Honest Bertha . . . I guess she was right. I know I can't live with this illness, let alone drive it out of my mind. It has destroyed me, nearly destroyed my family, and beaten down every doctor who tried to help me. No one will treat me anymore except Dr. Wakely, and he doesn't know what to do. He sounded relieved when he said I'll have to leave soon, that I can't stay here indefinitely without making progress, that I may have to commit to the state hospital or find some other institution that will take me. He had me visit a place called Community Care. But I'm afraid of making another change. Dad said he'd never send me to the state hospital. But his insurance may quit paying again when they realize I don't get therapy at mental institutions anymore, just controlled maintenance. So I may not have a choice. I won't go, though.

I wonder what might have happened if I had never started seeing psychiatrists. Did they make me sicker with all their theories, all their manipulations?

I'm alone and depressed most of the time now. There aren't any meadowlarks to listen to, and I don't get visitors, except Dad occasionally. Mom doesn't come; she's shunning me on advice of her doctor. And Dad and I don't know what to talk about, probably because nothing has been left unsaid. We don't even play backgammon anymore. Staff is always too busy. Dr. Wakely doesn't stay long when he comes, and we don't have much to talk about anyway. We're both tired of discussing the same terrifying flashbacks, the same fears he can't do anything about.

I'll skip lunch—staff won't notice—and write a note for Dad. I snuck off grounds for a few minutes this morning. The razor blades are hidden in my dresser. Dr. Wakely will be here at 2:00. He'll pretend to listen to me, keep looking at his watch, and leave fifteen minutes later. That should give me plenty of time, because the nurses have stopped checking on me in the afternoons.

God give me strong fingers and the courage to use them. There's no time left for me.

PART ONE
Searching for a Cause

CHAPTER ONE

Dieting for Lent

Jenny wasn't always sick. For her first fourteen years she seemed extraordinarily well. A gregarious and fun-loving redhead, she exuded energy and was constantly in motion. The rest of her family marveled at her frenetic pace. Then . . .

Jenny bounced into the kitchen. She stopped abruptly when she saw her mother at the counter telephone. "I don't know. Probably the same as last year. No afternoon wine. No coffee. Caffeine's not good for me anyway." Her mother turned toward her, smiled, waved, and left a forefinger poised in the air to signal "just a minute." Jenny smiled and waved back.

"Yes, I'll observe the church fasts, maybe diet some, too . . . No, it's not my weight, but I like to eat, and I ought to give up something I like, otherwise it's not much of a denial." Jenny tried to make sense of the conversation. "It's one of her church friends," she whispered to Thane, the family collie. "They talk forever." Thane wagged his tail in agreement.

Waiting impatiently, Jenny admired her mother's graceful appearance and handsome auburn hair, cut stylishly short and graying at the temples, gleaming lustrous in the sunlight. There was a natural cheerfulness to her mother's presence, a zest for living that everyone enjoyed. *She seems younger than forty-five,* Jenny thought.

Phone call concluded, her mother advanced to give her a hug, embracing both daughter and backpack. "How was school honey? Did—"

"Mom," Jenny interrupted. "You don't need to diet. You look great, even after five kids."

"Thanks, Jenny. But I need to give up something for Lent."

"Like what?"

"Desserts . . . between-meal snacks."

"Maybe I'll diet too, keep you company."

"That's a nice devotional gesture, Jenny. But you don't need to diet."

Jenny fidgeted. "I'd kinda like to. I feel fat. And I'd like to look beautiful like Nancy."

"Don't be silly. You're not fat, and you look like your own beautiful self."

"Wel-l-l-l," Jenny murmured, "maybe just a small diet . . . so I'll be lighter in the saddle."

"Would you like to ride today? I can drive you."

"No, not today. I have to study for a test tomorrow."

"Spring Charity show is next month, and you need to be ready," her mother admonished.

"I know, Mom," Jenny said testily. "I will be."

"Don't you have a riding lesson with Bob on Saturday?"

"I guess," Jenny responded listlessly. "I don't like him, Mom."

"You know he came out of retirement to coach you."

Jenny frowned. "It's just that . . . sometimes he gives me the creeps, and . . ." A glower from her mother suppressed the rest of Jenny's response. A ringing phone interrupted. "Sorry, honey," her mother said and turned to answer it.

Jenny scooted upstairs to the small corner bedroom she shared with Janis. From his bedside den, Pooh, a stuffed bear, welcomed Jenny with his perpetual grin. Jenny returned the grin, shucked her backpack, and surveyed the room. Her desktop was clear, her dresser drawers tightly closed. Carefully folded at the foot of her bed was a worn quilt, appliqued by her mother with favorite childhood figures—a clown, a monkey, an elephant, and a smiling hedgehog. Above her bed, a shelf neatly organized her prized possessions: a ceramic jumping horse, a complete set of *The Chronicles of Narnia,* three silver award cups surrounded by a dozen red, yellow, and blue ribbons, four photo albums, and a framed picture of her first horse, Little Dickens. At least *her* things were tidy. But elsewhere! The lower trundle bed was still extended, with its upper sheet and blanket piled in a heap and the lower sheet pulled back, exposing the mattress beneath. Janis's pet puppet, Frida the alligator, curled on a grease-spotted pillow next to a half-full bag of chips. On Janis's desktop an unfinished English paper lay under an empty Coke can and a fresh bag of sunflower seeds. At the foot of the bed, a dollhouse replicated the untidy nature of its free-spirited twelve-year-old owner. "You're such a pigpen, Janis," Jenny muttered. *No, I'm not going to clean up for her. It's not fair I have to share; Janis should live alone with her mess. That's so dumb . . . keeping separate rooms for David and Nancy while they're away at school.*

Through the south window, Jenny looked out on a suburban neighborhood wrested from arid Colorado plains. Two-story homes with two-car garages crowded along curving streets. Fences separated each backyard. Patches of melting snow mottled dormant brown lawns. A cold, gray sky withheld the promise of spring. Wistfully, she looked at a dilapidated barn across the avenue. Snow hung from a rickety north roof. When the barn manager announced that he couldn't renew his lease, Jenny had moved her horse to a new equestrian center 4 miles away. She was still unhappy with the change and wondered when the old barn and its riding arena would be torn down. *Progress! Soon only houses and people will surround us. No room for barns or horses. Or meadowlarks.*

Crossing the hallway, Jenny went into the children's bathroom and stared at herself in the mirror. *Puffy eyelids, like Mom's . . . but why didn't I inherit her pretty hair? Mine is long and limp and straight. At least my bangs cover some of my freckles. I've got more freckles than Janis and Brian combined, and I'm the only one who didn't inherit Dad's dimpled chin. I have really nice eyes though . . . at least I got Dad's blue eyes.* Then she frowned. *But I have fat cheeks in a fat round face.* She raised up on tiptoes and her frown deepened into a scowl. *More fat. I have a lumpy body. Chubby . . . pudgy . . . plain and short.* She turned sideways, inhaled, and stuck out her chest. *No curves yet. Just bumps. Mom says be patient, but she has no idea how gross I feel.*

Jenny stomped out of the bathroom and down the hallway. She paused briefly at Brian's doorway and eyed his clutter, as unsightly as

Janis's. His pet puppet, Fri, alligator twin to Frida, stared impudently at
Jenny from the top of a wrinkled sheet. "Only ten but he gets his own
room," she muttered and stuck out her tongue at Fri. She glanced envi-
ously into Nancy's room, which stood vacant and serene. Then she
flounced back down the stairs.

The season changed. Tulips bloomed and spring breezes rippled lilac hedges
heavy with lavender blossoms. Lent came and went. The Easter holidays
ended. Jenny's diet did not. Her food denials became obsessive and continued into May. The effects showed in her gaunt frame and tightly drawn
facial features. Head down, body slumped forward, Jenny trudged home
from school. Close by, a meadowlark called out in long double notes,
melodic and flutelike. From the field beyond a similar clear voice answered.
For a moment, Jenny's melancholy lifted and she smiled. *So dependable.*
Every spring they return and sing to me. Then a robin stuffed with garden
worms chirped from a freshly watered lawn. His happiness captured
Jenny's attention, and she stared at the bird's swollen belly. "Fat little
pig," she muttered. Her backpack straps cut cruelly into her bony shoulders, and she winced as she shifted her load. *Just carrying my books exhausts*
me. I'm so tired . . . only three weeks until summer vacation . . . hope I make it.

That night Jenny fidgeted in her chair at the dinner table as she listened to her mother's phone conversation. "Yes . . . I'm taking her to the
pediatrician tomorrow." *If she keeps talking to Mrs. MacGregor as if I'm not*
here, I'm going to scream.

Jenny sat alone at the table, feeling abandoned. With her fork, she
pushed the remains of a meager helping of three-bean salad around her
plate. Four spoonfuls of rice and a roasted chicken wing remained
untouched. She frowned at the four empty chairs around her. At least
Thane remained loyally at her side. *And he's just staying in hopes of table scraps.*

Jenny frowned at her sister's plate, littered with food remnants. *Why*
don't they make her eat everything? Janis always gets away with picking at her
food. More furrows lined Jenny's brow as she glanced at her mother's plate,

still nearly full. She lapsed into a deeper sulk. *Mom's stuck us with a deli special again. If dinner's not from the deli, it's one of those dumb soups—"swill stew" Janis calls them—or other Crock-Pot stuff.* Jenny looked at the two remaining plates, both empty. Laughter drifted in from the den where her father and Brian had adjourned to work on a ship model. She felt resentful that they could have a good time when she felt so miserable.

Jenny's mother returned to the table, smiling. "Mrs. MacGregor hopes you're feeling better."

"I'm not sick, Mom, just tired." Seeing her mother's smile fade to a disapproving glare at her plate, Jenny dutifully forced down a gob of rice and a bite of chicken.

"You know you're still grounded, riding too, until you start eating better," her mother said in a matter-of-fact tone.

"I know," Jenny sighed. "I just can't make myself eat this stuff." Defiantly, she placed her fork beside her plate and dropped her hands to her lap. "Why can't I just fix myself a nice green salad?"

"We've been over that." Her mother's voice grew impatient. "You know you can't get enough nutrition from salads alone. You should eat what the family eats."

"I feel guilty and out of control when I eat," Jenny murmured.

"I don't understand how you can feel guilty about eating," her mother snapped.

"I can't explain it."

"Well, we have an appointment to talk with Dr. Reneker tomorrow. Maybe he can help. He was very sympathetic when I talked to him. His daughter is anorexic."

The term wasn't new to Jenny. Her anorexic condition had been openly discussed. "So . . . so what can he do for me that he obviously hasn't been able to do for his own daughter?"

"I don't know, honey, but we have to try something. Oh, and Mrs. Meyer is coming over Saturday to talk to you."

Jenny's expression was still skeptical. "Why Mrs. Meyer?"

"She's anorexic, too."

"I know that, but what can she say to me, except 'don't do what I've done.' Why would she think I can eat big meals when she can't?"

"Not big meals. Just good meals. Maybe she knows of something that could have turned her around in the early stages."

"Okay, Mom. I really don't care." Jenny stared at her plate and grimaced, refusing eye contact with her mother. "But I'm not going to eat any more. I just can't . . . yeah, I know, upstairs to homework and bed."

Despite several appointments with Dr. Reneker, a kind and patient physician whom she liked and trusted, Jenny reduced her nutritional intake further—to apples, an occasional lettuce salad, and Diet Cokes. Her weight plummeted to 67 pounds. Too weak to take an interest in her horse or other activities, she drifted deeper into a languid depression. She wandered listlessly through her shrinking world, barely connecting with anyone or anything, an apparition of her former self. Her family looked at her and saw a fleshless wraith of skin and bone. She looked in the mirror and saw a chubby adolescent.

Jenny's eyes, once full of fun and mischief, now showed only misery—from a private torment she could not comprehend. What was causing her anorexia? How could she fight back against an adversary she couldn't see or touch? She rarely smiled, never laughed. Her siblings began to avoid her. Her parents held secret, whispered conferences late into the night.

Never denying her lapse into serious illness, Jenny knew she was killing herself in plain sight. She reasoned she would die if she didn't eat, but her will was impervious to reason. She wouldn't be forced to eat, no matter how severely her parents restricted her. She had no idea how to resolve the conflict. Her weekly electrolyte tests reported increasing deficiencies in sodium and potassium. When they dropped to a dangerously low level, Dr. Reneker insisted she enter Children's Hospital. Her exhausted parents readily agreed, and Jenny fearfully consented.

CHAPTER TWO

Yellow Roses

*C*hildren's Hospital didn't fit Jenny's preconception. It was a pleasant place, bright and cheerful, not dark and foreboding as she had feared. She didn't feel confined, either physically or in spirit. When she roamed the hospital corridors, everyone—patients, doctors, and staff alike— smiled at her. Such a welcoming environment eased Jenny's discomfort at being one of the hospital's oldest patients. Soon she didn't worry that others would stare at her and see only a skinny teenage freak with a distorted body image.

No illness can suppress the natural happiness of children for very long. Each day, laughter erupted from rooms and wards, flowed through hallways, and expelled fears and despair from all the nooks and crannies of the hospital. Only the oncology ward exuded a more subdued mood and hinted at something incurable on the premises.

Meals became tolerable. Jenny's electrolytes returned to normal as she gradually began to eat again. No parents hovered over her threatening reprisals if she didn't eat. As if awakened from paralysis, her hands and arms hesitantly resumed familiar feeding motions. She tried to eat until her tray emptied. Sometimes she couldn't, but often she succeeded, only to face a rush of conflicting emotions. Pride in accomplishment warred with undefined guilt. Growing self-confidence sparred with lingering self-doubt.

Days grew into weeks, weeks into a month.

June 29. My first journal entry. Dr. Westin suggested I keep a journal to help me deal with my thoughts. So here goes. It reminds me of the journals

I kept for sixth grade. They were fun. Maybe these will be, too. Four weeks in the hospital already and I'm kinda worried about how much longer I'll be here. No one can tell me. I just can't spend my whole summer here. I can't go back to school and face those stupid questions. "How was your summer?" What do I say? "Great, I spent the whole three months in the hospital, eating. And how was your summer?"

I like my doctor, though. So young and good looking. He's thoughtful and never hurries like other doctors who scurry around the hospital like nervous squirrels. Dr. Westin is easy to talk to—for a man. He listens patiently, even though he seems as confused about anorexia as I am. When I ask him a question, he asks me how I feel about it. I wonder if that's what talking to a psychiatrist is like. I'm glad I don't have one of those, although Dr. Westin says I may need therapy when I leave here. Who ever heard of a fifteen-year-old seeing a psychiatrist! Uggh. Revolting thought. What will we talk about? I'm only screwed up in one way—about eating. How much can we talk about eating?

June 30. We're having a little mystery here. I'm looking at six yellow roses in the crystal vase on my nightstand. Every weekday morning a fresh one arrives with a card bearing the same printed message. "From a secret admirer" it says, followed by a heart sign. Sometimes seven or eight roses accumulate before a withered one has to be discarded. I don't have a boyfriend, so I've asked the nurses who's sending them. "Sorry, Jenny," they say. "They're delivered and we don't know the source."

July 1. Well, mystery solved, I think. I asked Dad yesterday if he was sending the flowers. "My admiration of you is not a secret," he said. "So, how could I be?" He had that mischievous look in his eyes, and his answer was very evasive, so I'm sure it's him. Poor Dad. Why can't he tell me a little lie and just say no. I'll keep the mystery alive, though. It's fun pretending we don't know who's sending them. I wonder if Dad knows I know. I'm surprised how something so simple helps me feel good about myself and look forward to each day.

July 4. A holiday and a weekend. What a bore! Weekends make me feel sorry for myself. Dad comes by every evening after work but won't come on weekends. Dr. Westin is off duty on weekends. Even when Mom brings Nancy or Janis and Brian down with her to visit me on Sunday, they don't know much to say after, "How do you feel?" What a dumb question. If I don't say, "I'm fine," they'll get upset. Maybe I should try and make them understand how awful I feel sometimes, quit pretending to be cheerful when I don't feel cheerful just so I don't make them sad or angry about my problems. Why do I feel like I have to entertain them and make them comfortable when they come to see me?

It's no fun listening to the great things going on in their lives when there's nothing going on in mine. I'm tired of hearing about soccer games on Friday, Saturdays at the cabin, and what's going to happen at the July 4th block party. And I don't want to hear about what's happening to every family in church and in our neighborhood. Happenings are everywhere except here. Nothing happens here except eating and talking. Everyone's having a wonderful summer except me.

July 11. I actually had a fun Saturday. Nancy brought Thane down and we played fetch the tennis ball out on the north lawn. It felt good just to run around and laugh in the sun with my big sister. The nurses were terrified Nancy and I were going to sneak Thane into my room. Maybe we will someday. He can sleep under my bed, share my food.

July 18. Dr. Westin says I can go to church with my family tomorrow. I don't know if I want to. Mom put me on the prayer list, and everyone she hasn't talked to already will stare at me and wonder what's wrong. Those who know will ask if I'm better, and I won't know what to say to them. Why can't Mom understand how weird that makes me feel?

July 25. Next week I'm being discharged. Hurrah.

July 28. Mom and Dad are coming to pick me up. I know I eat better and I know I feel better and I know I have more energy. But, oh the doubts. And the questions that torment me at night when children's laughter isn't around to cheer me. Questions no one can answer. Am I well or just improved? Why did I do this to myself? What will happen when I leave? Why must I always feel so gross and fat? Why do I still feel guilty when I eat? How do I get rid of these feelings? Where do I get the right prescription? Why can't I be happy like my sisters, like everyone else?

Aug 27. I'm still bummed about seeing a psychiatrist. Mom and Dad insisted, and I only agreed because I was scared about leaving Children's Hospital. Both Dr. Reneker and Dr. Westin recommended Dr. Conley. He's supposed to be good with adolescents. I guess that's what I am. Dr. Conley was on vacation when I got out of the hospital. Then I went to the ranch with my family for two weeks. So yesterday was my first session.

It almost didn't happen. Sometimes I feel so ashamed. It's kinda like a bad dream—not really me who's sick but some foreign person inside me. Anyway, I was upset about going yesterday, so Mom and Dad both went with me, to help me feel more comfortable. I freaked out when we got there, started crying, got hysterical, and ran away from the car, across the field from the doctor's office and all the way down to Cherry Creek. Mom and Dad didn't know what to do, let me run free or chase me. They sorta trotted along behind yelling, "Jenny, please stop." I finally did and when they caught up with me all out of breath, I could see Mom was crying, too. We sat on a grass bank along the creek and talked until Mom and I calmed down. When we went back, I was twenty minutes late for my appointment. The doctor didn't seem to mind.

What I can't figure out, is if I'm so sick I need a shrink, how come I got along fine without one for almost four weeks? Well, almost fine (I'm supposed to be honest about what I write in here), because I'm still paranoid about what I eat and how fat I look and feel. I haven't lost much weight, but I'm worried about going back to school.

I didn't have the slightest idea what we were supposed to talk about yesterday. I don't think Dr. Conley did, either. He just kept looking at me, trying to appear serious and smart, waiting for me to say something. He made me nervous. So I talked about the ranch and all the families we've vacationed with there for so many years. I couldn't tell if he was interested. He didn't say anything about his vacation.

I didn't tell the doctor about my crush on Jimmy McGuire, the ranch chore boy. Jimmy is so-o-o handsome—for a sixteen-year old. No pimples or acne or scraggly chin hairs. Janis still teases me about falling for a gofer. I don't think Jimmy knew how I felt unless he could tell I was blushing around him. I won't see him for another year. Something to look forward to.

September 3. I like Dr. Conley, but I don't like going to see him. My sophomore year starts next week, and I'm really scared about going back. But Dr. Conley isn't helping. He wants me to explain why I'm scared, and I don't know why.

September 17. Well, my therapy with Dr. Conley may be about over. Mom and Dad went with me yesterday for a family session. We talked about eating being a control issue and how I use not eating as a way to rebel against control and to keep attention on me. Mom agreed with the doctor, but Dad was skeptical. He said the two theories were conflicting. I'm not sure what I think.

Then Dr. Conley said my siblings may have resented how my involvement with horses and show competitions took so much of my parents' attention. We talked about that for a long time, but I still don't know what that has to do with not eating. Our session was over before I could ask him.

When we left his office, I told Mom and Dad that Dr. Conley reminded me of someone. "Of course," Dad said. "It's Walter Matthau. The doctor's got a face like a basset hound. He's a dead ringer for Walter Matthau."

"The actor," Mom said. "Don't you remember, Jenny? He was the coach in Bad News Bears . . . the movie. He's really funny."

We all laughed, then Dad said, "I'm sorry, Jenny, but I could barely keep from breaking up in there. I don't think I'll ever be able to take Dr. Conley seriously."

"Should we tell him who he looks like?" I asked.

"Heavens no," Mom said. "We don't want to offend him."

"Maybe he'd be flattered," Dad said.

October 1. No session yesterday. Dr. Conley went to a series of meetings in Hawaii. Lucky man. I'm doing well in school. But I feel out of place. Cherry Creek is so huge—4,000 students—I feel kinda lost. And I'm not like the other students. I know I still look like a little girl who will never grow up.

October 29. I'm not doing very well with this journal. I'm too busy with school, and I can't get motivated to write, except after I see Dr. Conley and sometimes not even then.

I'm still having trouble eating and Dr. Conley isn't helping. I don't want to see him anymore, and I think Mom and Dad will let me stop. Mom is busy with needlepoint designs for the church kneelers, and sometimes she gets irritated about having to drive me to appointments and wait for me. Dad isn't impressed with Dr. Conley and wants me to see Dr. Corbin. Mom agrees. What do I want? I just want to be well and normal. Is that too much to ask?

I can't handle my bad feelings about eating. Not by myself. When I'm depressed, Mom can be really patient and sympathetic. Sometimes, though, she just gets angry with me. But it's almost impossible to talk to Dad. He doesn't get angry, but he says he feels uncomfortable and inadequate when I get depressed. When he's home he seems too restless, too tired, or too busy to talk to me.

Week after next we're going to Boulder to talk to Dr. Corbin. I'll see if I like him any more than Dr. Conley. Dad says Dr. Corbin has a full schedule and can't take me on a weekly basis until after the first of the year. Dad's going to teach me how to drive. I'll have my learners permit soon, so I'll be able to drive myself. Hurrah.

CHAPTER THREE
Not a Bad Girl

*A*s she left Dr. Corbin's office with her parents, Jenny felt less tense, more relaxed than she had in a while. She sought her mother's hand. "I like him, Mom. He's not preachy."

"I'm glad, honey. He's a sensitive and practical man. He already knows a lot about the family, and he was a godsend to your father."

"Jim helped me avoid a breakdown," her father added. "I'm grateful beyond words."

"You're sure it's okay for me to see your doctor?"

"Sure. I've told him there are no secrets about me. I think of him more as a family doctor than my psychiatrist." Jenny visualized a door sign, JAMES CORBIN, FAMILY SHRINK, and smiled at the image. Her father continued, "Are you okay with Jim's approach?"

"Approach?" Jenny's brow furrowed. She was uncertain what he meant.

"Remember the two alternatives he discussed and the one that he recommended?"

"Oh yes—he said we should deal with the present rather than analyze my childhood. I like that. I feel uncomfortable when I'm pressured to think about the past."

"Remember, Jenny, about the weight limit," her mother admonished. "You agreed to keep your weight up, and I'm not going to weigh you."

Lecturing me again, Jenny thought. "I know, Mom," she responded wearily. She let go of her mother's hand. "He won't see me if I can't keep my weight above 80 pounds. I know you don't think I can do it."

"Jenny, that's not true. I think you can do it if you have help."

"I'm really sorry, Mom. I'm still upset that I have to see another psychiatrist."

"You wouldn't have to see a psychiatrist if you could maintain weight on your own."

"I know—you think I should be punished for starving myself."

"Enough," Jenny's dad intervened. "Truce time. We have a doctor Jenny likes and we all respect. Let's do our best to make it work."

After seeing Jenny and her parents to the door, Dr. Corbin returned to his office. He sat quietly at his desk, absorbed in summarizing the previous fifty minutes in a few phrases of neatly penned script, an exercise he could complete in five minutes on one side of a piece of paper.

JENNIFER HENDRICKS read the tab on his new patient file.

Dr. Corbin began his first page.

- *Interesting family dynamics. First, Gordon develops free-floating anxiety. Now his daughter is anorexic. Any connection? Hereditary or environment? Age-old unanswered question.*
- *Any compulsive behavior patterns in parents? About eating?*
- *Anne feels she had enormous burden holding family together when G was sick. Why did she think his illness would split family? Why was G's illness so threatening to her?*
- *Mother/daughter conflict over J driving. Symptomatic of control issues? A's latent hostility and J's resentment are evident. Why didn't Children's or Conley see that?*
- *J feels guilty about being anorexic. Thinks she's being bad. Needs to be assured she's not being bad. Very important.*

Dr. Corbin closed Jennifer's file, opened a filing cabinet next to his desk, and inserted the new file next to a bulging folder marked GORDON HENDRICKS—INACTIVE. Would her father's file have to be reactivated? Perhaps not. Dr. Corbin pulled his former patient's folder and added to the summary page inside:

- *Asked G how he was dealing with stress of J's illness. G said it didn't make him anxious. Asked him why. Interesting but honest response. G said, "That's easy, I don't feel threatened." He also said he felt ashamed.*

Returning the folder and closing the drawer, Dr. Corbin smiled at a neatly framed certificate above his desk. "For the Third Consecutive Year," it read,

RECOGNITION AWARD FOR THE UNIVERSITY'S MOST POPULAR UNDERGRADUATE COURSE—TO JAMES B. CORBIN, M.D., FOR HIS SERIES ON HUMAN SEXUALITY.

Despite the ribbing he endured from his colleagues, Dr. Corbin was proud of his course and his award. Some doctors knew what was important to America's youth.

Dr. Corbin turned off his answering machine and the ringer to his telephone, closed the blinds over his expansive picture window, and stretched full length on his office couch, his 6-foot 2-inch athletic frame still nearly a foot short of filling it. With no more appointments for the day, he could close his eyes and empty his mind of the day's quota of human frailties. Programmed relaxation was an important ritual habit developed over twelve years of practice. It neatly severed each day into two parts, permitting him to return home with some semblance of his sanity intact.

Sometimes he wondered if he had jeopardized his own mental health when he switched from internal medicine to psychiatry. But for him, the mind provided greater fascination than the body. On Sundays, he preferred playing chess to watching football.

Dr. Corbin possessed a genuine compassion for his patients. In a time when other psychiatrists fiercely protected their diminished private lives, he encouraged patients to call him anytime. He recognized that emotional distress seldom shut down at doctors' convenience. He gained patient trust quickly through his sincere and pragmatic approach, his openness about himself, his intelligence and good humor, and his honesty about the limitations of his profession.

"Why the hostility between your mother and you?" Dr. Corbin asked gently.

"I don't know—seems like Mom started getting on my case after I got sick."

"Not before?"

"I don't think so." A fleeting notion to the contrary surfaced but was quickly suppressed. "It's worse when Nancy is away at school. Maybe Mom's upset because I haven't done well showing my horse since I've been sick."

"Does she say that?"

"No."

"Then why do you think she's upset?"

"I feel her disapproval. She has such high expectations, and most days I don't feel strong enough to work with Miss Roan."

"I think there's more to it than showing horses. Does your mom take time in the evenings to talk to you, encourage you?"

"Yes, particularly when I'm depressed. Most of the time she's really nice to me, and we sit on my bed and talk for a long time, until I feel better and calm down. But sometimes it seems like I can't do anything right. She scolds me a lot. I probably deserve it."

"Why do you say that?"

"Because everyone says what a wonderful person she is. So how could she be wrong?"

"Wonderful persons, even mothers, get impatient, particularly if they're stressed. And it may not be a case of who's right or wrong. Does her scolding make you angry?"

"Yes. It seems like she picks on me all the time, even when I try to be good. Nancy never does anything wrong."

"Doesn't Nancy get scolded?"

"No, she's always been Mom's favorite."

"What about Janis and Brian?"

"Those pigpens get away with everything. Janis does what she pleases and screeches at Mom if Mom scolds her. Brian's the baby and he's spoiled rotten. But he's such a sweet little kid, no one can get angry at him."

"Does your mom seem hostile in the morning—night—after school? Any patterns?"

"Not really—except one thing maybe."

"What's that?"

"When she comes into the house after being gone for a while, she seems angry, and I try to stay out of her way. Like when she comes home from church, from visiting neighbors in the evening, or from seeing James."

"Why do you think she's angry after church?"

"It's like church is her escape into a make-believe world of peace and perfection. Then she has to come back home to reality, to turmoil and flaw because of me, and she resents it—resents me."

"Does she go to church often?"

"Every day—she's in charge of a big needlepoint project. But she's almost always home when I come home from school."

"Tell me about James."

"A friend's son. He has leukemia."

"Your dad mentioned that."

"Mom stops by the hospital every day to see him. It seems like she spends more time with him than me. She's always telling me how brave he is, how hard he's fighting his disease."

"Does that upset you?"

"Yes. I'm sick of hearing about it. It seems like she compares me to him, and I come out inferior. Do you think I'm just jealous?"

"No, your resentment is natural. Is your mother driving you here next week?"

"Yes."

"I'll talk to her then."

"Please don't tell her I'm upset about James." Jenny felt disloyal and apprehensive.

"You haven't discussed your resentment with her?"

"No. I don't think that's what's making me sick, though."

"Probably not. But it makes it more difficult for both of you to deal with your anorexia. I need to talk to her about it."

"I'm afraid it will just make her angry."

"I'll be careful. You need reassurance from your parents, not just from me, that you are not a bad girl just because you are sick."

Jenny sat in the waiting room, wondering if she should feel resentful or relieved at sacrificing ten minutes from the end of her session. Dr. Corbin met with her mother alone.

Dr. Corbin began. "Are you aware of the hostility between Jenny and you?"

Anger flared briefly in Jenny's mother's eyes.

"Is that what Jenny said?"

"No. It was apparent from seeing the two of you together."

"It seems like she uses her anorexia to get back at me."

"For what?"

"That's just it. I don't know. But I think she has chosen to be anorexic, and when she chooses, she can be well again."

"In your view it's a teenage behavioral problem?"

"Mostly."

"You may be right about that. But when psychiatrists are honest with themselves, we all have to admit we don't understand this illness very well."

"So you can imagine how I feel!"

"I know the nature of your feelings, if not their intensity. Mothers feel intense pain with anorexic daughters, even more than with other illnesses their children may have. And I don't have a lot of good answers why that is, either."

"Thank you. Your honesty helps."

"Tell me about James." Dr. Corbin sensed a startled reaction to his query.

"He's only seventeen and dying of leukemia."

"Jenny told me. Both Jenny and your husband have mentioned how preoccupied you are with James."

"He's very weak but has such a strong spirit and a positive attitude. He's dying and wants so desperately to live. He's a fighter."

"And Jenny?"

"She's the reverse. She's strong physically but gets depressed and has a negative attitude. She's living but wants to die and doesn't seem willing to fight."

"So James is more deserving of your attention. I thought it might be something like that."

"I can help James. I don't seem able to help Jenny."

"I know how natural it is to address a need that responds rather than one that doesn't, to gravitate to where you are appreciated. But I do have a suggestion."

"Yes?"

"Try not to focus so much attention on James when you are with Jenny. Holding him up as an example to Jenny only increases her guilt and complicates her feelings about you and her illness. It creates a perception that you don't care as much about her. You need to reassure Jenny that she's not a bad girl, that she's not being bad just because she's anorexic."

Jenny's mother paused thoughtfully before responding. "I understand and I'll try." There was a wistful earnestness and a hint of tears in her eyes. "I'll really try—and thank you—thank you, Jim, for helping us once again. We're all very grateful."

Jenny's relationship with her mother improved. With Dr. Corbin's emphasis on helping her live with illness, Jenny remained functional, despite food and fat fears that still seethed inside her.

For the next eighteen months, Jenny felt like a committee of four—father, mother, doctor, and patient—managed her life. All joined together, generally cohesively, in efforts to improve her living environment, often in small but significant ways. There was better meal planning at home, and she moved into her own room, enrolled in a private girls' school for her junior year of high school, and reduced her participation in horse show competitions. With her allowance savings, she acquired Kelsey, a golden retriever puppy.

As Jenny completed her second year of coping with illness, Kelsey fell victim to an epidemic of the deadly parvovirus. That her beloved pet had died in her care was emotionally devastating to Jenny. Never a strong barrier against the powerful surge of her illness, Jenny's wellness resolves faltered. Her eating habits again deteriorated. Depression hovered over her, like a vulture sensing vulnerability. Her weight slipped below 80 pounds.

Dr. Corbin conceded a two-week grace period to Jenny for her to regain her weight. She couldn't. The pact with her doctor was broken, and Dr. Corbin refused to see her unless she was admitted to a psychiatric care facility. Her fears of being forced into a mental institution did not materialize. Much to her relief, the "committee," voting three to one, decided against institutionalization. The search for a new psychiatrist began.

CHAPTER FOUR

Voodoo Psychiatry

*N*ew beginning. New hope. Jenny sat alone in Dr. Weintraub's waiting room, clutching her spiral notebook and pen. She was winding down after a full day of classes at St. Jude's Academy and a tiring forty-minute drive through crosstown traffic. Her watch showed twenty minutes before four, and she knew from experience that appointments commenced precisely at the appointed hour. She was apprehensive but resolved. She opened her notebook and reviewed her last journal entry.

September 15. Next week a new doctor, and I'll do my best to make a fresh start. I like Dr. Weintraub, like her a lot. She's overweight but in tune with my feelings about being fat. I'm glad Mom and Dad let me decide about working with her. She doesn't use drug therapy, and I didn't like that doctor at the Med Center who said I should take drugs. Dr. Weintraub has such a quick wit and disarming smile, and she's cheerful and chatty—kinda like a pal. I think I'll be more comfortable working with a woman, although I'm sorry to leave Dr. Corbin. I feel badly that I let him down. He was so nice to me.

Dr. Weintraub's let's-get-with-it, no-nonsense approach was impressive. She picked up right away on my depression and seems confident she can help me. She's really smart, maybe smarter than the other doctors I've seen, probably smarter than me. Maybe I can finally turn control of this illness over to someone who's intelligent enough to deal with it. I'm tired of feeling awful and not knowing why I feel that way.

I really missed Nancy today. I walked by her room and it seemed so empty. Her being home in the summertime helps me a lot, and I wish Lewis & Clark College wasn't so far away. I miss talking to her, even though she's been critical about my being anorexic. Like Mom, she thinks I can get well if I want to. It's tough now that I'm the eldest at home, particularly when Janis is such a pretty girl and I'm not. Making friends is easy for her and difficult for me. Mom's been really hard on me lately, like she's missing Nancy, too, and taking it out on me. I can't seem to do anything right around the house. I try to help Mom, but she's rarely satisfied, almost always finding fault.

Jenny nervously checked the time again and began a new entry.

September 22. The doctor's three o'clock is going to walk out that door in a few minutes, look at me, and wonder what's wrong, just as I'll look at her and wonder what her problem is. I hope she's not another anorexic. I felt more comfortable waiting for Dr. Corbin. He separated his office and waiting room by a hallway to prevent patients from seeing each other. He always came into his waiting room to greet me, and I could tell he was glad to see me. He made me feel good, and he always had a minute or two for small talk as we walked back to his office. Dr. Weintraub wants me to knock, and she'll say "Come in" if it's okay.

Dr. Bertha Weintraub looked at her watch. There were no clocks in her office. She disliked clocks, and she didn't want patients looking at them or thinking about time. In an adolescent specialization, it was important to control everything. A cancellation had provided her with time to think before her next session, her first with Jennifer Hendricks.

Often the doctor felt like a mental voyeur. Each day her patients refilled her head to exhaustion with a stream of misery sourced in the human mind. And who suffered more than troubled adolescents! But it was worth the stress—to see young people, even the tough cases, come into her office unhappy and sullen and then leave fifty minutes later with smiles and animation restored to their lives. Rarely did that not happen. Her anorexia patients were among her toughest cases. Although many severe eating disorders improved, many did not. Eating disorders were epidemic, but psychiatrists saw only a fraction of those afflicted, just those who could afford treatment. Jennifer Hendricks was one of the lucky few.

Dr. Weintraub scanned her appointment book for the rest of September, then the rest of the year. Almost filled already, it reflected the progress of a neurotic society. Welcome to the decade of the shrink, it proclaimed. She stared vacantly at the dated pages in front of her as memory briefly turned time backward. Despite her concentration camp childhood, she had been fortunate. She had survived. She couldn't remember a lot about her early years and her family's privations, but she didn't have to remember much. Just mentioning concentration camps always humbled her patients whenever they started feeling too sorry for themselves.

Restored to the present, Dr. Weintraub turned to the previous week in her appointment book and reviewed an inserted sheet of notes covering her introductory meeting with the Hendrickses.

- *Jennifer—High school senior. Growth stunted. Can't hide this eating disorder in a sweater. Intelligent and hurting. Trusting and receptive, not into denial or fighting therapy like a lot of teenagers.*
- *Mother—Anne, does church work and sculpts clay figures—very strong emotionally. Liked her a lot.*
- *Father—Gordon, CPA—tougher read. Open about his anxiety problems, his father's alcoholism. Positive experience with therapy. Good insurance coverage.*
- *Causes—Middle child syndrome? Dysfunctional family? Enabling behavior by a parent? Intrafamily conflicts? Childhood illnesses or fears? Textbook case of family curse?*
- *Treatment—No drugs, everyone agreed. J badly depressed—see her twice a week, once a month with parents. Need to be more confrontive—Corbin too soft? Explore childhood and relationships. Dream therapy?*
- *Remember—This is a mind, not a body, problem. The mind always controls the body.*

After Dr. Weintraub closed her appointment book, she rolled away from her desk, looked at her bulky body, and grimaced. She reached down the side of her dress, bunched a roll of flesh under the fabric between thumb and forefinger, and then smiled. If only she could give some of her extra pounds to her anorexic patients.

The appointed hour arrived with no departing patient. *What is going on in there?* Jenny wondered. Better to interrupt than be late, she decided, as she screwed up her courage, walked across the room, and knocked on the door. A voice on the other side said pleasantly, "Come in, Jennifer." When Jenny entered, Dr. Weintraub gestured to an armchair in front of her desk. "Please sit there," she instructed. "It's quite comfortable."

Jenny sat primly with her back rigid and her body forward so her feet could touch the floor. She waited patiently for her new doctor to begin the session.

From her swivel chair, Dr. Weintraub peered at Jenny through horn-rimmed glasses, smiled, and asked abruptly, "How do you feel about working with me?"

Jenny spoke softly but without hesitation. "I feel good about it. I know I need help, and it was my decision to come here. Mom and Dad didn't make me."

"You're experienced with psychotherapy, so you know what we talk about is confidential?"

"Yes."

"I hope you will feel comfortable talking to me . . . about everything."

"I think I will."

"And being honest with me. Teenagers aren't always candid about their real thoughts. They learn it from their parents."

"I'll try," Jenny responded. She didn't think she'd held anything back with Dr. Corbin, but she knew what Dr. Weintraub meant. Her parents, particularly her father, seldom talked about their feelings.

Dr. Weintraub's smile faded as she leaned forward to emphasize her next question, one she asked all her new patients. "Are you sure you want to get well?"

"I'm sure." Although she didn't detect any skepticism in the doctor's voice, Jenny continued with some confusion. "Why wouldn't I?"

"To keep yourself the center of attention."

"I'm past all that," Jenny said firmly.

"Yes, I believe you are." Dr. Weintraub's face grew even more solemn—*like an owl*, Jenny couldn't help thinking—as she considered her next question, one she asked all her anorexic patients. "Are you willing to give up your anorexia?"

"Yes." Jenny resisted a temptation to quarrel with the doctor's suggestion that she had chosen her illness. "I don't know why I'm sick."

"Did you and Dr. Corbin work on why you're anorexic?"

"Not much. More like he tried to help me live with an eating disorder."

"Ducking the issues." Dr. Weintraub freely voiced her disapproval. "I'm not surprised. In here, however, we work on cause. If we can find the cause of your anorexia, I'm sure we can cure you."

"I hope so. I so want to be well—and normal."

"It won't be easy," Dr. Weintraub spoke sympathetically.

"I know."

"The process of your getting well will take a great deal of time. Much friction will develop between your family, especially your parents, and you as you come out of your shell and establish your own identity."

Jenny wondered what that meant. She couldn't think of an appropriate response and squirmed apprehensively.

Seeing her patient's uneasiness, which she had expected, Dr. Weintraub smiled. "Don't worry," she reassured Jenny. "It's my job to help you get well, and I'm good at what I do. I'll help you work through all the family issues."

What family issues? Jenny wondered if she should ask. She managed a wan smile in return.

Session number one of several hundred had begun—with psychiatric lesson number one: A healthy family must have conflict. Over the next several weeks, Dr. Weintraub shook recollections from Jenny with a bulldoglike tenacity and bombarded her with speculated causes for her anorexia.

Session 1. "There's a link, Jenny, between your childhood asthma and your anorexia, especially your stubbornness in not breathing through your mouth when your nose was stuffed up."

Session 2. "You sucked your thumb unusually long, Jenny. Find out when you were weaned. Your anorexia may be rooted there."

Session 3. "You know how your dad acts. Do you think you might be like him?"

Session 4. "Tell me about your recurring dreams."

"In one, my sister Nancy and I are fighting over a doll in the basement. Nancy shoves the doll at me, runs upstairs, and the doll blows up."

"It explains your lose-by-winning attitude, Jenny, even then, as a child."

"In another dream I'm in an elevator going up. The devil is there and looks in my eyes. He can steal my soul if my love is not stronger than his hate. I can look in his followers' eyes and bring them back to love, so he hasn't stolen my soul yet."

"Going up symbolizes growing up. The devil represents anorexia and its pressures trying to consume you. Your attitude is better because you are winning."

Session 5. "You have been selected to receive the Hendricks family curse. Your dad's dad and his dad both had nervous breakdowns around age forty. Because you were sickly with asthma as a child, your dad identified with you and loved you best of all his children. Then your dad had abdominal surgery, complications, and a breakdown. Do you remember any change in his attentiveness to you?"

"Yes. He was less involved with me and the horse shows after he got sick. Mom was always there, but Dad wasn't."

"That's because he didn't want you to be like him and tried to ignore you from then on. He ignored you so you wouldn't get the curse. You viewed this as rejection, became very angry, and turned your anger inward, resulting in depression."

"I was depressed even back then?"

"Of course."

Session 6. "Your lose-by-winning attitude is part of the family curse."

"Like when I won at horse shows, but my friends said that I didn't deserve it?"

"Precisely. You're a very stubborn, determined-to-win person. You think you're a winner, but you're a poor sport about it. That's the sick Jenny."

"If I think I'm a winner, why am I sick?"

"Being sick was ingrained in your upbringing to be most like your dad, to inherit the Hendricks family curse. Although the real you is a determined winner, the expected you is a sickly kid."

"I remember I always had this fear that something awful was going to happen to me, particularly when I got my first horse. Everything was so great, but then Dad got sick, and I was sure I'd get cancer someday."

"Your fear was a result of your following your father's generational fault and receiving his transmission as the designated recipient of the Hendricks family curse."

"But the curse has been a middle-aged male thing. Why didn't he transmit it to my brothers?"

"I think you know why."

"But I don't, I really don't."

"Because you were his favorite."

"I didn't think he had a favorite. I know Nancy is Mom's favorite."

"Believe me. You were his favorite. I've talked to your mom. She thinks so, too."

Session 7. "Have you thought more about the family curse?"

"Yes. Maybe I was Dad's favorite. It's kinda nice to believe that. And I think Mom helped transmit the curse too, although she will deny it."

"Your mom? How?"

"My theory is she had a subconscious fear that I would get the curse, which allowed the curse to be transmitted even against her conscious thought processes."

"Very good, Jenny. Do you see how both parents' involvement makes the curse very strong inside you, so strong that it prevents the winner personality in you from overcoming your sick personality that insists on weighing 75 pounds or less?"

"Yes, I think so."

"And how this fits perfectly with your devil dream? The devil is the curse waiting for you to give in to it. It's always there waiting to get you."

"Yes."

"Do you understand your fear of cancer?"

"No, there's none in my family."

"Anorexia is your subconscious cancer. Don't you see that all the symptoms, like weight loss, are identical?"

"I guess."

Session 8. "Did you discuss the family curse with your mom and dad?"

"Yes. Mom understands. Dad's not convinced. He says you're practicing voodoo psychiatry."

"Your father isn't knowledgeable about well-established psychiatric concepts. Was he upset about being identified as the cause of your illness?"

"No. He thinks there might be a genetic connection, and he feels badly about it, but he doesn't agree with the curse theory. You've got too many generations involved. His grandfather didn't have a disorder. He said it doesn't make sense to connect his anxiety and his father's drinking problems to my eating disorder through a selection process. He thinks it's nonsense to suggest I was chosen as this generation's sick person."

"Does he acknowledge that first you were his favorite and then he ignored you?"

"He says that's absurd."

"He's just being defensive."

"That's what Mom thinks, too."

Session 9. "Here are my thoughts about school, written down like you asked me."

I haven't been to school since Wednesday, and even though I'm feeling physically better today there is no way I will go because mentally I'm a mess. School terrifies me. I know most kids have an aversion to school, but once they are there they don't feel so negative about it. That's how I used to be. I usually even enjoyed school. Not so anymore. I am a nervous, terrified person at school. I HATE it, and I mean with a passion.

Here's why I think I hate it: I leave home at 7:00 A.M. and work nonstop until 2:30, when I get home. I have no friends. I have a headache and am exhausted when I get home; all I can do after school is homework and sit around. I am usually weak and all I can think about is where I can sit down next.

I don't know why I'm afraid at school. It could be because every day I go there I see all these people my age enjoying life and it reminds me of how abnormal I am. I don't enjoy one thing about school—it is a chore and I detest it. School adds a lot of pressure on me and I really can't handle it. So much energy is going into fighting with myself (my depression) that I have no energy left for anything else. I'm so depressed I wonder if a hospital, no matter how awful, would be better. HELP!

"You need more friends, Jenny—to help you get through the day."

"I know, but why can't I make more friends?"

"Does your dad have a lot of friends?"

"I don't know. His best friend died while on a fishing trip with him last summer."

"I suspect he has very few friends. Have you talked to him about friends?"

"Yes. He said the number of friends isn't important, it's the quality that counts."

"See how obvious it is, Jenny. Friends are not one of his priorities, and your inability to make friends or become close to others is just like Dad."

"I do want friends, though."

"Of course. And friends you will have, just as soon as we can get you cured. In the meantime, what about a tutor to help with school?"

"Kinda sounds like the answer I've been looking for. But I don't think a tutor is acceptable to Mom and Dad."

"You know I'm leaving next month for two weeks in Hawaii . . . to lecture?"

"Yes, and I'm worried about what I'll do while you're gone."

"I've arranged for you to tour Willowcrest Sanitorium next week. If you aren't less depressed by next month, I may have to admit you there."

"I know."

Session 10. "Why do you want to be different, Jenny?"

"Different?"

"Yes. Your thinness. Does it make you feel special?"

"Sometimes, yes. Sometimes, no, because I wish I could eat normally like everyone else. And I get tired of Mom telling me I'm not everyone else."

"The neighbor family you spend a lot of time with, the Fultons, were they attracted to you because of your different looks?"

"I don't know."

"But you like their attention?"

"Yes. Their family always seems so perfect."

"Even though they are so materialistic?"

"I never thought of them that way until you pointed it out to me."

Session 11. "When your dog died last year, how did you feel?"

"Like something terrible would happen to me."

"You know you didn't transmit the family curse to him?"

"Yes."

"It was okay to grieve over him, but it wasn't okay to make his death symbolic of some greater tragedy ahead for you."

"I know. I should derive strength from hardship."

"Yes. Like we've talked before, my childhood in the concentration camp made me strong. It's why I am what I am."

Session 12. "Why do you want to stay a boy?"

"I don't—I mean I'm not a boy."

"Of course you are. Something in your mind is holding you back from maturing into a woman."

Session 13. "At your age, your close relationship with Mom is abnormal. It's caused by your fear of breaking away from the family and growing up."

"But Mom's still angry a lot. She's hostile to me sometimes. Dr. Corbin saw that right away and tried to help her overcome it and help me deal with it."

"Maybe Corbin did accomplish something. I haven't seen Mom's anger or hostility."

"Most of the time it doesn't come out when we're with others."

"It would be better for you to hate Mom at your age. It would make it easier to break away."

Through the remainder of Jenny's senior year in high school, Dr. Weintraub continued to weave past and present circumstances into psychological profiles of dysfunction. Biweekly therapy sessions continued, and Jenny's role as designated inheritor of a family curse played to exhaustion without beneficial effect. Although most of the doctor's diagnostic hip shots fired wide of the mark, she diligently sought to meet Jenny's need to confide in someone outside the home. Jenny responded with her trust and loyalty. She found the doctor sympathetic and supportive of the "well Jenny" but unrelentingly intolerant of the "sick Jenny," characterizations used by Dr. Weintraub to distinguish appropriate (normal) from unacceptable (anorexic) behavior.

The doctor's separation of Jenny into two identities, one implicitly good and one implicitly bad, became a persistent theme. Dr. Corbin had bolstered Jenny's self-esteem by reassuring her that being sick was not synonymous with being bad. His reinforcement collapsed under Dr. Weintraub's battering-ram assertions to the contrary. However, Jenny remained functional. She stayed out of the hospital, and a best-friend relationship blossomed during her senior year of high school.

CHAPTER FIVE
This Evening's for You

May 20. I made it. But the meadowlarks didn't—the first spring they didn't return!

Only one more week of school. And here is the best part—Dad is enthusiastic about taking me to the annual father/daughter dinner and dance, a St. Jude's tradition. Mom is helping me find a new dress. I'm excited.

"Over there, Dad, I see them." Jenny tugged at her father's arm as they entered the school gymnasium. "Diane and her father are saving us seats."

Jenny beamed as he turned toward her and smiled. He surrendered easily to her direction, as if to say, "This evening's for you." Tonight would be a rare interlude of unspoiled happiness. No anorexic thoughts. No stressing over last week's session with Dr. Weintraub. No anxiety about difficult sessions still ahead. High school was over; tomorrow she would graduate. And tonight she was determined to enjoy herself. She had two other accomplishments to celebrate: a best friend, Diane, to share the evening with, and—notified just this afternoon—she would graduate number one in her class, an achievement she had once thought beyond her reach.

"I'm proud of you, Jenny." Her father spoke softly, his arm resting lightly across her shoulders as they walked across the dance floor. "Not just for your academic recognition—I've always known how smart you are. I'm proud of how you've persevered, and I'm very proud of how pretty you look tonight in your new dress. Like a young woman. It's so good to see you happy and relaxed . . . and self-assured."

"Thanks, Dad." Jenny blushed. Compliments from him were not a frequent occurrence, and she occasionally mistook their absence for parental disapproval, particularly because he also rarely criticized. She needed his approval, especially tonight.

Diane jumped up, hugged Jenny warmly, backed away holding on to Jenny's hands, and looked earnestly into her eyes. "Jenny! Congratulations! I knew you could do it! I know how much this means to you! I'm so happy for you!" First acquainted as high school juniors, Jenny and Diane had become best friends during their senior year, before they knew they competed for top academic honors. Competition had enhanced their friendship.

Jenny squeezed Diane's hands. "You know how easily it could have been you."

"Nope, you were always better in math," Diane laughed.

For most of the evening Jenny and Diane disappeared into the private, exclusionary world of close friendship. Because of her waiflike appearance, many of Jenny's classmates were uneasy in her presence. They instinctively shied away from her illness. Only Diane seemed naturally at ease with Jenny, and only with Diane did Jenny feel comfortable enough to be open about her illness and mental distress.

As the evening progressed, Jenny danced a slow dance with her father, then another, as she overcame her initial awkwardness with an unfamiliar activity and began to enjoy moving with the music. "Why won't you do the faster stuff?" she teased, knowing how self-conscious he was on a dance floor.

"No sense of rhythm," he confessed.

"You're doing okay with slow steps."

"Slow steps don't offend my dignity. But my feet tangle when they have to move fast . . . or maybe it's my brain that can't move quickly."

"Well, you are trying. Poor Diane. Her father won't dance at all!"

"What can you expect from a history professor!"

"Not much, but at least as much as from a CPA!"

At the end of the evening, the drive home gave Jenny a rare opportunity for private time with her father. She curled up in the front seat of the family station wagon. "Thanks, Dad."

"Thank you, Jenny, for such a nice evening. I really enjoyed myself." He reached over and squeezed her hand.

"Even the dancing?"

"Even the dancing. The band wasn't as noisy as I feared."

"Was it okay that I spent so much time with Diane?"

"Sure. I'm a big fan of hers. She's sensitive to others and obviously very fond of you."

"Did you like her father?"

"A bit stuffy, but I enjoyed him once we found something we could both talk about."

"And my teachers?"

"I had a long talk with Sister Anne Marie. She told me how highly regarded you are at St. Jude's, for your attitude and work ethic as well as your scholarship, but she was cautious when I asked her how she felt about your going to Carleton College. She didn't exactly endorse it."

"She knows I've struggled with school this year." Jenny elected not to elaborate.

"About Carleton, are you sure we haven't bitten off more than you can chew?"

"Yes, Dad," she responded with irritation, "and Dr. Weintraub has been very positive about my going there."

"Sorry, honey." Then he teased, "Have you and she run out of other things to talk about?"

"No way," Jenny laughed. "She still wonders why you don't get angry at me, like Mom and my siblings do."

"Get mad at you because you have an eating disorder?"

"Yes. She thinks it would be healthier."

"For me or for you?"

"For both of us."

"Does she say you are behaving badly when you are sick?"

"Yes."

"I thought Dr. Corbin assured you that being sick wasn't being bad."

"He did. But maybe he was wrong."

"What do you think?"

Jenny paused for a moment. "I know I feel guilty sometimes, so maybe I am bad."

"Or do you feel guilty because the rest of your family suffers, too?"

"Whatever."

"It's important, Jenny. It's okay to feel badly that others hurt when you are sick, but don't let anyone lay a guilt trip on you just because you contracted a poorly understood illness."

"Are you angry at me now?"

"No, Jenny. More like disappointed with your doctor."

"Why don't you get angry at me?"

"Do you want me to?"

"No. But why does the rest of the family get mad at me and you don't?" Jenny persisted.

"That's not so complicated. For twenty-five years I've been trained to judge actions, what people do, not who they are. I can separate you from your illness. Your mom can't, and your siblings tend to follow her lead. I can't find it in my heart to blame you for getting sick."

"But Mom can?"

"Maybe it's harder for her, because if you're not at fault she fears she and I might have to acknowledge some kind of parental failure."

"And you don't fear the same?"

"No."

"But why does Mom think there has to be blame?"

"I'm not sure I can analyze that deeply."

"Dr. Weintraub thought I might be trying to get back at Mom for something, like I'm intentionally hurting her. Does Mom think I'm sinning when I don't eat?"

"I don't know, honey."

"Do you think I'm sinning?"

"That's not for me to judge. I think your mother is convinced you can end your anorexia if you really want to, but I don't think it's that simple."

"Because of your experience with anxiety?" Jenny barely remembered the scary period when he didn't smile at her—or anyone else. Years of job stress and a complicated surgery had produced an immobilizing anxiety, one which left him fearful and withdrawn.

"Mostly. I know what it's like to have my mind push me in a wrong direction and be unable to alter that by strength of will. I know I can't make myself not be anxious, so I can accept that you may not be able to rid yourself of food fears."

"But you don't seem anxious now. You seem at ease with yourself."

"Thanks to a lot less job stress, I've learned how to control my anxiety better, how to adapt to the condition. It took me a long time to understand, accept, and live with limitations."

"And you think I can do the same?"

"I'm sure of it."

"But I need professional help to do it?"

"Yes. And I did, too. That's why I've been encouraged by your willingness to stay in therapy, even though I may occasionally disagree with your doctor."

Their conversation lapsed, and Jenny smiled contentedly into the darkness. She felt tired from a good time. Not worn out from food fears, depression, or frustration. She gave in and shut her eyes. It was nice to rest, free of any thoughts.

The car lurched as it turned into the driveway. Jenny stirred and reached out to rest her hand on her father's shoulder. "Thanks, Dad. Thanks for being with me tonight." He covered her hand with his. Warmth spread from the gentle pressure of his touch.

In August Jenny joined her family for their annual two-week summer vacation in Montana. In her only journal entry of the summer, she recorded:

August 1. *Our last ranch vacation together? Dad says it's the emotional glue that attaches us to a common place, bonds us to each other, and keeps us connected—to our past and into our future. David says it even better: "We make our own good times here." How much longer can the tradition continue?*

Bolstered by good feelings from a successful holiday and a resounding vote of confidence from Dr. Weintraub and her family, Jenny entered Carleton College in September. She was determined to succeed on her own and without weekly psychiatric counseling. By Thanksgiving, however, Jenny felt too sick to continue at Carleton. Away from home and professional help, her food obsessions worsened, as episodes of binge eating and purging—her first bulimic experiences—began to cycle with periods of food denial. She returned home for Christmas, resumed seeing Dr. Weintraub, enrolled for the spring semester at the University of Colorado, and arranged for dormitory housing in Boulder. Despite psychiatric counseling through the winter and early spring, Jenny continued to decline, and in May she moved back home from Boulder to study for final exams. Desperately seeking help beyond the boundaries of her therapist's office, Jenny began counseling with a diet and fitness expert. With Peter, a recovered bulimic, Jenny experienced a flicker of hope that she might actually learn how to eat healthily without fear. If it wasn't already too late.

Distressed but undaunted by Jenny's weight loss, Dr. Weintraub watched her patient drop to 65 pounds before she finally requested a family meeting. Fresh input from Peter wouldn't be enough. Something had to change.

CHAPTER SIX

Confrontation

May 20. Only the second entry since exactly a year ago! We're leaving for Weintraub's office soon, and writing in here should help me relax. I'm so weak. Yesterday was the first time I couldn't drive, first time I couldn't think. Dad took an afternoon off and drove me to Boulder, but I nearly passed out during the last final exam and couldn't finish. Dad had to carry me back to the car. I'm sure Weintraub will find something to criticize him for, some kind of enabling again.

Maybe I should admit to the mental hospital, like Weintraub suggested. I feel drained of everything—no energy, no purpose, no idea of what to do next. And I'm afraid Mom and I will fight again if I stay home this summer.

I'm so tired I couldn't finish my meal log for Peter last night. I really admire him—so enthusiastic and positive after overcoming his eating disorder. And his girlfriend is beautiful—what I want to look like someday. Although he only started with me three days ago, I've been able to follow Peter's diet plan without any problems. Mom's excited about using him, and Dad says Peter has the most rational approach to eating disorders he's encountered. Weintraub is skeptical. She says my problem is not what to eat but whether to eat.

As Dr. Weintraub waited for the knock on her door, she reviewed the notes she'd made for the family meeting.

- *Dad—a bit testy, less trusting since family curse episode. He's supporting J's sick behavior, keeping her chained to anorexia. Force to surface! How?*

- *Mom—staunch ally. Agrees D is enabler¿*
- *Peter—an opportunist¿ Is J following his plan¿*
- *J—weight dangerously low. Too ketotic for effective therapy. Have to identify cause of anorexia soon.*
- *Hospital—insists J needs intense structure of the Therapeutic Community Unit. Physical rehab first. M and D object¿ Probably not. M not comfortable with J home this summer¿ D might go for lower-cost angle. Make sure he knows he pays less if J hospitalized.*
- *Insurance co.—precert required. J's weight should scare them into agreeing.*
- *Duration—eight to ten weeks if we're lucky.*

As usual, Dr. Weintraub directed the seating arrangement in front of her desk so that Jenny sat in the middle, as if to symbolize that she and her illness separated her parents.

The doctor assumed control of the session by quizzing Jenny about her new nutrition program. "Are you following Peter's recommendations¿" the doctor challenged.

"Yes," Jenny replied softly.

"Every meal¿" Dr. Weintraub's skepticism was conveyed in a mocking, unpleasant voice.

"Yes." Jenny's voice was apprehensive.

"And keeping a daily record of what you eat¿"

"Yes."

"Same-day record¿"

"Yes." Jenny paused and then remembered. "But only through lunch yesterday. I didn't record dinner last night."

The doctor had the opening she sought. "You're cheating on the program already," she bellowed.

"That's not fair," Jenny responded. "I was too tired last—"

"No excuses, Jenny," the doctor hammered in, cutting her patient off. "You know you're supposed to keep a daily record. You're feeling guilty because you've done something wrong."

Jenny struggled to formulate a response. She looked first to her father, then to her mother, then back to her father, appealing with a look that said, "Please say something—she's being unfair." Her mother remained impassive, but after some initial hesitation, her father intervened, as if on cue. "You're mistaken, doctor," he said. "You're being unreasonable, and Jenny's showing understandable anger, not guilt. She has no—"

Before he could finish, the doctor shifted her arsenal to him and blazed away. "And why are you so protective?" Her small eyes grew larger and flashed with combativeness.

"Because you're sabotaging Jenny's new nutrition program," he retorted. "Like retracting a lifeline just tossed to a drowning sailor. I won't let you do that."

"You mustn't be protective. She's cheating and should feel guilty."

"And I don't like your laying a guilt trip on her when she has no reason to believe she's done anything wrong."

"Come now, Mr. Hendricks, you know it's important to have accurate records." Dr. Weintraub changed tactics to friendly persuasion.

"Accurate, yes. Not necessarily precise."

"Time delay in keeping records detracts from their accuracy."

"No argument."

"Then, shame on you, Mr. Hendricks. You shouldn't encourage Jenny to break the rules."

"Slow down, doctor. Peter made no rule about timing. I was there. She's merely to keep a daily record. Peter said the quantities don't have to be precise. When to make the record is discretionary, a matter of judgment, not some rule. There's no reason for Jenny to feel guilty."

"It's not a matter of judgment. It's a scientific rule. Doesn't Peter know all anorexics are terrible liars? They should have no discretion."

Jenny winced but was relieved when her father elected not to divert into another argument. "So, you want to hold her to a higher standard than her nutritionist?" he asked.

"There's a scientific rule about records. Of all people, you should know that."

"I don't think there is such a rule."

"You're too stubborn and protective."

"Meaning I always have to agree with you and go along with your attacks on Jenny?"

"Meaning you are supporting Jenny when she is wrong. You're encouraging her bad behavior, and that's unhealthy."

"I'm too tired for this," Jenny muttered, a confused bystander to the conversation.

Her father turned to her and asked, "Did you post the record this morning?"

"No, Dad. I haven't yet," Jenny answered glumly.

He smiled and said gently, "That's waiting too long, Jenny."

"I know," she sighed.

"But I still can't fault you for last night."

"Thanks, Dad. Thanks for that." Jenny looked at her doctor and waited.

"Good compromise," the doctor said. Her eyes continued to telegraph disapproval.

Jenny wondered why her mother had remained silent during the exchange.

Discussion of an eight-to-ten week hospitalization for Jenny proceeded more compatibly. Jenny and her parents agreed when Dr. Weintraub insisted her patient needed more intensive care, a program only a mental hospital could provide. The doctor explained that she would see Jenny daily and that her billing rates carried a 30 percent inpatient premium.

"On top of your 40 percent outpatient increase six months ago?" Jenny's father asked. "That's pretty hefty inflation, isn't it?"

Jenny winced again. Her father rarely discussed the cost of her illness and had never complained, but sometimes she felt guilty at the mounting price tag for her treatment.

The doctor expanded. "Actually, your cost will decrease because insurance will pay for all rather than only a portion of my charges."

"Interesting paradox," he said.

"Why do you charge more in the hospital?" Jenny's mother asked.

"More intense program." Dr. Weintraub responded to Jenny's mother but looked at Jenny's father. Seeing skepticism, she smiled and added, "Maybe you should look at it as a rate break when Jenny goes back to outpatient status."

"And my insurance company goes along with this absurd double disincentive, to you and to me, for Jenny to be treated outside the hospital?" he asked.

"Yes. Most insurance companies do the same."

"So all psychiatrists pad their inpatient rates?"

"I wouldn't call it padding, but most psychiatrists do have higher inpatient rates."

"How can you be objective in recommending hospitalization when you're paid less for outpatient care?"

"We're professionals." Dr. Weintraub's eyes grew larger again.

"Of course," he said cynically.

"Believe me, hospital care management is one of the toughest things I do."

"I believe you just made my point," he said. "What a backward system—an extortionist's delight actually—and we're all trapped in it. No wonder mental health care costs are out of sight."

"Costly, but unfortunately sometimes necessary." As she claimed the last word, the doctor looked at her watch, signaling an approaching end to the session. "We're agreed then, to admit Jenny to Willowcrest?"

"Yes," Jenny's parents responded together in subdued voices.

Jenny's lips opened, but for a moment she remained voiceless. She finally murmured, "Yes," feeling shamed by the word's utterance. She had just acknowledged a condition that terrified her. Her lips trembled as she fought to hold back tears.

"Fine." Dr. Weintraub clasped her hands. "Today's Friday. You'll need tomorrow to pack. I'll schedule Jenny for Sunday admission." Abruptly, she rose from her seat, leaving no opportunity for questions, for easing of the obvious anxiety that had filled the room.

As they left the doctor's office, Jenny clutched at her parents fiercely and turned them so they faced her. Her lips still trembled and her earnest face pleaded for reassurance. "Am I mental?" she asked. "Am I, Mom? Am I, Dad?"

A lost child's anguish spilled out in her simple question. She felt four arms embrace her. "No, Jenny," her mom said gently, not smiling. "You're not crazy."

"No more than the rest of us," her dad added, his smile forced.

Their words were hollow and insufficient, and Jenny's body shook with uncontrollable sobbing.

Looking wan but well groomed, with a bright blue ribbon in her hair, Jenny waited for her parents to catch up as she stared apprehensively at Willowcrest Sanatorium. It looked drab and lifeless. A converted four-story brick and cement apartment building, with no outside grounds, Willowcrest blended inconspicuously with dozens of surrounding buildings identical in design, all vintage 1950s. Nearby sprawled an enormous health care complex, extending for block after block in all directions from its core facility, the University of Colorado Health Science Center.

Jenny felt detached from the moment, as if she acted a stranger's role. She couldn't clue in to the reality of checking into a mental institution. Could this really be happening to her? Overnight bag in one hand, she held the door to Willowcrest open with the other. Her father struggled in with her suitcase and an armload of clothing on hangers; her mother followed, carrying a box with more of her belongings. Both looked haggard. An empty waiting room greeted them as they approached the reception desk.

"Jennifer Hendricks," Jenny identified herself in a tremulous voice. "Dr. Weintraub's patient . . . for admission to the Therapeutic Community Unit."

They stood patiently while the receptionist searched through some papers. "Sorry," she said, "it will take just a minute. No one's in admissions on Sunday."

"Dr. Weintraub preadmitted me on Friday," Jenny said.

More paper shuffling. "I'm sorry, Jennifer, but we have no record of your preadmission. You're not on our schedule for the TC Unit and there's no room assigned."

Jenny struggled to suppress a rising fear. "What should I do?"

The receptionist tried a reassuring smile. "It won't be a problem, Jennifer. We'll admit you now and find the paperwork later. But you may have to share a double room. It will be a few minutes before I can find a nurse to take you up."

The three took seats and stared ahead. Jenny slumped, her resolve wavering. "What happened?" she asked.

No one had an answer. "Nice beginning," her dad muttered.

"Should I call Dr. Weintraub?"

"If it will make you feel better," her mom responded sharply.

Jenny flinched at the hostility in her mother's voice. She fished some coins from her purse and disappeared into a phone booth in the corner. She returned, hands nervously squeezing her purse. "I left a message. There's no one home."

"Typical," her dad said. "Where is the doctor?" he queried the waiting room. "Shouldn't she be here?"

"Of course not," her mom admonished. "It's Sunday. I'm sure she's out with her family."

"Admission to a psych hospital has got to be a traumatic experience for anyone. And we don't even know if Jenny's problem is mental. You'd think Dr. Weintraub would be here, to help Jenny feel more comfortable."

"That's the staff's job."

"They're not off to a good start."

Jenny sat down and wrung her hands. "Why didn't Dr. Weintraub arrange this on Friday? She said she would."

"Maybe she did," her mother said.

"And it's just an administrative foul-up." Her dad offered a small consolation.

Feeling abandoned, Jenny sat on the edge of her chair. Relaxing was impossible. She turned in appeal to her mother. "But Dr. Weintraub promised a private room. Now I have to share with someone who's crazy."

Her mother frowned. "You'll just have to wait and straighten it out tomorrow."

She's scolding me, Jenny thought. *And what for? I haven't done anything wrong.* "I'm really scared, Mom. And ashamed I have to come here. I'm terrified about being in a mental institution for so long . . . two months. It's . . . it's hard for me."

"Don't you ever think how hard it is for the rest of your family?"

Jenny swallowed an angry retort and fought back tears. *Mom's mad at me again, for bringing this on the family and myself. She still thinks I deserve any pain I feel.* She glanced at her father. But he sat glum and impassive, staring straight ahead.

Awkward silence dissipated into action as a nurse finally appeared. Conversation remained stifled. Unresolved fears and angers crowded into an elevator that seemed to take hours to creep up to the fourth floor.

CHAPTER SEVEN

Gain Weight—or Else

May 23. If I ever write a book about anorexia, I'm going to entitle it "All anorexics are similar, but that doesn't mean we're the same!" Most of the staff here treats me with suspicion and mistrust. For example, last night when she weighed me, my nurse asked if I had weights in my pockets. That pissed me off ROYALLY. Maybe some anorexics come here and continue to play their games of deception, but I'm here to work this out. It's my fourth year into this disease and I've gone beyond the initial compulsive crap. I've had it with throwing up, laxatives, the bag of it. I don't intend to do that ever again. I've got to give my body the full chance it deserves.

May 24. I can't believe I'm here. I don't like it, can't stand it, but I'm afraid of what might happen to me if I left and went back home. I cannot comprehend staying until August! I feel the same general terror I felt when I started at Children's. Apparently I'm the only anorexic here. Everyone else has some other mental illness.

This morning I went to my first agenda meeting. Patients are supposed to identify a communication problem they have and then the group discusses it and works on a solution together. The meeting was held in a tiny room where eight out of ten people were smoking. When people smoke around me I get bad headaches and can't think clearly through the pain and smog. The leader of the meeting was a male nurse who makes me uneasy. I can feel his dislike. He is egotistical and lofty, as if he is pretty damn proud of himself being head nurse. Not once have I seen any expression come to his face or eyes. He stares you up and down and talks in a raspy monotone. I can't stand the guy. The agenda meeting didn't work for me because it seemed like a bunch of theatrics. Everybody was nice and polite and controlled. The group leader made sure everyone stayed within the boundaries of the only topic allowed: communications. I was amazed how conveniently he could see similarities in different patient's problems and redirect group comments from one focal person to another through those similarities.

May 25. One of the dumbest things they do here is weigh you every day. Everyone's body weight fluctuates daily, and it is ridiculous to reward or punish me based on my daily weights. Today the scale reported I had gained 3 pounds in two days. It would be physically impossible for me to consume 10,500 calories beyond those needed to simply keep me functioning. Therefore, my gain must be excess water and when my body sheds the excess in a few days, I will be punished.

It's upsetting stepping on the scale every morning and fearing how bad I'll feel if I've gained or the punishment I'll receive if I've lost. Either way I lose.

The practice of daily weighing, reward and punishment, presents a control issue: I feel like I need to control my weight gain and loss. These are old feelings that are very real to me and must be dealt with. Knowing that my weight gain isn't permanent doesn't help. My problem seems to be that since I didn't gain all this weight on purpose, I lost control, which makes me feel disgusted and angry. Misplaced anger maybe, but still anger. So where does this anger belong? Dr. Weintraub says it belongs to my dad. Try as I might, I cannot follow her analysis. Usually when Weintraub comes up with a theory like this, in time I can see its truthfulness. However, I cannot feel, see, or imagine this hypothesis. I have no anger toward my father. If anything, I'm angry at Mom, almost all the time.

May 26. Today is a family meeting. I have a feeling Dr. Weintraub will attack Dad. She says our relationship is abnormally close. Same thing she said about me and Mom two years ago. All I know is I do love him intensely. He is the only one who has loved me for better or for worse. My mother and siblings gave up on me eons ago. However, I suddenly see something. Maybe if he had shown displeasure, anger, and disgust toward my illness I wouldn't have felt so comfortable maintaining it. He's sort of saying, "It's okay by me if you stay sick." I don't think Dad has done this consciously (in fact, I don't know he's done it at all). I know he wants me to gain weight. Also, in his own way, he seems positive about my treatment. Nonetheless, I have hesitated to let him see the extent of my emotional distress. When I try to discuss my emotional problems with him, he shakes his head, laughs a little, and says that anyone in my physical condition would feel depressed, inadequate, etc. Granted, my physical condition impacts gravely my havoc-filled emotions; but what he doesn't seem to accept is that it was my emotions that brought me to this degenerate state, not vice versa.

I don't want this to sound as though I'm agreeing with Dr. Weintraub's hypothesis, or even that I think the above is significant. For all I know, if Dad had said, "I won't tolerate your illness," I might have gone and thrown myself off a cliff.

May 27. Yesterday's family meeting was more like a Weintraub sparring with Dad meeting, with Mom and me as spectators.

As if she had achieved an exciting breakthrough, the good doctor said, "You know Jenny has an Oedipus complex with you." Although I had expected it, her announcement really startled Dad. He got that irritated expression where he screws up the corners of his mouth sorta in disgust. "A wh . . . what?" he said.

"Oedipus complex. You're familiar with the term?"

"Yes. But Jenny with me? You're serious?" Dad looked at me, and I had to nod my head up and down in agreement, because Weintraub has been so convincingly insistent that my relationship with him isn't normal. He got a hurt look in his eyes, which made me feel bad for having to agree with the doctor, and then he looked at Mom. "I've thought so, too," she said.

"Whew, that's heavy," he said. "How do you know?"

"From yesterday," Weintraub answered, looking smug. "When you came to see her, I watched from behind as the two of you walked down the street."

"You could tell from our backs, our butts?"

"No. I could tell by the way she looked up at you."

Dad got that irritated look again. "Sounds like a snap judgment. Are you sure?"

"Yes." Weintraub actually smiled, as if in personal triumph. I felt sorry for Dad. He looked sorta . . . well . . . confused, and he's not easily confused. "Is it serious?" he asked. "I mean, she wants to kill her mother and marry me?"

From that point they both started talking about me like I wasn't there. "She's not pathological about it," Weintraub said. "But it is serious. It's part of the unhealthy relationship the two of you have, the umbilical cord that still connects you to her."

Although Dad muttered a passive "I see," I could tell he wasn't convinced.

Weintraub said, "She feeds unhealthily on your sympathy and reassurance. Then she gets upset and loses weight when she doesn't receive that support from you."

"Is there something I can do about it?"

"Yes. Cut the umbilical cord. Quit feeding her."

"And that will end her Oedipus feelings?"

"Yes."

"I'm sorry," Dad said. "But I don't get the Oedipus connection. I didn't think the queen encouraged her son." I wasn't sure I got the connection, either. Even Weintraub looked a little confused. Like she does when I get nailed, Mom seemed to enjoy watching Dad squirm. "Shouldn't I give Jenny sympathy and reassurance?" he asked.

"Not when it reinforces her bad behavior, her illness."

"Sounds like a quit-beating-your-wife type of issue," Dad grumbled. "I didn't think I was reinforcing bad behavior."

"You are, and it must stop."

"And what if you are wrong? It's obvious from your own premise and your patient's present condition that Jenny has been getting damn little from me. If I cut back to zero, is she more likely to die? Maybe she needs more feeding—let's call it love and understanding. Isn't there a better chance that might help bring her back?"

"No. Jenny can be cured only when her umbilical cord to you is severed."

Dad mumbled something about "emotional blackmail" and then said, "So, what should I do? You obviously have no confidence in my judgment or my ability to react properly in a given circumstance with my daughter.

Should I never give Jenny any sympathy or reassurance without checking with you first to make sure I'm not supporting bad behavior?"

"Mr. Hendricks, your obvious bad attitude is also part of the problem. You have to quit being sympathetic with Jenny's negative feelings about her treatment."

"Even when her feelings are justified?"

"That's not for you to judge."

"Sorry. I've been trying not to interfere with or criticize your treatment. How is it you're so sure I'm doing these things you want me to stop? You're rarely a party to conversations between Jenny and me."

"I've seen enough of your interactions. I can tell."

"Like you can watch Jenny and me walking for a minute or two and know she has an Oedipus complex?"

"Yes."

"Amazing insight."

"It's like Helen Keller and her family. Are you familiar with her story?"

Dad looked puzzled. "Yes, but Helen Keller wasn't anorexic. I don't follow the connection to Jenny." He looked at me again and this time I shook my head side to side. Weintraub's Helen Keller analogy was something I hadn't heard before, and it didn't make sense to me either. When Dad looked at Mom, Mom smiled and nodded her head up and down in agreement.

"Behavior problems," Weintraub explained. "Helen Keller was a terrible spoiled brat, unmanageable and nonfunctional . . . until her family quit coddling her, quit pitying her."

"You think Jenny's a terrible spoiled brat?"

"Yes."

That was the second time Weintraub had condemned me in front of my parents. I felt wounded and ashamed but didn't say anything. I knew Mom wouldn't defend me, and I hoped Dad wouldn't come to my defense and make matters worse. He didn't. He just asked, "And you think her family is coddling and pitying her?"

"No. Just you. And it has to stop for Jenny to get well."

"I don't like my support being characterized as coddling or pity, and—"

"Believe me, it is, whether you like it or not."

"Your analogy still doesn't seem valid. Helen Keller's whole family coddled her, and apparently you've concluded I'm the only coddler in Jenny's family."

"Although you are the only one, Jenny will hang on to her illness as long as you continue to validate it."

"So you think I should join the let's-beat-up-on-Jenny gang? Piling on, I think it's called."

"If you must put it that way."

"I have trouble keeping up with you, you take such giant steps. You say love and understanding equals coddling equals validating her illness?"

"Yes. The way you practice it. You're too permissive. Do you realize Jenny's progress with me is zero?"

"At last you said something I agree with."

Weintraub's eyes were really blazing. "Jenny cheats, and her parents won't confront her. Even the hospital staff won't confront her. I'm the only one who will."

"Sounds like I have company in the doghouse. What should we all confront her about? How is she—"

Weintraub got red in the face then and sorta lost it. "It's the way the two of you conspire," she screeched. "You and Jenny want to run away together. I know it. You can't fool me. Neither one of you listens to anything I say, and all you do after our sessions is challenge my conclusions. I know the two of you are out to get rid of me. You and Jenny want others to do all the work for you, and we can't be effective until you quit feeding her illness."

I was stunned by Weintraub's attack, more embarrassed than angry. Even Mom looked shocked. I heard Dad mutter the word paranoid. He looked angry, and I was afraid he might validate part of Weintraub's suspicion and fire her on the spot, even though she's wrong about us conspiring and wanting to get rid of her. But for some reason Dad quit being argumentative and said, sounding flustered, "Perhaps you could help me by going back over some of my recent interactions with Jenny and explain what I did wrong and what I should do differently."

Weintraub looked at her watch and said, "Sorry, time's up." She ended the session just like that. Dad said he'd think about the doctor's comments, go back and analyze how he'd been reacting to me. He said he'd try to be more careful in the future. I hope that doesn't mean he'll quit coming to see me. I wonder if we'll talk more about this in the next family session. Often there's no continuity at all from one session to the next. I don't think the doctor takes good notes.

May 28. *Diane came last night. It was great to see her. She is one very special, intelligent person. She's gonna help me pick out a new wardrobe when I regain my weight. I hope someday I can look as grown up as she does.*

After spending time with a friend who genuinely cares, it's hard to accept the artificial caring here—or rather, "controlled" caring as I call it. I understand the nurses have paperwork and other duties that pressure them and keep them from being able to sit with every patient who needs to talk. However, nothing is more irritating than to be in the middle of something really important to you and be interrupted and told, "I'm sorry, I can't talk now. Would you like to schedule a time to discuss it this evening?"

Another disgusting thing is that your every move, every word, is reported to your doctor. Dr. Weintraub says it's for my benefit, but, damn, I might as well be talking to a tape recorder. It pisses me off when Weintraub comes in and reads nurses' reports on me aloud. Disgusting. How can you feel at ease talking to someone if all you say flows in the ears and out the pen! I am much more careful of what I say now, although I refuse to be untruthful or allow myself to hide. I know I must verbalize even if it lands me in trouble with Weintraub. I also read on my chart yesterday that my room is to be checked daily for laxatives and signs of vomiting. That adds to my uneasiness. It feels like they are crawling under my skin.

Today we discussed my fixation on my parents, friends, etc. Dr. Weintraub said that I cling to them through my illness. I fear if I am well they won't be interested in me or care for me. What she stresses is that growing up and letting go doesn't mean having to say goodbye, and when it does, it will feel okay to say goodbye. I guess I feel that when I am on my own my family will be so glad to be rid of me that it will be "goodbye for-ever," and that scares me.

May 29. Today I lost half a pound, no big deal, unless, of course, you are anorexic in which case you've done something wrong. The excess water I've been carrying around finally realized it wasn't needed and made its exit. Peter said this would happen; yet the staff insists I purposely lost weight to express anger because my family went away for the weekend.

At dinner this evening I wanted to throw my food, binge and barf, or not eat at all. I felt disgustingly angry. This anger appeared suddenly and departed in just one minute. It scares me when I am overcome by these emotions and can't pinpoint what causes me to push the panic button. It's like some controlling force grabs me and throws me off course until Dr. Weintraub or I can slap me back into a better frame of mind.

May 30. Today I lost more than a pound and Weintraub is gonna nail me. They're sure I'm doing something purposefully to make myself lose. I'm not, I'm just nervous. I can't sleep and I'm restless. I was upset about Dr. Weintraub's threat of "if I did worse this weekend"; that alone was enough to keep me jumpy the past two days.

Well, I have resolved to tell Weintraub the brutal truth. I'm sure it will land me in a pile, but I am going to tell her I may not have eaten all I should have. Yes I was angry, yes I was upset, and yes I'm scared to death.

I was truthful and she was wonderful. She said she is excited to give this (diet plan) with Peter a try, but I've got to pull my weight (ha-ha, what a pun) and make sure I keep gaining. She said it is impossible to commu-nicate when I am this low and she wants me to gain to 75 pounds, she doesn't care how. If we don't do it with Peter's plan, she says she'll be forced to go full-fledged behavior modification.

May 31. Well, I did it. I weighed 69½ this morning, a 3-pound gain in one day. Now all I feel is anger.

Why does it unnerve me so to have a change in my weight? Why is it so damn important to stay skinny? I say I want to be a doctor, success-ful, beautiful, smart, etc., yet why do I continue to be so obsessed that I will never realize those goals? Dr. Weintraub says it is to maintain my rela-tionship with her, my family, and especially my dad. I'm painfully aware that

I couldn't deal with life without them, and so I force their interest in me by staying sick.

A psychologist who works for Dr. Weintraub just called to tell me he's giving me a test this week. He was surprised the doctor hadn't told me about it. Also Mom is coming tomorrow to give the guy a family summary. No one explained that to me either.

The kitchen is screwing up. I'm supposed to have wheat bread, but they keep sending white. I've had chicken for lunch three days in a row and fish for dinner two nights in a row. They don't balance food exchanges either. They send me a whole head of broccoli and only an ounce of protein. They drown the fish and potatoes in butter, which they neglect to figure into the day's plan. Today I haven't had any snacks and for lunch I got white bread, cauliflower, an ounce of cottage cheese, mayonnaise, and mustard. What the hell am I gonna do with the mayo and mustard? Spread it on bread I'm not supposed to eat in the first place?

I'm upset that everyone thinks I'm lying. I'm lying that my pee is truly my pee, I'm lying that I haven't touched a laxative or vomited since I've been here, I'm lying that I'm following Peter's diet. Dammit, I haven't lied once about any of those things! No one believes.

June 1. *This morning I worked on a letter urging P.M. Magazine, 20/20, or 60 Minutes to do a story on Peter. While I was writing, a nurse came in and commented that I sure was busy. So I read the letter to her to get her opinion. She didn't say anything, not a word. In here silence means disapproval, and I can just see it written in my chart, "Jenny has outrageous and unreasonable hopes of getting public recognition." But it's not that way at all. I don't expect anything to materialize out of this, but it doesn't hurt to try, and it damn well could help. Maybe I can help Peter get the publicity he deserves. He's got such a good idea and a great attitude and approach to go with it. Trying to help him help others like me is better than doing nothing.*

Weintraub told me to beware of clinging to Peter.

June 2. *Dad found an article in the newspaper about hormonal deficiencies in anorexics. I wonder if the hormone shots the doctor at the University of Colorado gave me to induce my period were responsible for my sudden plunge into self-starvation and depression again. If I try to* pinpoint when I started going bonkers it was definitely around that time. My compulsive feelings were present before the shots; however, they became uncontrollable and more irrational after them. Maybe they knocked me down so far that by the time they wore off I couldn't climb back up. Hormones may have more to do with my problems than Dr. Weintraub gives them credit. I've wondered how much of my mental problem is mental and how much a physiological result of four years of malnourishment. I suspect it's about half-and-half. Weintraub says it's all mental.

June 3. Yesterday's family session was hard but good. Dr. Weintraub asked my dad if he could ever say to me that he had lived with my mother longer and if push came to shove I would have to leave. (Something he once told David, I guess when David was causing a strain on the marriage.) Well, Dad said he couldn't, and I admitted if he ever told me that, I would feel as if someone dropped the bottom off my world. Then he told Weintraub her analogy wasn't valid because I wasn't causing a strain on the marriage. Afterward I cried and felt guilty.

Today Weintraub and I explored my self-pity and desire for others to pity me. It is despicable but true. That I want people's pity and really thrive on it wasn't clear to me until now.

Our community meetings and agenda groups are all so protected that everyone avoids confrontation and no one risks saying something important. Nothing is ever resolved. Mostly what I get from them is boredom. I thought the purpose for working in groups was to learn how to deal with others' judgments and differences. Here that stuff is off limits. Patients aren't allowed to discuss what's really bothering them, why they are here. Staff says only psychiatrists can work with patient feelings. Problem is psychiatrists generally aren't available when we need them and most sessions with them are short. Then they send bills for triple the time they spend with us. Dad says that's because insurance won't pay for case management time. We get more professional avoidance than professional help. I think this is contradictory to the purpose of coming to a mental hospital. Other patients feel the same.

A common problem here is the deep depression most of us feel. Although I have some ideas about how to help myself, most patients are at a loss *about what to do with themselves. They don't communicate. Often drugged, they just sit around in stupors.*

Today I took the Rorschach inkblot test. It was the pits. You go through a set of ten inkblots, seven black and white, three in color. You turn the picture any direction and say what you see. Then you explain where you saw what you saw and why that part of the blot made you think what you saw. It was a real effort for me to see anything in the blots. I wanted to say on a couple of them, "Dammit, all I see is a fucking inkblot, you fool."

Last night another patient and I had a long talk. She has the same relationship with her parents that I do. It was comforting to know that someone who isn't anorexic can feel superclose to her father and alienated from her mother, by her own fault as a child.

June 4. I knew Willowcrest wouldn't be fun, but it's part of my character, maybe my problem, to make tough experiences enjoyable. Right now I hate Willowcrest. However, I have broken my binge/purge cycles—something I couldn't do at home. Otherwise, I'm still the same mental mess.

Today I drew a horse for the first time in years. I picked a foal from an old Quarter Horse Journal. He is scratching his face with a hind leg, not an easy position to draw. I am very pleased with how realistic it looks. It's given me an amazing feeling of accomplishment all day. The most positive treatment I've had in two weeks I prescribed and executed on my own.

I really miss Mom today. I'd love to go out and spend some time alone with her, get our relationship back on its feet. She is a wonderful lady and it's time I start acknowledging that, start emphasizing her good qualities rather than her shortcomings. Same with people in general.

June 5. Mom, Janis, and Brian came over after church. I'm hurt because they know I have full privileges and a pass, but they didn't offer to do anything with me. It makes me feel rejected. I'm sure they felt revulsion and wanted to get away from me. I wanted to scream, "Don't you realize I'm not locked in here. Everyone else leaves and spends the day with their families, yet you come and go and brush me off as if I were a fly. My fault or not, I feel DISCOUNTED!" But if I told my family how I felt, Weintraub would come down on me like a ton of bricks.

June 6. *Right now Dr. Weintraub is holding a staff meeting about me. As usual I'm excluded, even though Willowcrest's literature says patients participate. I'm afraid something unpleasant will be decided and enforced without my having any say in the matter.*

I just got the meeting results. The head nurse explained it in a nasty, vengeful way. No privileges anymore. I thought I wasn't here to be punished. Also, I have to eat with a nurse and after I eat I have to be around people for thirty minutes. No problem, except it implies that I've been doing something bad, which I haven't. They say they want to make eating more pleasurable for me, but they're lying. Why don't they tell me the truth?—that they're policing me. I feel so deceived by Weintraub. She promised me getting well would be a good experience.

At dinner a nurse sat with me and criticized my eating. Afterward, we walked and I told her it was ridiculous and juvenile to make me sit for half an hour when throwing up isn't my problem anymore. She explained that in the future I might want to and this will help me then. Her explanation is also ridiculous. Conditioning me to a monitoring program that disregards my feelings isn't going to help me deal with anorexic or bulimic feelings I might have later when no one is looking over my shoulder.

The best thing that happened today is that David called. I don't think I've ever been as honest and at ease talking to him. He invited me to go over to his apartment, have dinner, and watch HBO with him some night soon. He made me feel a lot better about myself.

I'm going to make this a positive experience no matter what. If I can't be outside running around then I'll be in here writing. If I can't go to the park and read, I'll go to the patio and read. I'll take this time to relax and learn and grow. I'll be like that man who was in solitary confinement for forty years and became a renowned expert on birds. I'll put extra energy into positive things for me. Somehow I'll learn to tolerate and get something out of those disgustingly boring groups—that'll be hardest of all.

June 7. *The doctor ordered two half-hour, supervised walks a day, but the nurses are always too busy. They need to write a chart, they need to take vitals, they need to go to dinner.*

In the community meeting, Karen brought up her sexual abuse as a child. Immediately the staff cut her off and proclaimed, "We only deal with the here and now." They squelched her topic despite the fact that the whole community was quite ready and willing to discuss it with her.

I'm angry about losing privileges yesterday. I don't understand what's going on and I wonder, what's next? It bugs me that Mom got a warped sense of satisfaction from seeing me punished. That dynamic constantly aggravates me. She loves it when I get nailed. It's like punishing me is something she would like to do herself, but that would be un-Christian, so she rejoices when someone else does it for her. I think her delight stems from her feeling that she has been avenged. Mom doesn't seem to comprehend my pain. It's like as long as I deserve my pain and it doesn't happen to her, why should she be sympathetic?

June 8. None of the nurses have time to take me for a walk this morning, and I know from my experience last night it's going to take a lot of organizing on my part to get a walk this evening. Shifts change at 4:00 and the new shift immediately does vitals, starts charting, and does rounds. Then it is dinnertime. Then it is group time. Then, don't look now but there are thunderclouds coming in. And after the rain: it's dark now, Jenny, no walks allowed in the dark. Funny how they follow the doctor's orders to a "T" when it comes to my sitting in their sight for a half hour after meals; but they completely disregard doctor's orders that I walk for half an hour.

Here is the law. If Jenny gains, she gets full privileges. If Jenny doesn't gain, she is confined to the unit with no privileges.

June 9. Another family meeting. This morning we talked about my feelings surrounding my relationship with Dad in four stages of my life: pre horses, Dickens, Miss Roan, post horses. I felt loved in the first stage, dismissal in the second and third (I think he had less of a negative attitude toward my riding when I first started), and loved again in the fourth. Dr. Weintraub said my illness may have been designed to punish him, and in so doing, I gained more attention and love from him—as he admitted today. It is a vicious thing, then, that I do with this disease. She says I punish him by deteriorating physically (again verified by him: "it breaks my heart to hug you"), but then I gain his love and attention because he identifies so well with my emotional struggle. She says I compromise my views to agree with his as a way of protecting him.

This afternoon was a family interview with the psychologist. It didn't feel like a family interview, more like a Jenny interview with the family as spectators. He confused me and backed me into corners. He said if I was so smart and understood my illness so well, why didn't I cure myself. The truth is, I don't know why I can't. Nothing has ever been resolved about my disease. He made me realize I'm no closer to understanding the whys of my self-starvation than I was when I entered analysis four years ago. Despite all I've learned about myself and about anorexia, I still don't understand why I have this fucking impulse and how I'm supposed to lose it.

June 11. Last night I went home for the first time. Dad came to get me around 7:30 and I stayed until 10:15. I worried that I would want it to be too perfect, that I would want lots of attention and expect my family to entertain me. I was afraid I would end up depressed and disappointed. Well, nothing upsetting happened. I got no special attention and that was okay. I looked at our new sunroom, talked with Ma and Pa awhile, watered my plants, and watched Dallas. When that lonely, self-pitying, abandoned mood snuck up on me, I went upstairs to talk to Janis. We painted our nails and then walked down to Kings to get some Lubriderm lotion and gum. Then I came back, ate my snack, and took a walk with Dad. Except for that brief period prior to seeking out Janis, I didn't feel "out of things" at all. I was relaxed and happy in my own home for the first time in a long time. Don't get me wrong, I haven't progressed far enough that I could pull that off every time, but each step forward is a positive gain on my road to recovery.

June 12. I gained a pound from yesterday and GOD, I'm terrified. I was worried my weight was down so I drank four glasses of water this morning. Now I'm confused as to what is real weight and what is water weight. Tomorrow I'm not water loading, even though I'll be paranoid about being confined all day. I suppose this conflict is necessary in order for me to get well. For some reason, today I feel grosser and guiltier than I have yet. I'm so afraid, so out of control. I feel grotesque and bloated. HELP, how do I deal with this FAT feeling? Mommy, I'm scared.

June 13. I lost a pound; that means I sit here all day. Even though I was upset yesterday I still ate everything on my diet, just as I have the past six days. Nonetheless, I get punished. Damn this system. I lose no matter what I do. If I gain, I feel like shit, if I don't gain I feel like shit. It's obvious they understand this and are trying to make me feel shittier when I don't gain.

June 15. My feelings only get worse as my weight goes up. Why does Dr. Weintraub have to go on vacation right now? She is the only one I've ever trusted enough to believe it when she says, "Hush, Jenny, it's not even real. Quit looking at the symptoms and tell me something about the problems." I admire her probably more than anyone in the world.

June 17. Tonight I had dinner with Peter's girlfriend. Then we went over to Peter's and bugged him and made him watch The Sound of Music. "Five times I've seen this already," he said. "Only once by choice." He gave me a Shamitoffs 100 percent natural coconut and chocolate bar. It was supergood, but afterward I felt that old compulsion for more, more, more. Luckily I was with people who care about me, so that feeling passed. As I ate that bar I anticipated the disgust I would feel if my weight goes up tomorrow. That is such a pissy way to start a day; I begin preparing for the emotional shock of weight gain hours before I step on the scale.

My feelings for Peter and his extended family are similar to my feelings for the family who boarded Little Dickens. Both families had confidence in my ability to do well, to win. Both were taken with the "well" Jenny's sense of humor, her drive and determination. I've looked to both for feeling worthy. Not good, Jenny. I've got to find that in myself—somewhere. I can't go on depending on others to make me feel okay. The only person I've got with me for life is me.

June 18. My grandfather, Daddad, is in the hospital with an old prostate cancer problem they discovered is spreading again. They think he's dying. Mom will talk to Meme tomorrow and then she'll call and let me know what's going on. I never thought about him dying, at least not for a long long long time; he always has seemed so strong. What will Meme do without him?

June 19. I have an antsy caged animal feeling. Like I'm stuck and can't go forward and can't go back. I've been here four weeks and I'm still the same mess. If I went home now, all the work I've done would go right down the drain. I've gained some weight, but the feelings that made me lose it in the first place are still there, and I have no idea how to make them go away.

I'm mad at Weintraub. How am I going to deal with her absence? I see no hope for progress, other than weight gain. I also feel abandoned by Dad, but I'm unsure if I'm mad at him. At first I was, when he told me he was going to Idaho to fish with my uncle, but then I looked into his blue eyes and couldn't be angry. He was just like a child, so excited about his trip. He told me now was my chance to prove I could fly. Now that makes me mad. How does he know I can fly? Take away all my supports and then assume I can do it on my own?

June 21. Mom wants me to come home; I think I will. She also wants me to spend the night; I think I won't.

June 22. Daddad died last night. It was the weirdest thing. All day I felt tired and out of it. At home yesterday afternoon, I was moody and cold to everyone. When I got back here for dinner, I felt guilty about how I acted at home and frustrated because I couldn't pinpoint why I behaved that way. During the community meeting I had the worst sense of fear and loneliness since my first night in the hospital. It was like I'd been abandoned all over again, but by whom? Mom called at eight and said Daddad had died near seven, which was exactly when I was most upset. I'm not saying I have mental telepathy, but why else did I feel so bad yesterday?

June 23. I'm mad. Somehow I got myself so fucked up that I have to spend my whole summer in a psychiatric institution. My life is so up in smoke that I can't be around to comfort my family when they need it, or have a good time as occasion affords it. My family is on the outside, free to go and come as they please, lead normal lives, but I'm stuck here like a black goat in a cage. It doesn't matter that they played a role in this illness. I'm the one who must work through it. I know that I got what I deserved, but Lord, life really goes on without me. That's it, the problem is I don't ever seem to go on. Everyone changes but me. I hang on so tight, and when I start to slip I try desperately to get back the ground I've lost. It's like I want to go back to the protective shell of childhood; I feel I have an identity there. Yet there is no way my family will have me back, so then what do I do with myself? I have nowhere to go. It's so confusing.

June 24. It's funny how I don't feel complete until I ride my bike. I can't relax without it. Exercise is my compulsion. What I've got to do is this: If I exercise lots, I should eat enough to compensate. I can do that.

Mom and Dad are leaving tomorrow to go to Florida to help Meme. Dad cut his vacation short and came home; seems like he never gets to relax. I'm upset because that's one more week without him and Mom. I'm feeling left out.

June 25. I weigh 76½ pounds and I feel awful. I'm gaining weight and I don't know how to deal with it. It makes me feel like screaming, yelling, tearing my hair out, and crying. I am so disgusted with myself. What happens when I get to my "ideal" weight? What do I do then?

June 26. I'm sick of depressed people and I'm especially sick of trying to communicate with old, deaf, depressed people. It's like talking to a wall that blinks and licks its chops every once in a while. Staff says it's my fault for not communicating, but dammit they are SO OUT OF IT. Debra sleeps day and night; her doctor has her on so many drugs she barely functions. Then there is Janet, a hypochondriac who is sure everything wrong with her is physical and is driving us all crazy with her constant whining and self-pity. Let me not forget Ted, a new patient who is about as open as a bolted door. He never talks or comes to meetings.

At least I can talk to Kathy. We had a good conversation about whom we get well for. I seem unable to do it for myself. Kathy says she has decided not to do it for anyone but herself. She is twenty-two, used to be a model, and is gorgeous—that's her good qualities. She derives massive pleasure from being sick and sampling every form of mental illness. She makes sure everyone knows she's been here nine months and has tried to commit suicide three or four or five times, who knows the latest count. She wears a suicide attempt like a badge of courage.

June 27. I was so negative yesterday I forgot to mention Harry. He is one patient I really like. I met him and right away I knew we were compatible. He speaks with his eyes. To me that's a sign of sincerity. Harry was very depressed and two weeks ago tried to commit suicide. Unlike Kathy, he's ashamed of his attempt. Since then he's made remarkable progress. I think his success is due to his truthfulness and his willingness to avail himself of every opportunity for self-improvement. Of all the patients here, and some of the staff, I consider him the sanest.

I'm worried about our family ranch vacation. Will I go and then have to come back here? (I couldn't stand that.) Will I be pronounced well enough to leave here permanently? (I'll be terrified to put myself to such an advanced test.) Will I stay here and not go? (I'll be lonely and feel left out.) Staff suggested I make columns and write the pros and cons for each situation. I'll start that today.

June 28. This morning I went outside to ride my bike and found a dying baby bird. He looked like he had been born malformed and his mother had pushed him out of the nest. He was lying on the sidewalk with his insides oozing out of a huge hole in his stomach, obviously in a great deal of pain, probably more dead than alive. Once in a while he would open his beak and push his little limbs out from his body as if attempting to push away the pain. Well, that totally undid me. The poor thing was in agony and nobody could help him. I told one of the nurses, and she had maintenance do something—God only knows what. I cried a good cry. Lord, I felt impotent. Why can we fly to the moon, sail across oceans, understand volcanoes, hurricanes, etc., but when it comes to helping a fellow creature out of pain we are basically ineffectual. Maybe that's why it upset me so very much. This society never helps or touches each other—WE DON'T KNOW HOW TO. When it comes to the very essential in life, the creatures of God, we don't know how to let ourselves love or help each other. Instead, we put all our energy into other matters, which by comparison seem so very trivial.

CHAPTER EIGHT
Therapeutic Relief?

July 1. I tried to tell Weintraub how frustrated I am. The problem is she doesn't know any better than I do how I got here or how I'm gonna get out. I've gotten nowhere. What I have to show for six weeks of work is 8 new pounds and nothing else. I feel worse now than I have ever.

I told Dr. Weintraub about feeling ignored by Dad when I'm talking about positive things. She kept pressing me to say that I think Dad has an investment in my being ill. Well, to be honest, I don't know. I can see a difference in the way he responds to me when I am doing "good" vs. "bad." Maybe in order to regain the special recognition I received from him in childhood I decided to play sick. This gets me to another point. I'm still not convinced my problem is with Dad. Do I really see questionable things in our relationship or do I contrive them because Dr. Weintraub insists there are abnormal encounters between him and me? I don't know why she's so certain. She's even persuaded the staff. I could come up with as many facts that might trace the blame to Mom or my horse trainer even.

Our Montana ranch vacation is looming on the horizon, and I've been cleared to go. But I don't know what I'm gonna do. Weintraub just returned from two weeks there, and I feel violated, like she stole something precious from me, from my whole family. What right did she have to go there, to OUR special place! She told me the ranch owners think I am a rotten, weepy, spoiled kid. What right did she have to talk to them about me, use them to validate her judgments?

July 2. I'm still the only anorexic on the TC Unit, but that's about to change. Paula, who's spent sixteen months on the third floor locked ward, will transfer here to be in a less restricted environment before she's released.

When she saw me today she stared at me, as usual. I don't like her staring at me all the time. She has no compunction. She may as well take out her tape measure and measure me, so intensely does she size me up. Also, Kathy has seen Paula bingeing in the cafeteria several times. I'm not sure I'll be able to deal with a manipulative, secret, bitchy anorexic. I don't want to feel compared to her in any way. I don't need to be around someone with the same obsessions I have. The further away I can get from those unrealistic attitudes, the better chance I'll have to get well.

When I mentioned my feelings about Paula to Dr. Weintraub, she said unless others facilitate my needs, spoil me, or help build my ego, I get angry and jealous and feel betrayed by them. She scolded me for not being able to see past my fear that Paula might steal my place in the limelight, for not realizing I should be happy for her, happy that she's progressed to a less controlled unit.

July 3. I feel like throwing in the towel. I can't deal with all the crap. I tried to explain to Mom how depressed and confused I'm feeling, but I couldn't seem to talk to her rationally. At one point I got hysterical and couldn't stop crying. I can't explain what a hell I'm in now, and she can't grasp any fragment of what I'm saying. This makes her mad 'cause she can't help me, and it makes me mad 'cause I can't tell her how to.

July 4. Happy Fourth! Paula transferred yesterday and we had a good talk. She's not convinced anorexia is bad. I think she still considers it a fun game to play. She told me she can remember the exact day she sat down and made a decision to starve herself. "I was watching a television special on anorexia," she said, "and I thought it would be an exciting thing to do."

Well, the good doctor really socked it to me today. She told me I can't go back to Carleton until I return to the University of Colorado for a semester. She also scolded me for my stunned reaction to her decision. She says when I feel backed into a corner, angry, and unable to cope, I put on what she terms a "Yoda" face and cry. She says my Yoda reaction (1) makes the confronter feel guilty, (2) shuts off further communication, and (3) keeps me happy in my selfish illusion.

July 6. I weigh 79½ pounds and I am FREAKING OUT. Everybody has forced me to gain weight and all I'm getting out of it is a lot of shitty feelings. I feel gross, terrified, and fat. I've kept my end of the bargain. I've gained all their weight, but no one is helping me feel any better. Ironic that gaining weight keeps me alive but makes me want to be dead.

I'm jealous of Paula because her doctor hasn't forced her into a big weight gain. Paula is supposedly working on everything I'm working on yet she gets to stay as skinny as she pleases without punishment. She food-binged the past two nights without any interference. I don't know if she throws it up, but I know I could never digest what she eats in one sitting.

Weintraub waltzes in and out of my life pulling strings that never seem to be attached to anything or going anywhere. All she does is make me hurt.

We've had only three family sessions, and Dad still doesn't see that he might have a role in this. He says some of Weintraub's conclusions aren't rational, just blind stabs in the dark. Nancy is even more critical than Dad. After coming to a session, Nancy said, "She's rude and she's a tyrant, Jenny. So controlling. I don't see how you can stand her." Some days I can't.

July 10. I knew I couldn't always have a private room, and now I'm gonna get an anorexic roommate—Jane—about my age. I'm not sure how I feel about it. Paula and I get along pretty well, so maybe I can be friends with Jane without feeling threatened.

July 11. All through high school I couldn't see that no matter how earnest my resolve never to be bratty to Mom again—no matter how good, kind, and helpful I was to her—it could not negate the damage I did to our relationship each time I threw up, starved myself, and in general refused to love and take care of the body she gave me.

July 12. Dr. Weintraub says I have the attitude that the world owes me homage because I am intelligent and special. She says I owe the world. I need to help people. I need to be a good Christian. I need to be selfless like Ghandi, not selfish like I am now.

July 14. Yesterday Dr. Weintraub revealed how my anorexia started. She said most adolescents go through a period of being picky about their food.

Usually they will get away with it for a while and then, if it is carried to extremes, their parents nail them and they stop.

When my eating habits became extreme, Dad was off in his own world and Mom was fanatically observing her Lenten denials. I utilized Lent as an excuse not to eat and although Mom may have realized what I was doing was unhealthy, she condoned it because it showed my dedication to the church. I think a lot of the anger I have toward Mom and her fanaticism is because she placed her church above my health even when my life was slowly being threatened. It was like I was saying: Look at me, I can be real bad, I'm doing something terrible—what do you think of that?—and I was expecting them to say, "Cut it out." Instead, I got free rein to be as much of a shit as I wanted, which led me to greater extremes to see how long it would take them to say, "Enough." They never said "Enough" until I almost died this year.

Dr. Weintraub suggested Dad's reaction to anorexia would not have been so passive and permissive had it been David pulling the strings. It's my opinion that if David had become anorexic when he was my age, Dad simply would not have allowed it. I'm less sure that Dad would have so adamantly opposed it had David gotten sick at the time I did. Dad was too inside himself and withdrawn to really care about what went on with any of us during those years. Although initially there was no doubt in my mind that had I been a boy, anorexia would not have been allowed, now I am semiconvinced that it would have because Dad was so uninvolved.

July 15. Jane was into her food all night long. She has these little bags of food stored somewhere, like a squirrel, and they make loud crinkling sounds every time she opens one.

July 16. Jane is human only after she's thrown a fit and gotten a lot of attention for it.

July 17. Jane is still throwing up; sometimes I think she is doing it in our room.

July 18. Dr. Weintraub and I talked about how I handle anger at others. She says I throw my anger at others, but maintain they're angry with me and then, because they started it, I feel justified when I fly off the handle. She says I never give in to authority. I always want to fight. I wanna be in control and insist I know more than even an expert.

July 21. Staff still won't let me participate in my treatment plan.

July 22. My depression is unbearable right now.

July 24. To preserve my privileges, I've water-loaded so much before they weigh me that I lost track of my real weight eons ago.

July 25. Yesterday I felt like bingeing worse than ever. Today I found a note on my dresser that Jane is asking for a new roommate. She didn't even talk to me about it. I'm sure it's about our confrontations. I'd asked Stan, the ward nurse, what could be done about Jane throwing up in our bathroom. He urged me to confront Jane, so I did last night. What worries me is that Weintraub is going to accuse me of making it unbearable for Jane to room with me.

Well, I was right. Even though she knew none of the facts, Weintraub accused me of burdening Jane with my jealousy. She assumed I was at fault. Stan was there and the coward didn't say anything—Weintraub had him too intimidated. He wouldn't acknowledge that my confrontation with Jane was prompted by his advice, nor did he tell Weintraub the issue with Jane was her throwing up in our room. He just sat there and let me get nailed.

July 26. This morning Jane followed me down the hall, looking like a rabid dog. Her eyes were filled with hate. Finally I said, "What are you going to do, Jane, hurt me?" She said, "No, I'm just going to follow you around and make you uncomfortable." So I decided to ignore her. I went to our room and she followed me in and started a harangue. Here are some of the things she said: "You are a spoiled rotten brat. I hate you and it's no goddam wonder your family hates you. I hope they never forgive you, because I never will. You've ruined my whole fucking life, you goddammed bitch. I hope you suffer and feel twice the pain I'm feeling now because of you. You are the first person I trusted since eighth grade and you betrayed me. You are responsible for ruining my whole life—I hope you know that." I guess she's still a little upset I told Stan she was throwing up. I'm glad she's moving out, and I'm even gladder I'm leaving for two weeks' vacation. I need to get away from all these crazy people.

August 17. I'm back at the hospital after two weeks at the ranch in Montana. Because I lost weight while I was gone, Dr. Weintraub says I've gone backward. She says if I couldn't maintain my weight on my own, then I have to accept that I've regressed. Why can't she ever admit the problem is that the program here doesn't move me forward? Why is progress measured only by the weight scale? Now I'm never gonna get out of here.

I'm gonna describe what it's like being back here. It is first and foremost depressing. Everybody around me is depressed, and we all feed off that in each other. I don't think it's possible for anyone to maintain a good outlook here, much less someone who was upset to begin with. I don't think a psych hospital is the ideal place for relieving depression—however, I have no suggestions how else it might be done. All I know is I want to avoid all those people. I don't want to get back into all the head-game crap. I'm sick of everything meaning something supersignificant psychologically. Talking with some of the patients is like talking to robots. They have a down-pat psychological explanation or term for every one of their behaviors. My problem is that I have no explanation. I don't understand what makes me constantly feel fat and like I'm going to freak out. Being here makes me want to cry and cry and cry.

August 18. Dad was supposed to be here forty minutes ago, and I am terrified Weintraub told him he is not to see me anymore. Today's was the hardest, most humiliating, most awful session I have had with her ever. "You are a spoiled, groveling, sniveling, ungrateful brat," she screamed at me. "Just a lying, dependent twelve-year-old narcissist consumed with self-interest. You're against everyone. You try to control everyone. Well, you've succeeded. Now what are you going to do? Why don't you go home and torture your family? If you stay around long enough you'll be the only one left. Janis and Brian will grow up and go away. That's what you want, isn't it? Jenny is Queen of the Universe?" She harangued me for forty minutes and then just got up and walked out. I have never felt so ashamed and angry and confused. Deep inside me I know most of what she said about me is true. But screaming at me doesn't accomplish anything. It just gets both of us upset.

I'd like to talk to staff, but Weintraub told me something that keeps me from doing so. She said the staff feels that I am concerned only about me, my selfishness, staying Daddy's baby, and not letting anyone penetrate my stronghold.

August 21. *Dr. Weintraub said I have a "paranoid personality." That label makes me feel like I really am crazy. Weintraub seems to think if I tried harder, I wouldn't be paranoid. I've never been aware that I'm any more paranoid than your average person. She also said I look for the negative in people, in school, in relationships, in everything.*

I am so confused lately. I'm not sure what Weintraub says is bullshit and what is honest injun. I only know life is damn hard and I've got to keep trying.

August 22. *Paula discharged yesterday so she could go to college. She's not even close to being cured.*

August 24. *I feel out of touch and worthless here. I'm angry at everyone. I'm locked up in this little jail where I'm expected to perform and get better yet no one can tell me how.*

I'm like a blind person groping frantically for answers, and the more I'm compelled to find them, the more they elude me. Dr. Weintraub says I know the answers. She says I know the source of my illness and that I am hiding it from her. Try as I might, I can't think why I am so determined to remain abnormal. Some of my thoughts are:

(1) Every time things get tough, scary, or not the way I want them to be, I retreat to a hideaway where people take care of me, especially my dad.

(2) It seems like it all started when I moved from Open showing to Quarter Horse showing and stopped winning as often. Suddenly the one area I felt outstanding in evaporated. I hated facing the possibility that I wasn't as good as I had thought. At that time, Dad was so far into his cocoon he was nonexistent in my life; all my parental reassurance came from my mom—when I won. The less I won, the more critical she became. As I lost and lost and lost, I lost my confidence and the "show business" became more pain than pleasure. So much work and very little reward—for Mom, too. Perhaps my anorexia was in part an effort to see if I could be

loved and admired without performing. Instead of saying, I'm sick of only feeling worthy when others notice I'm a good rider, I made it so I couldn't perform while at the same time punishing Mom for allowing a performing charade to go on and on and on. It was all so screwy—winning was entirely dependent upon how the judge saw me. Maybe that's why I judge my self-worth according to how others perceive me. Maybe that's why I've become a compulsive achiever.

(3) When I was a child, Mom refused to get me the clothes I wanted to keep up with my best friend. I wanted cute, short outfits, grown-up clothes like my friend used to get on her birthday, each new school year, Christmas, etc. Mom's response was, "You don't have to be like everyone, Jenny." That made me angry, but I'd just swallow it and say okay, I guess I won't be like everyone, I'll be better. I won't care about anything but my horse, and I'll be best at that. Then I wasn't best at that any-more. All those years other girls were curling their hair, doing their nails, and chasing boys, I was developing the best show horse. When I stopped doing horse things I was so far behind socially I felt I could never catch up—and I never have.

August 28. Guess what? Last night Paula called me from college. She was in shambles; she already feels like she's reverting, and she's only been there three days. My hypothesis is her doctor never got to the root of her problem and never made her gain up to a normal weight.

September 1. Yesterday I went running for the first time in nine days. I ran for thirty minutes—fast—and damn, I felt wonderful and ecstatic.

September 5. Here's what Dr. Weintraub told me: (a) She and I have no more of an alliance than she and my dad because I thwart every con-frontation with either pure submissiveness or crying, screaming, and falling apart. (b) I've made no progress, in fact I've regressed, from two years ago—I'm not in school, I'm sour and depressed and resistant. (c) I look at her and Peter as saviors to pull me out of the wilderness without my having to work. (d) I care about no one but myself; I only love people for what they can do for me.

September 7. *Our morning session was deferred until afternoon because I was gone when Weintraub showed up half an hour early for our appointment. Then this afternoon, she attacked me for screwing up. "You purposely avoided me this morning," she railed at me. "Bullshit," I said. "You know it's your fault for being early. I've never avoided you."*

Sometimes I think Weintraub fabricates situations like this, setting me up just in order to nail me. She said "It would be nice if once, just once, you could admit to your passive fuck-you attitude. You've been confronted about this bad attitude before." Well, she was wrong about that, too. "More bullshit," I said. "That's one of the few bad attitudes I don't have that I haven't been accused of." That really made her mad. "Jenny," she screeched, "you're trying to ignore an uncomfortable event by sublimating it." I didn't give in to her then although sometimes I do when I think she's wrong—because she's such a bully. And now I'm worrying maybe she was right, maybe I am crazy and won't let myself remember unpleasant confrontations.

Anyway, she kept ranting. "You're the most self-righteous person I know," she said. "It's time you stopped being angry." Me angry, what about you? I thought but didn't say. I said, "One of the things stressed here is you can't stop feelings, you can only learn correct ways of dealing with them." She said, "Yes, but not for someone who has let anger consume her to the extent you have, someone who has hurt everyone who ever cared about her through her angry, punitive ways. You ought to start caring and be more human and loving and forgiving."

Well, I can see her point, but what do I do with my angry feelings? I just can't say, "Stop" and assume they will. She knows that. Sometimes I don't comprehend her at all.

Before she got up and stomped out she said, "I've reached a conclusion about you, Jenny. Either I'm nice to you and treat you compassionately and carefully, in which case I will never cure you, or I'm confrontational and hostile with you, in which case I will lose you—because your father will put his foot down and say, 'Enough.'" Either way I lose, and I feel disillusioned that she's presented me with that kind of dead-end setup. How do I reply to her? This type of confrontation doesn't ever accomplish anything except spiral me into a suicidal slump.

September 8. In today's family session, Weintraub lectured us about having to accept the reality that therapy is hurtful and confrontive and if I'm ever to be "cured" I've got to go through it—we all do. She said the most necessary step in curing an anorexic is to make her and her family hate the therapist, so that all the anger and frustration can be confronted and resolved, until all involved say, "Enough" and give up this shitty disease. She said she hates my sickness and the behaviors and attitudes which accompany it. She likes and cares about the "well Jenny," and she wants that side of me to be set free.

September 11. Mom's birthday!!! I'll call her before I do anything else.

Dr. Weintraub is letting me eat in the cafeteria. I have no restrictions, and she is giving me a week to prove I can eat responsibly before she puts me back on a behavior mod program.

September 13. Weintraub's so damn sure she knows exactly how I am: "rotten, spoiled, and manipulative," she kept saying today. I'm tired of spending our time being lectured about how improperly I answer her questions. If I'm silent, she says I'm refusing to cooperate. If I talk, I'm just filling in the gaps to appease her. If I agree, I'm trying to shimmy out from under her confrontation. If I disagree, I'm bullshitting her. It makes no difference; we just don't communicate anymore. The only way I can tell her anything is by gaining weight.

September 14. Weintraub asked, "What if your father died—who would take care of you? Your brothers? Your sisters? Certainly not," she taunted me. "Just you, and you've done a hell of a job screwing that up. If your father died that would be the end of you or the end of your illness. You would have to choose. For too long a time you have shown you would choose the end of you."

September 16. In the family meeting Dad said if he ever felt the anger Weintraub says he's supposed to feel toward me, he'd kick me out. That scares me because according to the good doctor, before I can get well, he's supposed to feel that anger, as a result of his being emotionally and financially ripped off by me. He spoke so assuredly that he'd never feel such a threat from me. He said he resented the doctor's attempt to emotionally blackmail him into feelings he doesn't have.

September 19. Weintraub says I'm angry because I wanted to win with my horses, discovered I couldn't, and pitched a five-year temper tantrum. I think she's wrong. If there is horse-connected anger, it's that Mom wanted me to win so damn bad and when I didn't I let both of us down. Also anger at Mom that she felt if she had all the opportunities I had, she'd be better than me.

September 21. First Weintraub changed our appointment time and made me miss my class at Denver University. That seems stupid and juvenile to me. Then, right out of the blue, she started our session with, "How can you go to church every week when you are breaking every tenet?" How do I answer a question like that? She accused me of wanting to stay sick, of liking the special feeling of being in the hospital. As usual she's 180 degrees off—she hasn't a clue.

September 27. Today I feel vulnerable, scared, and lonely. We just had goals group and my goals were to study, work on some issues I've been looking at all week, and make sure I eat enough. I knew I blew it when I mentioned eating goals, and I'm sure to catch it from Weintraub. Although my program revolves around weight gain, I'm not supposed to set goals about eating!

September 28. I've got to come up with an agenda. What should I do? I could talk about feeling disassociated lately, like I'm not here nor there, like I don't have a "peg," like I just want someone to hug me and say you're gonna survive, Jenny, you really are. I feel I need to be punished. Isn't that weird! I feel I deserve to be hurt and hurt and hurt to pay for all I've done.

Dr. Weintraub says I should be honest and accept her number one premise: I want to be perfect so I delude myself that I am.

September 29. Dr. Weintraub told me my behavior and feelings are contradictory to what I say. I say, "I will do it, I want to get well," but my actions say I don't want to. My heart says: Don't you dare get fat. Don't change, don't change, it screams at me day after day and especially night after night.

She said I'm dishonest about this issue—that I still won't talk about these feelings but continue to hide them, cultivate them, and not change them.

October 5. I'm totally freaking out. I started selecting my own food today. I'm terrified I won't like what they're serving, and I won't get enough to eat.

October 7. I'm so very down lately, because I feel inadequate and don't have anything to offer. Weintraub said when I catch myself feeling this way I ought to tell myself I'm making more manure and detour around it. Well, I tried and I still feel bad. I don't feel like being alive. No self-pity here, just anger. I feel like a fat blob without anything to offer myself or anyone. I'm at the point emotionally where I always return to anorexia. I don't know how to pick myself up when there's nothing to pick myself up to. I'm empty. HELP.

October 9. I'm sick of this unit. I'm sick of the far-out people running around up here.

October 20. I'm not writing in here very often anymore. Because I'm getting better? Anyway, I just had an interesting experience. I was sitting in the park enjoying being outside on a warm autumn day, and this great-looking guy who'd been playing basketball came over to talk to me. His name is Ben, and he graduated from college a year ago. We talked a long time, just shooting the breeze, and then he asked the inevitable—where I lived. Well, I gave him the cold, hard facts. I'm sure he was shocked, but he was super about it. Even though he didn't leave immediately, I was thinking I won't see him again.

October 27. I went back to the park and guess who was there! Ben was sitting in the exact same spot where we met. It was the same time of day, and I'm certain he was waiting for me. I wondered if he'd waited every day this past week. I didn't want to seem obvious, so I sat by a tree I knew he had to pass on his way back to his apartment. We talked a long time. I like him.

I mentioned Ben to Weintraub. She was adamant. "Don't ever speak to him again," she ordered. "Or anyone who makes advances to you out there." I'm too stunned to react now. I feel even more like a prisoner denied *contact with the outside world. She doesn't have any idea what Ben is like, and she won't take time to let me tell her.*

Tonight I will cry myself to sleep and mourn the end of what might have been.

Jenny stretched up on her tiptoes and frowned at her body image in the bathroom mirror above the sink. What she saw confirmed successful weight gain; her unhappiness at what she saw confirmed unsuccessful therapy. She returned to sit on her bed and wait for her parents' arrival.

Conflicting emotions swirled inside her. She felt elated by her discharge in time for Christmas, but uncertainty about her achievements nagged at her. *I must be better,* she rationalized, *otherwise why would Weintraub let me leave? She says I'm better, and I trust her, but she still insists I see her every week. How much better am I if I've become dependent on a doctor to keep me functioning?*

Jenny was excited about going home to resume a life suspended. But she was fearful of her ability to be accepted again, to interact normally with people who weren't crazy. *What if they all think I'm crazy? Even if they don't say it, I'll see it in their eyes. Will they welcome me, genuinely be glad to see me, or will they ignore me, only pretend I'm okay now? I'm afraid I'll be like a displaced person, not belonging anywhere, not attached to anything or anyone.*

A nurse interrupted Jenny's thoughts to announce her parents' arrival. Shaking with nervousness, Jenny trotted to the ward door to greet them.

Willowcrest discharged Jenny two days before Christmas. The basis for her discharge was a medical fantasy: weight gain equals progress. During seven months of confinement, Jenny gained 25 pounds, a cruel delusion of improvement. Her temporary weight gain masked a lasting reality: therapeutic failure. She left Willowcrest with a heavy burden of unresolved and untreated problems, all enhanced rather than diminished by her stay. Nourished by her treatment program, Jenny's anorexic feelings continued their rampage within her. Distorted body image, food obsessions, terror of weight gain, latent depression, and shrunken self-esteem all accompanied her discharge. Causes of her anorexia and how to cure it were still unknown.

And the causes of failure? Uncooperative patient? Enabling father? Misfocused therapeutic approach? Emotionally abusive therapy? Or merely a poorly understood, intractable illness?

Jenny had entered Willowcrest with a positive attitude, a strong desire to recover, and a willingness to work hard to do so. She had been fearful and frustrated but not resistant. Her doctor presumed Jenny's anorexia was self-inflicted, a behavior problem, an illness of choice. Dr. Weintraub placed primary responsibility for cause and resolution on Jenny and her parents, insisting that Jenny's father kept his daughter ensconced in an anorexic state. Using a patient-belittling approach to psychotherapy, her doctor battered Jenny with regular assaults on her self-esteem, using name-calling as a favorite cudgel. In the process did Jenny somehow become "junkie" to the demeaning confrontation "pushed" by Dr. Weintraub?

How terribly wrong the doctor was in her approach would not come to light until Jenny's next hospitalization.

CHAPTER NINE
Unpleasant Memories

*A*fter Christmas, Jenny struggled to reconstruct a normal life and restore her place in the daily rhythms of family and friends. Feeling detached from reality, as if just wakened from a long dream, she nevertheless plunged into frenetic physical and social activity.

She contacted a number of health clubs, joined one, and started a daily exercise program. A busy schedule of church youth-group activities helped fill her calendar. She continued a social and professional relationship with Peter and his girlfriend, reconnected with some of her friends from horse show days, and spent Saturday evenings dancing or going to the movies with Diane, now a sophomore in college.

At the wedding of a childhood playmate, Katy MacGregor, Jenny sat beaming with her family in a front row pew. During a lull in the proceedings, she nudged her father and whispered, "I suddenly feel sad, like I've missed out and will never catch up." Her father smiled encouragingly. "There's still plenty of time left for you, Jenny," he said.

Another era ended for Jenny when her horse, Miss Roan, was sold at auction. It was not as stressful a separation as she had feared. "Anticlimactic really," she explained to Dr. Weintraub. "I haven't ridden in months, and memories of my horse show years are all conflicting and confused. I'm relieved all that is finally over. I cried when we said goodbye, though. Miss Roan even nuzzled my ear like she used to."

Jenny studied help wanted ads and contacted prospective employers close to home. Barely three weeks out of Willowcrest, she started a job at Children's World, a day care center.

But hyperactivity could not long block Jenny's distress. Her pain was too sharp and insistent. Weekly sessions with Dr. Weintraub didn't help. Nor could she find a sense of peace at home. There she felt awkward and misplaced, more like a visitor than a resident family member.

Physical problems plagued Jenny. Her teeth and gums, badly damaged by regurgitated stomach acid, required painful oral surgery. Then she fell victim to daily exposure to the ailments of small children, contracting a succession of nasty viruses, whose raging fevers left her exhausted. Then a different virus attacked her, this one mental. Shadowy, unpleasant memories began growing inside her.

Seeing her patient's physical regression and deeply concerned about Jenny's continuing emotional distress, Dr. Weintraub prescribed more therapy, increasing sessions to twice weekly.

"Something's happening to me." Jenny sat tense and anxious.

"Something's always happening to you, Jenny," Dr. Weintraub teased. "Tell me about it."

"It's the way I feel at work. I'm uncomfortable with the little kids almost all the time now."

"Do you know why?"

"It's like I'm afraid for them . . . afraid they'll be abused." Jenny's voice was barely audible. "When a policeman visited Children's World, I wanted him to talk about child molesting. I'm always interested when a news broadcast has a story about child abuse, and I've always been curious about abused children. I . . . I seem to identify with them."

Dr. Weintraub's brow furrowed in concern. "We need to focus on your childhood recollections," she insisted gently. "You've repressed something bad. Your work with children is eroding your repression, reconnecting you to something that happened a long time ago, probably the cause of your anorexia. What was it, Jenny?"

"Do you think I was . . . abused?"

"Probably. When did it happen, Jenny? Who did it?"

"I don't know," she sobbed fearfully.

"There's too much resentment and anger inside you. We have to find out what happened . . . so those emotions can be released."

"But how?" Jenny wrung her hands. "I can't remember."

"Get your baby book, photo albums. Go through them carefully. They will help you remember. You've mentioned conflicting feelings about your horse show years. We'll start there."

Thus, Jenny began a long, dark journey upon a turbulent sea, where she would drift besieged and lost, without a sense of destination or safety. She bound herself to that vague, contradictory world of last year, five years ago, ten years ago, even back to infancy. Like a python squeezing life from its intended victim, Jenny's haunting childhood memories, once unleashed, would never relinquish their tenacious grip on her mind and emotions. The more she probed her recollections, the more venal their response, the more unresolved their implications.

"What about the horse shows, Jenny?" Dr. Weintraub quizzed. "Have you looked at your photo albums?"

"Most of them. I'm still looking."

"Tell me what you remember."

"Just scraps mostly, like pieces to a jigsaw puzzle. Occasionally whole scenes. Some with Bob, my second horse trainer. A lot with Maria, one of my best adult friends. We went to horse shows together."

"Tell me about Bob."

"It was after I got Miss Roan. I was twelve. Bob was old and his breath smelled bad. He came out of retirement to coach me. He and Mom never let me forget that, as if they demanded I feel forever grateful."

"Did you feel grateful?"

"Until he started pawing me." Jenny's face showed her disgust.

"Did you complain?"

"No. Mom thought he was wonderful, and I was afraid my complaints might be my fault."

"Can you remember more? What did Bob do?"

"He tried to fondle me. It was grotesque. He tried to touch my breasts, and I had to push him away politely. Some of his desperate maneuverings occurred right in front of Mom. They were just hugs then."

"Did Mom intervene?"

"She was oblivious. Bob called it needin' some lovin'. He had his hands all over me at horse shows. I found a picture Mom took of me right after I fought him off one time. The picture helped me remember, like you said. Maybe nothing drastic happened, but there was a lot of hugging and patting and squeezing. I got damn tired of trying to dodge his gestures of affection."

"What about Maria?"

"She was a lot older than me, maybe twenty then. I really admired her. I remember my first horse show with Maria. I wanted to go but was sure Mom wouldn't let me, because she hadn't met Maria. But she surprised me and said yes. Maria's niece came too and shared a bed with Maria. I wore my cowboy boots, dried manure and all, to dinner because I forgot my shoes. We all laughed about that." Jenny shook her head as if clearing cobwebs from her recollection. "Then it's night and I'm watching TV with Maria, tired, drifting in and out of sleep with the lights still on. Then there's noise and I'm awake again. Maria is in the bathroom throwing up. I'm scared. I'm tired and want to sleep, but there are too many distractions. Maria won't turn off the TV or turn down the bathroom lights. 'What's going on?' I ask. 'Go back to sleep, Jenny,' she says. And, oh yes, there is junk food everywhere."

"Maria was bulimic?"

"Yes, but I didn't know what bulimia was then. She always traveled with a lot of Snickers bars, M&M's, and a box of Dunkin' Donuts."

"Anything else about Maria?"

"Some, but not whole scenes." Jenny grimaced, squinted her eyes, and looked above Dr. Weintraub's head as she struggled with incomplete recollections. "Maria driving her car up a narrow mountain road. Me saying I'll walk, thank you. Road getting skinnier and skinnier till they can't turn around. Both Maria and her niece laughing and laughing."

"Laughing at you?"

"I don't know. Then I remember another show, being locked in the back of the horse trailer and Maria wouldn't let me out. It's confusing, because I also remember being thrown out of the trailer. Then I'm lying down in Maria's car coming home, my head in her lap, feeling an awful depression. This memory gives me a weird feeling. I see a barn on top of a hill, and the barn gives me a scared feeling. I remember a show in Wyoming, when Maria and I stayed with her friends and shared a sofa bed. When we got home she took me, Janis, and Brian to the movies. I wore strawberry Lipsmacker. I felt bad about myself, jealous of her attention to Janis and Brian, but then I felt good." Jenny paused, looked at Dr. Weintraub, and shrugged her shoulders.

"That's all?"

"All I can remember . . . about Bob and Maria."

"Keep digging, Jenny. I'm sure there's more. Look through old records, like school notebooks or diaries."

"Any more memories from horse shows?"

Her mind reeling with partial memories, random fragments from her past, Jenny shuffled several pages of notes she had brought with her. "Nothing complete. Gary Lander—he was my first trainer—making me jump Dickens 4 feet when I was more terrified of Gary than the jump, then telling me I'm riding like a bag of shit. He used to make me ride and ride and ride, until I was exhausted, then criticize me for overriding."

"What else?"

Jenny blushed as she read from her notes. "Memories of hands on my breasts . . . can't place who, where, when . . . maybe they're not real at all. Then I remember laps. Seems like I was always sitting on laps, sometimes of people very close in age."

"What happened on laps?"

"I just remember being there, nothing that happened."

"Other memories?"

"Once on a trip I saw this other horse I wanted desperately, but Mom and Dad said no."

"Any more trips without Mom or Dad?"

"I remembered another trip with Maria, after I left Children's Hospital, when I swam and ran. I've tried to remember why I went running. It seems I had a reason, because I remember feeling really crazy, but it could have been ketosis."

"Jenny, your relationship with Maria sounds unnatural. Could something bad have happened with Maria?"

"Maybe . . . I just don't know." Jenny focused again on the bare wall above Dr. Weintraub's head, as if searching there for a window into her past. "There was a trip with everyone from the Landers' barn. A hotel where Marge Lander didn't want her daughter to sleep with Jimmy Hopkins—he was thirteen or fourteen. So I did . . . different beds, I think. The old fear of not being able to sleep crept in, but I pushed it away, told myself I was safe in a hotel. The next day at the show I was afraid of Jimmy."

"You mentioned an old fear of not sleeping?"

"Even before the horse shows I was afraid of sleeping away from home, which makes me wonder if I was abused by horse people, or if it—the abuse—just plain didn't happen."

"Maybe you only experienced normal apprehension when separated from Mom and Dad."

"Maybe. Mom told me David had the same fear."

"Did you tell Mom about something happening to you when you were showing horses?"

"Yes, and I got really angry at her. She said, 'Maybe nothing bad happened to you, maybe it was a fear that it might that scared you.' She's already denying anything happened. She just brushes it off, not concerned at all, and meanwhile I'm losing my mind over our discoveries. I feel she should be distraught too or else there's no merit to my anxiety."

"Have you told Dad?"

"Not yet. I imagine Mom did, but I don't know his reaction."

"We'll have to end early today, and I see you have a lot of notes left."

"That's all I have on my horse years. Should we start on the earlier stuff? It rambles a lot."

"Save it for next Tuesday. We have a few minutes, though. What about now . . . the present? Anything currently upsetting you?"

Jenny paused, then started again thoughtfully. "The repulsion and rejection I feel at family times. And—I think you'd call it my identity crisis—the guilt I feel about who I am."

"Tell me about family times."

"When we are together in church or on holidays or at the cabin, it's like a farce. I don't want to have anything to do with those times. I'm always angry at not feeling part of my family. But I don't want to be part of my family because that would be acknowledging the myth of its unity and storybook perfection. Before I would binge. Now I don't do that. When I have to face family times I RAGE inside. Maybe the rage comes from feeling like my place is to point out the screwiness of my family, but the way I do it makes the shit land on me. I go as an anorexic, fucked up, and that way I deny our family's perfection."

"Can you explain your guilt feelings?"

"It's like, lookit what I'm doing when I've been given everything."

"You weren't given the new horse you wanted."

"No, but I worry that others think I have everything."

"Do Mom or Dad say that?"

"No."

"Your brothers and sisters?"

"No, but they might have been jealous of my horse and the time Mom spent with me."

"Did they complain about it, call you spoiled?"

"No. They're busy with their own lives. You're the only one who's called me spoiled." Jenny said it without resentment.

Dr. Weintraub looked at the notebook open on Jenny's lap. "More recollections for me?"

"When I went through my baby book, I found a picture of a clubhouse David, Nancy, and I shared in the basement. A scary feeling came over me, like the clubhouse caved in on me, and I tried to climb out the windows . . . to escape? I can't remember. My mind shoves it away."

"What else from your baby book?"

"I was potty trained by two because I wanted to swim, but I sucked my thumb for a long time after that. Mom says—in the book—I'd get wildly excited, wound up like a top, and the pitch of excitement at my third Christmas was almost unbearable. Three must be the worst age, she says, because then is when the tears took over so quickly. She says I was very gregarious, disliked playing alone, and would always play with other children if given the opportunity. Apparently at three-and-a-half years I said, 'I'm not queen of the castle, I'm just the mother.'"

"Mom recorded that?"

"Yes. She writes that I said, 'I don't want to turn out to be a lady.'"

"Interesting."

"It's not in my baby book, but I remember being sick and staying home from school. Just Mom and me together. I see dark, feel dark, but also feel good. I'm confused because I fantasize about this being a time with her I yearned for. On the other hand, I remember feeling boxed in, caged and controlled and really unhappy. I remember Mom yelling at me, being terrified of her and hating her but at the same time wanting her desperately."

"What did she do besides yell?"

"I remember she washed my mouth out with soap, me feeling that it was normal, my due. Then she had a paddle she used on me until Dad made her get rid of it. So after that she used a . . . a hairbrush. I have definite memories of being beaten repeatedly with a hairbrush."

"Dad didn't make her get rid of the hairbrush?"

"I don't think he knew."

"Any food memories?"

"I remember watching *Blinkey's Fun Club* on TV and looking forward to a snack but not being able to have one until they did on the show. I was thinking about food and being fat even then. When I was ten, I remember feeling fat when I visited my grandparents."

"Let's talk about unhappiness and anger. Can you remember when that started?"

"I know I've been angry for a long while at my family for treating me like I'm a bitch, but my unhappiness started before that." Jenny shuffled through pages of her notebook. "Here's a poem I found that I wrote in sixth grade, around the same time I got Miss Roan:

> *You sit in your room—alone*
> *The cold seeps into you*
> *You look out the window*
> *Snow is falling*
> *You feel the warmth of your body, the cold of the pane*
> *Two different worlds*
> *For a fraction of a second*
> *You feel as two, but you're still one*
> *In your room—alone.*

I think I was unhappy then."

"Not too unhappy to write a beautiful poem. Anything before?"

"When I was little I had a favorite toy, a stuffed swan, that Mom took away because I was allergic. It made me very sad."

"You keep coming back to Mom."

"I know. It seems for a while Mom wants me to stay tied to her. I get angry, get anorexia and cut off from the rest of the world. Then suddenly she's pushing me out of the nest to go to college. She's so sick of me by now she wants me gone. But now there's no focus to my life, because all has been forsaken for her, and Jenny has no identity left. So the harder she pushes me to go, the more determined I am to stay.

"Sometimes I'm jealous of her devotion to church. There was a time when birthdays and Christmas were not letdowns, but now they are because of all her church involvements. Like on my sixteenth birthday, she basically ignored me because so much was happening at church. She doesn't do that to my brothers and sisters."

"Have you talked to her about it?"

"She says I'm too demanding. She denies there is any difference between how she treats the others and how she treats me. I want to believe her, but all the evidence is so different. I must be crazy. She says one thing and I feel another. And . . ." Jenny hesitated.

Dr. Weintraub prompted, "And . . . what else about Mom?"

"I don't know if I should tell you. I've agonized all week if it—the abuse—has something to do with Mom." Jenny stopped abruptly, as if fearful of some terrible retaliation.

"It's alright, Jenny, you can tell me."

"But you and Mom seem so close. I feel disloyal."

"You really must tell me. "

"Well . . . I remember being at my grandmother's and finding out how Mom used to terrorize her little brother when they were young, hitting him and everything. When Meme told me this, I had a sick feeling in my stomach like it made sense, as if I knew it all along. Meme talked about catching Mom in the act and Mom denying it and how afraid Meme was because Mom had come very close to seriously hurting Uncle Bret. I've thought maybe Uncle Bret was Meme's favorite, and when I became Dad's favorite, Mom wanted to hurt me. The book you gave me says you marry men who treat you like your mother, and maybe Dad rejected Mom for me like Meme rejected Mom for Uncle Bret."

"So by being sick, you're getting back at Mom?"

"Confusing, isn't it. I know I've wanted Mom to hurt like I hurt. I remember how pleased I was when she tried to ride Little Dickens and he dumped her. But then I seem so obsessed with Mom, always wanting her approval, and the book you gave me says abused children often cling very tightly to the abusive parent."

"What's THE important question then, Jenny?"

"Like, why is Mom's opinion so important to me? Why am I willing to forsake my own life for this screwy relationship?"

"I couldn't have said it better. Something for you to think about for next week. Keep remembering. Let's get all your troubling memories into the open where we can deal with them."

CHAPTER TEN

An Abused Child, Perhaps?

Although Dr. Weintraub helped Jenny drain her reservoir of anguish, it refilled faster. Jenny struggled under increased pressure to find answers to her anorexia in childhood events. She remembered something. Then she and the doctor analyzed together. Jenny remembered more, and they repeated the process. Accepting Dr. Weintraub's latest diagnosis of abused child, Jenny searched for verification as she recycled the past in her mind over and over again. She also sought validation in the present.

"I'm like the abused kids at Children's World."

"In what way, Jenny?"

"My baby book repeatedly describes me as hysterical and excited. Same behavior as three abused kids at work. One has always reminded me of me. She cries and hurts herself by inviting the other children's nasty comments. It's a cycle. They make fun of her, and the more she misbehaves, the more they make fun of her and the more obnoxious she becomes. I've often felt caught in this with Nancy, Mom, and my anorexia. They complain about my body size. I get mad, vent my anger by eating less, and then they complain more."

"Is it painful for you at work, continually reminded of what happened to you?" Dr. Weintraub spoke as if Jenny's abuse were already an established fact.

"Yes. Too painful, and the kids are too demanding. There's so much stress in my life I have nothing left to give them. I gave notice yesterday."

"You seem more distressed today than last week. Any reason?"

"It's like two parts of me are fighting each other. One part says I have to go back, find out what happened to me. The other part insists I forget the past and go forward."

"You won't be at peace until we resolve your abuse issues."

"I know that."

"Have you remembered more?"

"Some . . . mostly fragments." Jenny scanned her journal notes. "Feeling abuse from others . . . being picked on in seventh and eighth grade . . . terrible feelings about our cabin . . . getting lost with a bunch of kids I was responsible for . . . something happening on the cabin stairs . . . something really bad happening in a ditch. Crying . . . needing Mom. Maybe that's why I'm such a pity monger. Mom is nice to me only when she pities me. I remember being very sick once, and Mom read to me and made my lunch for me. She took care of me, made me feel loved after all."

Jenny turned a page. "Like Linus from the comics, I had this security blanket, 'blankie.' I cried and cried when Mom cut it into one small square and took the rest away from me."

"Do you know why she did that?"

"Because it was dirty?"

"Maybe to wean you."

"Or to punish me? I can't remember."

"We always come back to Mom, don't we?"

"When you picked up on the weirdness in my relationship with Maria, I think I was really trying to tell you about Mom. I have so many troubled memories about her."

"Like?"

"Like having a friend's mother ask me why Mom didn't buy me pants that fit. Mom making me feel guilty about asking her to braid my hair. Mom forgetting me at preschool. Mom making me iron my Brownie uniform, a hand-me-down, of course. Going with Mom to antique shows, waiting hours and hours for her. When I had to be picked up or taken anywhere, she was always late and never, ever without a logical excuse, making me feel like I had demanded too much of her and was lucky she was doing anything for me. She screwed up so many of my birthdays, not being there, and then gave me an ugly old trunk for high school graduation. Mom used to wash our hair, mine and my sisters,' and then comb it out for us. Mine was long and tangly, and she'd rip that comb right through till I almost cried out from the pain. Once she put me in our collie's doghouse, then put dog poo on my bed."

"Why did she do that?"

"Maybe to punish me for something?"

"Jenny, I have to ask . . . could you be overreacting?"

"I've worried about that. But my feelings of being mistreated are so intense, and what I can remember is very clear. I think she may have . . . abused me," Jenny hesitated to use the word, "only when I was bad . . . for punishment. I think she stopped when I started showing horses."

"Why did she stop?"

"I don't know. After she stopped, it's like I took all my anger at how she used to treat me, chose to forget it, and pretended I was sweet and docile. And that's when my anorexia began. When I first started starving myself, I remember Mom yelling and screaming at me, then crying and praying with me when she tucked me in at night. I remember saying, 'Please don't hate me for this, Mom. I couldn't live if you hated me.' Yet my very actions were asking for her hate."

"Maybe you were trying to recover the old relationship."

"The abusive one?"

"Yes. Maybe your anorexia began when it did because you weren't receiving the amount of abuse you needed to exist."

"You think I was an abuse junkie?"

"Maybe."

"When I was little, I was spanked about once a day and wondered why my friends weren't spanked that often. I decided I was just a difficult kid."

"Did Mom say that?"

"I just accepted it from the way she treated me. She hurt me, and even now, after remembering what she did, I want her pity and care."

"Jenny, your pity trips are just your way of getting people to like you again after being angry with you."

"I know, but I still want Mom to validate my feelings."

"Have you talked to Mom about them?"

"When I bring up remembering bad stuff, she always asks if it has anything to do with her, and I'm afraid to tell her it does. How can I tell her? Everyone else thinks she is so wonderful. I must be crazy to think otherwise. She seems relieved thinking we are focusing on Maria and other horse people. She thinks she is off the hook."

"Have you talked to Dad?"

"Some, but he doesn't know yet that we are discussing Mom."

"Have you finished reading *My Mother, Myself*?"

"I'd almost finished when Mom saw me reading it and asked for it. She feels very threatened. I'm sure she saw the parts I underlined, particularly the section which tells how you take bad mommy hate and turn it into bad little girl hate."

"Jenny, for your sanity and Mom's, we need to confront her. Don't try it alone. We'll have a family session, so I can help. But not yet. We need to work through all your memories first."

Dr. Weintraub folded her hands on her desk, her customary signal that a patient's fifty minutes had expired. "We have to stop now, Jenny. You know I'm gone all next week?"

"Yes, and I'm really worried. It will be a tough week for me. I'm having nightmares and not sleeping well, and I start a new job Monday. At least I'll be away from all the kids."

"I want you to stay focused on your memories. Go through your pictures again. Talk to your pediatrician and Dr. Corbin about any indications of abuse. And call Don Marin. He's the psychologist who tested you at Willowcrest last year. See if his test results suggested any abuse."

Jenny slumped in her chair, her eyes dull and lifeless, her appearance frail and emaciated. Dr. Weintraub spoke gently. "Tell me about last week."

"I read about that schoolteacher who was indicted on ten counts of child molestation. It really upset me, and then I remembered something major, something really significant, I think." Jenny talked with little inflection or emotion in her voice, despite the subject. "I was looking through one of our family albums. There's a picture of me on Tony's lap. He's Mom's stepbrother, whose daughter also showed horses. He used to visit us several times a year when he was here on business. He's kissing me. On the mouth. When I saw the picture I froze. It's like I knew instantly something bad, something sexual, happened with Tony. I think he molested me when I was little. I got hysterical and couldn't stop crying."

"Why do you think he molested you?"

"It was this feeling I had when I saw the picture. I even screamed 'This is it!' Somehow I knew this was what we have been searching for. Here, I brought the picture for you to see."

Dr. Weintraub looked at the picture carefully, frowning at the portrait of her patient with a handsome, dark-haired man in his early forties. She shook her head disapprovingly as she returned the photograph. "This is not a picture of a niece and uncle greeting each other. My God, Jenny, you do look like lovers. Can you remember when the picture was taken, who took it, anything else about that day, or any other time with Tony?"

"I was ten or eleven, and I remember Mom had been drinking wine that afternoon when she took the picture. Something bad happened before that. I think Mom had gone to the store, and it happened when Tony showed me how to clean my saddle. I can't remember any details."

"I'm sure you will remember eventually. It takes time."

"Did you talk to Mom or Dad after you found the picture?"

"It was Saturday, and Mom had gone to church. But I told Dad what had upset me and showed him the picture. Dad was shocked. He said he liked Tony, but he believed me and held me until I quit crying. He said as terrible as it was, maybe there finally was something specific we could all work on and help me overcome."

"Did you tell Mom about Tony?"

"No." Jenny grew more animated. "Mom had a big crush on Tony, and I was afraid to tell her. I asked Dad to decide whether or not to tell her. I told him I was afraid Mom wouldn't believe me. But I was still upset when Mom got home. She noticed and asked what was wrong. I told her I had remembered something major and her very words were, 'Does it have to do with me?' I said no and that I didn't want to discuss it yet. Then at breakfast on Sunday she was still acting so threatened that even Dad remarked about it. Mom said I act like I blame her."

"Did Dad tell Mom about Tony?"

"Not until Sunday night. Mom brought it up. My whole body was shaking. She was apologetic, saying she was sorry it had happened and especially sorry because it was believable; but it was like she was trying to humor me. It happened, Jenny. I'm sorry and that's that. Then she told me when she was little, one of Daddad's friends tried to get into bed with her. I felt she was saying, 'You think you've got it bad, Jenny. Nobody knows the troubles I've seen.' I flew off the handle, and she said no, no, she didn't mean it that way, she meant I was believable because she'd experienced the same type of thing. But her nonverbal message to me was: Look at what I've come through and I'm not a failure like you. I felt judged by her, like I shouldn't feel bad, life goes on . . . but I do feel bad and life doesn't go on.

"I felt suicidal after that . . . for the rest of the day . . . for most of the week, actually. Last night I heard Mom, Dad, and Janis downstairs laughing. I couldn't believe they were having such a good time when I was so miserable, and all I could feel was lots and lots of anger."

"Were you resentful because you were excluded?"

"I suppose. But I don't understand why I get so angry when Mom, Janis, and Brian all goof off. I get furious at their frivolity. It seems so phony to me."

"It's called *depression*, Jenny. And that's why I'm here. So you can have someone who's not emotionally involved to talk to about it."

"Sometimes I think I should take antidepressants."

"Talking about it is better. Don't you see how important it is that both Mom and Dad validated your feelings that Tony molested you?"

"I suppose I do."

"Did you talk to your other doctors about abuse?"

"The doctor who did my first Pap smear said my hymen had been broken. Mom and I had speculated it was because of riding. Last week I asked the doctor if horseback riding would break it. He didn't have an opinion. He did explain that some hymens aren't real functional anyway.

"Then I talked to Dr. Corbin. He explained that his approach to my therapy was different from yours, more supportive than analytical, more coping with today than exploring yesterday. He said he remembers nothing specific, but he has an overall feeling that we are right, that I was abused. He said he might have had some concerns about the relationship between Mom and me when I was little. When I got off the phone, Mom was sitting at the bottom of the stairs. I don't know how much she overheard, but she spent the evening at the MacGregors.' That's where she goes when she needs to escape from the house. I woke up at 1 A.M., and she and Dad were still awake talking. I had a terrible foreboding they were plotting to put me in the state mental hospital. I'm still terrified something is going on, and I'll be the last to find out. Paranoia?"

"Probably. What about Don Marin?"

"He called back on Friday. He said he looked again at my test results and saw no indication of abuse, only my obvious dependency on Mom. He suggested I look at what I resent in Mom now and quit trying to find something in the past to justify my resentment. I was angry he didn't support our theory.

"So, now I'm even more troubled and confused. Part of me says, Jenny, you're just a spoiled brat looking for reasons for your bad behavior, and you were never hurt at all. Then I have more nightmares and can't remember them but wake up feeling angry at Mom. So another part of me says it's true, it's true. If we can't prove abuse, I'll finish myself because I can't deal with it anymore. I'm tired of emotions that scream yes, and an intellect that argues no, because we have so little proof."

"Jenny, it's hard to prove abuse after so many years. We rely on your feelings and memory fragments to draw rational conclusions about what happened, not necessarily prove it. There are more recollections hiding inside you, and we must be patient, wait until they come out."

"If I can stay alive that long."

"Which brings us to Willowcrest. We should decide this week about returning to the hospital. I'm worried about you."

Jenny's eyes filled with tears. "I know," she said, slowly nodding her head.

"More memories for me?"

"A few. Remember how sure you were last year that I fantasized about having Dad to myself if Mom died?"

"Yes, when we discussed your Oedipus complex."

"Well, you sorta had it backward, cause I remember fantasizing that if Dad was killed, it would be okay as long as we still had his savings, but Mom's dying would be unbearable for me."

"Maybe you switched your obsession from Mom to Dad."

"I don't think so. I'm still obsessed with getting Mom to like me."

"Why do you think she doesn't?"

"Despite the nice things Mom says or does for me, a lot of her actions make me feel disliked. She loves to find fault with me. Like last year when my therapy centered on what an obstinate brat I was, Mom seemed to get intense gratification whenever you scolded me."

"And how do you feel toward her?"

"Anger. Disgust, sometimes. When she's at church or on the phone, I sense that it's not always the real Mom I hear . . . false is the best word for it. It's like Mom denies the reality that once she hurt me and is still mean to me. After all, how could a good Christian woman mistreat her child in any way?"

"What about your other resentments toward Mom?"

"I wrote them down after I talked to Don Marin." Jenny shuffled back through her notes. "I resent that Mom never seemed to love me unconditionally like Nancy and Brian, or at least passively like Janis. I resent Mom getting involved in my horses as much as she did . . . like she

pushed me out of my own life . . . she was so controlling. I resent Mom's
devotion to the church to the point nothing else has much importance.
I resent she never taught me about femininity . . . shaving, washing, tampons, nail care, clothes. Especially clothes. I resent not being given a
wardrobe I felt confident wearing. I resent her constant intrusion into
parts of my life: haircuts, friends . . . 'You shouldn't see Diane, she just
uses you.' Bullshit . . . Diane's my best friend. I resent her giving me
things that suit her taste and not mine. I resent that when I try to talk to
Mom about troubling memories, she constantly says, why do you have
to remember, why don't you just face the fact you were scared and go
on with your life?"

"She may feel she has no other way to cope with your memories. It's
hard for us, too. Remembered fears spill out of you like a flood sometimes."

"I don't know which to analyze, which not to pursue. Like what I
remembered yesterday about an elderly baby-sitter."

"Tell me what you remembered."

"It connects to my fears about basements. Mom used to take David,
Nancy, and me over to Mrs. Herbert's house. I remember Mrs. Herbert
would put me in a cage in her basement while she baked cookies, and
David and Nancy played upstairs on the kind of toy trucks you sit on.
I was terrified and wanted Mom to come and rescue me."

"Did Mrs. Herbert hurt you?"

"I don't know. I think she may have. I can't remember anything more
about her."

"Have you remembered anything more about Tony?"

"He came into my room once and showed me pictures. I sat on his
lap, and . . . and he touched me." Jenny dropped her gaze from Dr. Weintraub to the floor, as if in shame. "But there was something worse that
happened at some other time. But I can't remember. It's unclear, buried
in darkness. Every time I try to remember, all I see is the dark, and I
become very frightened. I even talked to my grandmother about him . . .
she's Tony's stepmother. She said Daddad, Tony's own father, had a poor
opinion of him. She said Tony borrowed money from Daddad and never

paid him back, that Daddad had a good sense about men, so that if he was negative about Tony, he had good reason to be."

"Tony sounds like the key. Keep trying to remember. Now, how do you feel about going back to Willowcrest?"

"I know it will be terrible in some ways. Willowcrest is so sheltered and unreal. I'll have to face nurses who assume I'm anorexic because I'm a persistent bitch. I won't like feeling abandoned by my family, confined and controlled by others again. My parents, particularly Dad, are skeptical now if Willowcrest can help me. On the other hand, I'm terrified of how poorly I'm functioning lately and what will happen if I don't go back to the hospital. I know at Willowcrest I can rest and be safe. Maybe I can break my self-destructive routines, and I'll get help from nurses I really like, like Marybeth. I know she can help me with the feelings that might cause suicidal impulses."

"Our first priority will be to resolve your abuse issues. Can I set up an admission for you next week?"

"Yes, I'm ready. But I can't remember any abuse other than the stuff I've mentioned. I can't remember anything really bad and that scares me. I'm afraid I may be wrong and leading everyone off track."

"I know you're right, Jenny. Trust your feelings. You have so many of the classic abused child characteristics: your loss of self-esteem, your feelings of guilt and shame, your extended period of thumb sucking, all your terrible fears when you were young. Nearly half of abused children also develop changes in eating habits. Don't you see what happened? You hurt so badly but didn't know why. You needed someone to see your pain and take care of you, and your anorexia was the way you tried to express your need. Your anorexia didn't work at home, because the responses all geared into your eating disorder, the symptom, and not the underlying cause, which was your abuse. Because your therapy hasn't focused on the right cause yet, it hasn't worked either. Now that we know why you're broken, we can fix you."

CHAPTER ELEVEN

I'm Sorry, Jenny

*T*hey embraced awkwardly. "Bye, Jenny," her mother said.

Then Jenny held the front door open, while her mother slipped through with a suitcase. "Bye, Mom . . . give Meme my love."

"I will. I'm sorry you have to go back, Jenny . . . and I'm sorry we'll miss your birthday."

"Me, too," Jenny said. She knew her parents' quick trip to visit her grandmother was long overdue.

"Are you sure you're okay with admitting yourself tomorrow?"

"Yes. I'm not afraid. I know Willowcrest is best for me right now."

Afterward, Jenny trudged upstairs to pack for her journey of a different kind. *Will I ever have a vacation again?* she wondered. Simple decisions about what to take overwhelmed her. How could she pack when she didn't know how long she'd be gone? A month? Two months? A year? Jenny stared at her suitcase lying open on her bed next to a stack of neatly folded sweaters. *I'll finish later,* she decided.

The next day, Janis offered to take her sister to Willowcrest, but Jenny had already arranged to drive a family car. They said good-bye in the driveway. Janis hugged Jenny fiercely, wincing at her sister's fragility. "I'm sorry, Jenny. And I'm really sad you have to go back."

Jenny smiled bravely. "At least you won't have to worry about me messing the bathroom."

"Yup. That'll be nice." Janis kept her hands on Jenny's arms, as if unwilling to let her go. "I'll bring Brian with me to see you on your birthday Wednesday . . . after school." She hesitated, wanting to say more, fearing a flood of tears if she did.

"That'll be really nice. Now let me go before I start to cry."

"Bye, big sister."

"Bye, little sister."

Their moment of tenderness passed. Janis stood and waved as Jenny backed out of the driveway. Jenny flashed one of her old carefree smiles and waved back. Her tears didn't begin until she turned the corner.

April 11. 73½ pounds. My blood work came back and Weintraub is worried. Not good birthday news. I have a very low white cell count—from the high-fever infections. She says my body is so depleted of its natural defenses that a mild infection could kill me. Willowcrest is also concerned about my heart. They think it's greatly weakened, and they fear an attack or failure if I overexert. I think they're wrong, but they control. So no passes or exercising. How will I stand it? Have to. Particularly today. Mustn't disappoint my visitors. MacGregors here for lunch. Janis and Brian, also Diane, this afternoon. I'm twenty today. No longer a teenager. Feel like I never was a teenager. Jenny's missing years.

Memories—Treasuring any gift Mom gave me: birthday clothes, knitting and drawing materials. It's like they became magical and by loving them I could love her, or if I loved what she loved, maybe she would love me. Corned beef, it's gross, can't eat it, my gag reflex won't let me. Mom standing above me making me eat it no matter if it chokes me. Tony and I looking at pictures in Mom and Dad's bedroom. On bed. Then darkness again . . . and terror.

April 14. 73½ pounds. Mom and Nancy here at 11:00. My great-grandmother and Brian later. Utter hopelessness. Don't care if I starve myself into oblivion because I'm skeptical getting well is going to be good. I cannot fathom going home again, much less being on my own. I feel so utterly stripped and unreal, like I'll never get to the point where I can just live life. In a way I want to give up my control: eat, relax, gain weight, focus on problems. But I don't know how to deal with the self-destructive rage I feel when I give up control.

In her second week at Willowcrest, Jenny began a new behavior modification program. Despite a flurry of visitors spilling over from a farewell party for David, soon bound for Australia, her agitation and depression deepened. Jenny continued to lose weight, strength, and cognizance. As Jenny's mind continued its relentless search into the past, Dr. Weintraub fought to keep her patient connected to reality. Abandoning her previous reservations about using drugs, Dr. Weintraub prescribed Librium and Tofranil, Jenny's first exposure to hospital meds.

Jenny's therapeutic focus on her relationship with her mother continued. So did its concealment from her parents. Dr. Weintraub pressed Jenny for a family meeting. "It's time we talked to Mom and Dad."

"Can we talk to Dad first?" Jenny asked fearfully. "Mom's gone until next week. She's at a Catholic monastery on her annual retreat."

"Will Dad be defensive?"

"No. He knows Mom is hostile sometimes. I don't think he'll deny my feelings."

Using her notes and journals to stay organized, Jenny spoke hesitantly about her mother. Apprehensive about her father's response, she glanced up several times, trying without success to read a reaction on his face. *Why does he seem so calm?* she wondered. Even his questions were subdued, almost impersonal. Dr. Weintraub watched them both carefully.

"So, what do you think, Dad?" Jenny concluded. Her expression was earnest, hopeful.

He answered carefully. "I've always thought your mother started to find fault with you after you got sick. We've talked about that before. But I didn't see anything abusive in how she treated you when you were younger. It's hard for me to think of her as physically abusive—ever. She's stern and inflexible sometimes. But physically abusive? I don't think so."

Jenny was close to tears. "Yes, Dad, physically abusive. It's hard for me, too. Really hard. I wish you could support our theory."

"I'm sorry that I can't, but I'm not convinced she hurt you when you were little. I understand your other resentments. They're valid."

Dr. Weintraub intervened. "Did you know, Mr. Hendricks, that the nonabusive parent is generally unaware of a child's abuse at the hands of the other parent? Jenny has talked about your being somewhere in the ether when you got sick, and . . ."

"But Dad was sick and out of it after I started showing horses," Jenny interrupted anxiously, "not before, when I think Mom was abusive to me."

"Just because Dad didn't see anything doesn't mean it didn't happen, Jenny." Dr. Weintraub's manner was reassuring, not critical. She turned back to Jenny's father. "This must be distressing to you—to hear Jenny talk about your wife this way. Why do I see so little emotion?"

"I've spent twenty-five years in a profession very unlike yours, where I've been conditioned not to show emotion, even in situations that are supercharged emotionally. It doesn't mean I don't have emotional responses, it just means you're not likely to see them. I'm also used to absorbing and reflecting on a lot of facts before making judgments."

"Can't you tell me how you feel? Shocked, disgusted, angry, sorry?"

"Will you settle for upset? I feel badly that Jenny was abused by others, maybe Anne, and I wasn't there to prevent it. Hell, yes, I'm upset."

"Maybe you're feeling negligent?"

"Whatever you want to call it. I also feel like I'll have to tell Anne."

"Let that happen in open session next week."

"I can't. I need to talk to her first."

"It's your decision." Dr. Weintraub shrugged her sloping shoulders.

"I'm concerned for Anne as well as Jenny, and I'm worried how anyone can tell Anne, or any mother, she may have abused her daughter. There's no good way to do that."

"I'm worried, too." Jenny clasped and unclasped her hands nervously. "I know Mom will deny hurting me, try to make it into a bad me against a good her and get Dad to side with her."

"Don't sell Dad short." Dr. Weintraub smiled wryly. "He's a very independent thinker."

"I'm feeling suicidal," Jenny confessed to Dr. Weintraub the following Monday. "I can't but think about anything except how hopeless I am." Her haunted facial expression, drawn features, slumped posture, and her general listlessness defined her state of mind as clearly as her words.

Fearful that she was losing her patient, Dr. Weintraub fought to keep Jenny focused. "I know you're anxious about confronting Mom. If you don't feel better after Wednesday's session, we'll move you to third floor RTU for better supervision."

Another symbol of failure, Jenny thought. "For my own protection, you mean," she said. "At least that's better than restraints."

Dr. Weintraub pressed on. "Did Dad talk to Mom?"

"Yesterday when she got home. He came down to see me afterward, but he didn't want to talk about it. He said we would just have to see how our session goes."

"What's important is to release the resentment built up in you, regardless of how well you can remember or analyze its source. Your feelings are undeniable sacred truths. Mom will have to accept that."

The conference table was rectangular, with six chairs. Dr. Weintraub sat at the head with Jenny on the right. Jenny felt her body begin to tremble and fought to suppress her fear. Her mother took a facing seat across the table. Her father paused, uncertain where to sit. Dr. Weintraub noticed his hesitancy. As she expected, he finally settled into the end chair between Jenny and her mother. All faces were grim.

Dr. Weintraub began, "You've heard most of this in bits and pieces, but let me summarize first. And then Jenny needs to unburden and talk about her feelings.

"Jenny's anorexia is tied directly to childhood abuse. She displays the classic behavior of an abused child with repressed memories. As is typical, her recollections are sometimes precise, but more often they are hazy and uncertain. However, her overwhelming feelings of self-hate, fear, and resentment are genuine and must be respected. Here is what we know or reasonably believe.

"As a small child, Jenny had a traumatizing experience with a baby-sitter who confined her in a dark place and may have physically abused her. During preadolescence she had improper experiences with horse people, ranging from repeated fondlings by her elderly trainer, to sexual play with Maria and others, and at least one incident of oral sex with a young farrier who—"

"He forced me, Mom," Jenny interrupted tearfully. "It was Billy Calhoun. It happened in a stall in the barn. I only remembered yesterday."

Mrs. Hendricks winced. "It's okay, Jenny." She spoke gently and with compassion.

"No, it's not okay, Mom. That's the point."

"That's not what I meant . . ."

With a loud "I'd like to continue, please," Dr. Weintraub regained control of the session and fixed a solemn gaze on Jenny's mother. "Also during this period, Jenny was sexually molested by your stepbrother. This was a primary triggering event to your daughter's illness, and I know it may be devastating for you to accept."

"I've told Jenny it was believable."

"She needs to know that you believe it. That you say it's believable isn't enough."

Turning to Jenny, her mother spoke with genuine anguish and without hesitation. "I do believe it, Jenny. And I'm so sorry it happened."

"There were at least two instances," Dr. Weintraub continued. "In the first Jenny was only fondled or pawed. You've seen the picture you took that evening?"

"Yes. But I don't remember that evening, and—"

"Of course not, Mom. You were drunk."

A mother's angry eyes scolded her daughter. "I don't get drunk, Jenny."

"Okay," Jenny shrieked. "You had a zillion glasses of wine but weren't drunk yet."

"Whoa!" Dr. Weintraub intervened. "Drinking habits are not at issue here. There was another incident with Tony, and it torments Jenny beyond her ability to deal with it rationally. Whatever happened . . ."

"I can't remember, Mom," Jenny sobbed. "But it was something really, really bad."

"I'm afraid she's right, Mrs. Hendricks. What happened isn't clear. But it's obviously too terrible for her mind to release. I'm confident she eventually will remember."

"Is it so important for her to remember?" Jenny's father spoke for the first time. "She suffers so much anguish giving birth to her memories. It's killing her. Trying to resurrect specifically what happened, when we all believe Tony molested her, doesn't make sense."

"I don't think she can rest easy until she does remember. And that's why she's here . . . to have professional help dealing with memory search and its consequences."

"I want to know, Dad," Jenny added.

He shrugged his shoulders, grumbling, "Damn cure is worse than the disease."

Dr. Weintraub peered at him disapprovingly over her spectacles but remained focused on her summary. "Before we get to Jenny's most difficult recollections, I must caution everyone that others could be involved. Only time will tell how complete Jenny's recall may be."

Jenny's father asked, "Should we go after those who sexually abused her? I suppose that's a good reason to remember specifics. Can we punish them after all this time?"

"My recommendation is not to consider sanctions now. Jenny's health is too precarious to divert time or attention away from improving her condition to punishing her offenders. I'm not sure we can prove there were punishable acts." Dr. Weintraub again turned her attention to Jenny's mother. "Now . . . Jenny's feelings about you." Dr. Weintraub paused, as if expecting a reaction. Other than a barely perceptible stiffening of her body, Jenny's mother gave no outward sign of response and remained silent. "Jenny has terrible fears and angers that center on her relationship with you and stem from childhood events, some of which she remembers clearly, many of which are shadowy and unclear. She is terrified of discussing these with you, and she still shrinks from using the word *abuse* in describing them. I know your husband tried to discuss this with you, and he is skeptical that there was anything abusive in your early relationship with Jenny. However . . . and I cannot overemphasize the importance of this . . . Jenny has intense feelings that you abused her both physically and emotionally when she was very young. Her feelings are beyond the typical adolescent resentments I have to listen to on a daily basis. I insist that her feelings be respected. They must be dealt with and resolved. To do that we have to get at the conflict that continues between the two of you, and we can't do that without bringing Jenny's feelings about the past into the open and dealing with them in a nonantagonistic fashion. I know that's a difficult order, but it's necessary. It's not a conflict that has to have a winner and a loser. And it's not a question of who's right and who's wrong, who's good and who's bad, or who's supported and who's denied. It's a question of acknowledging a badly damaged relationship between you and your daughter, being honest that you are both responsible, and deciding if it can be repaired or needs to be repaired in order for Jenny to break her devotion to anorexia before it kills her."

Dr. Weintraub folded her hands in front of her and leaned back in her chair as if to say, *I've finished. Now, it's up to you.*

Emotion-filled gazes of mother and daughter remained fixed on each other. Neither anger nor hostility nor resentment was present in either's eyes. Only grief and pain. Jenny wept openly, uncontrollably. Tears welled over her mother's swollen eyelids. Jenny's tortured face was that of a silent supplicant, wanting, needing, waiting.

In an instinctive response to her child, Jenny's mother reached across the table with her palms up. Jenny brought up her hands, clutched so tightly in her lap as to turn her knuckles white, and hesitantly extended them toward her mother. Fingertips met. Mother's hands slipped under and closed over daughter's. At that moment there were no others present in the room, only a lost mother and a lost daughter holding on to each other as if connected by a lifeline.

"I'm sorry, Jenny. So sorry. I wish I could go back and change it. All of it. I regret beyond any words I can speak that others I was fond of hurt you. I regret anything I've done that hurt you. I never meant to hurt you. I only wanted to love you."

"But, *did* you love me, Mom? *Do* you?" The plea of a wounded child.

"Oh-h-h, yes." A wounded mother's wailing lament. "How could you think otherwise?"

"I didn't feel it, Mom. Most of the time, I still don't. Mostly I just feel your hostility."

"I'm sorry, Jenny."

"Why did you let Tony do what he did?" Jenny's pleading voice was agony, not anger.

"Jenny, I didn't . . . I didn't know."

"How could you not see the weird relationship with Maria, how Bob couldn't keep his hands off me?"

"I didn't know." Her mother sobbed and then regained her composure, breaking physical contact with her daughter by withdrawing her hands. Their bond of mutual need severed easily.

A floodgate opened in Jenny—to a torrent that surged through it. "And all the times growing up. Did you have to beat me with a paddle . . . and then . . . then a hairbrush . . . every day? It made me feel—"

Old patterns of entrenched behavior reasserted themselves. Anger returned to her mother's louder voice, as she interrupted. "Jenny, it wasn't every day, and—"

"—so certain I was a bad girl. Was I that bad?"

"Of course not," her mother snapped.

"You almost never bought me clothes and those you did never fit. It made me feel—"

"Your clothes—"

Jenny continued to fight submission. "—so unimportant to you, more like . . . like an inconvenience than a daughter. Was . . . was—"

"Jenny, that's not fair."

"—was that punishment, too?"

"Of course not. Don't be absurd. I—"

"You were so involved with my horses, so controlling. It made me feel—"

"Jenny, I was not. The horse shows were—"

"—like I wasn't a *me*, just an extension of you."

"Jenny, you're not letting me finish."

"No, Mom, you're not letting me finish. I'm not going to let you shout me down this time."

"I am *not* shouting you down."

Jenny spoke in haste, avoiding her mother's glare. "I want you to know how terrible it feels sometimes to be your daughter, how terrible it feels when you are too busy to spend time with me on my birthday or—"

"Jenny, I've only missed one of your birthdays."

"—when you give me hideous gifts, like that ugly old trunk for my graduation, that reflect your taste without any thought to mine. It sends—"

"You never told me you didn't like the trunk."

"—me a different message from what you say. It makes me feel like you hate me."

"Of course I don't hate you."

"Because a good Christian woman like you could never do the unthinkable . . . hate her child? Then why didn't you help me with femininity, teach me about shaving, washing, tampons, nail care, clothes? I felt like every step I took toward growing up was met with your resentment."

"But why would I resent your growing up?"

"I don't know, Mom."

"And why would I hate you?"

"That's just it. I don't know why you treated me like you did. I don't know why I have such a strong feeling that you hurt me when I was too little to understand what you were doing. I feel like I wasn't then and I'm still not the child you wanted me to be."

"That's absurd, Jenny. I can't help how you feel about the past. What do you expect of me? What do you want me to do?"

Drained and listless, Jenny closed her eyes and slumped in her chair. Then she leaned forward. Her hand crept across the tabletop toward her mother, but it did not find what it sought. Jenny bent her forearm back and nestled her head into the inside vee of her elbow. "Love me, Mom, just love me," was her muffled, emotionless response.

Realizing the conflict had run its course, Dr. Weintraub intervened, ending the session. "I think everyone has had enough for today. Mr. Hendricks, please stay a moment."

Jenny and her mother left without speaking further. Dr. Weintraub said to Jenny's father, "I'm sorry I didn't see their awful conflict sooner . . . or recognize its significance."

"But why isn't Jenny mad at me?" he asked in a husky voice. "I'm the father. I'm supposed to protect my children. Obviously I didn't do it."

"We'll discuss that later. Right now we have to work on the conflict between those two. I want you and Mrs. Hendricks to meet weekly with Dr. Langley. I finally saw your wife's hostility revealed today. Her initial response and apology were wonderful, very sincere. But then she refused to hear Jenny's pain, only heard Jenny's accusations. She's not dealing with the situation. She needs help to do that, to acknowledge the broken relationship with her daughter. She also needs reassurance that a failed relationship is not an indictment of her entire life or her relationships with others, that she isn't a bad person, just as Jenny needs the same reassurance."

"Can't we do that with you? Together with Jenny? Try to heal their wounds together?"

"No. I don't have time. Jenny's condition is too critical. It will take all my energy to save her. Until she is substantially improved, I'm going to cut off all contact with her family. It's too unhealthy. She has to separate from her mother. Don't worry, I'll brief Langley. I've already counseled with him about your daughter's case."

Rather than relieving Jenny of her burden, the confrontation with her mother had intensified it. Drained of emotional strength and exhausted physically, Jenny no longer had the will to fight her mind demons. She gorged on despair, became hysterical, and roamed the hallways wringing her hands and sobbing, "I can't stand it. I'll never get better. I can't take it anymore." No one could talk her down this time. She had simply run out of cope. She was placed on suicide alert.

Dr. Weintraub moved Jenny to the third floor and ordered her sequestered in a quiet room devoid of hazard—or comfort. "I'm sorry, Jenny," she said, "but we have to do this."

Too tired to protest, Jenny docilely accepted her first consignment to modern medicine's alternative to the straightjacket.

Alone in the quiet room, Jenny sat on a cot, heavily medicated, unfettered, and unhappy. A ruddy face appeared at a small observation window built into the door. It made an effort to smile as it peered in at Jenny. Knowing not even a scream could penetrate beyond her walls, Jenny mouthed the words "come in." The nurse unlocked the door, entered, and switched on a single overhead light. "I have a telegram for you," she said gently and left, carefully locking the door behind her.

Jenny opened the telegram and read slowly, without emotion.

> *Dear Little Sister . . . you are flesh of my flesh. Remember*
> *that I always have and always will love you. Hang in there.*
> *Love . . . Nancy*

Jenny reread the telegram, let it slip from her fingers to the floor, picked it up, read it again, bemoaned the absence of a pillow or sheet to tuck it under, and placed it on the floor. Then she rose, turned off the light, and returned to the cot. She lay on her side, knees drawn to her chest, back to the door, eyes wide open, staring at the empty wall, unseeing, uncaring. As she lay quietly in the darkened, windowless room, a single tear formed in each eye.

CHAPTER TWELVE

You Are the Rat

*I*n her fifth week at Willowcrest, Jenny's weight slipped to 70 pounds, and Dr. Weintraub started her on a program used by Johns Hopkins Hospital. New program, same emphasis. We are going to refeed you, reward you when you gain, punish you when you don't. A rat-in-the-cage behavior modification approach: you are the rat. Here are the privileges you are denied and can regain only by gaining weight. You cannot plan or select your food, eat unsupervised, go to the bathroom unsupervised, deviate from a rigidly prescribed caloric intake, exercise in any way, have passes, go off this third floor, have visitors except clergy, or make phone calls without prior approval. Your friends and family may write but not visit or call. You must sit still for one hour after meals.

Progress measurement remained the same—daily weight gain. The method changed; Jenny would now be weighed standing backward on the scale. She would no longer know her precise weight; however, she would know whether she gained or lost from changes to her restrictions. Unchallenged by the facts, Jenny would be free to inflate her guesses about how much she gained simply by looking in the mirror. She would still have to endure an awful feelings paradox. To gain privileges she would have to aggravate her fatness anxieties. To calm her fatness fears she would have to remain restricted. A classic no-win situation.

And her therapeutic program? It remained mired in the conviction that Jenny's anorexia was caused by childhood abuse. Validation was sought in further analyzing the past. Talk therapy remained parent preoccupied and intensely introspective.

May 12. All of my nightmares end up with Mom trying to kill me and then someone else comes and she acts like she loves me. I read an article in Cosmo about a girl who hates herself because her mother hates her. It could have been written by me, only she has a boyfriend.

"Do you think Mom hated you when you were a baby?"

"Yes, and only me. When I was born, David was six, Nancy four. They were in school or preschool, so for two years until Janis was born, I was home alone with Mom, and she had plenty of chances to hurt me."

"As a teenager, why didn't you question your sense of impending doom, analyze its origins, rather than seeking relief from your feelings by avoiding food?"

"What could have happened is that no one understood there was an early childhood source to my hysterical feelings, so I accepted that the true origins . . . Mom hurting me . . . the sexual abuse . . . were unreal. The mother who took care of me when Dad or my brothers and sisters were around was a false reality. Even though Mom was mildly abusive verbally when they were present, that was nothing compared to what I sense she did when they were absent.

"Or . . . because no one else saw me being hurt, and Mom doesn't acknowledge hurting me, maybe my feelings about her are totally imaginary. Since I can't justify my feelings, I beat myself with them."

"But why punish yourself?"

"I think I decided I was a bad girl for having such terrible feelings about unrealities . . . being hurt. If being hurt was real, people would have seen . . . but they didn't . . . no one saw . . . so I must be crazy and deserve to die."

"No, Jenny, you don't deserve to die, and you're not crazy. What people didn't see, you being hurt, was real. They just didn't see it happen. It's like a cut you might have. No one sees how the cut was inflicted, but the wound and its bleeding confirm the cut's reality. Your wound and bleeding are emotional, less visual but still apparent in your behavior and feelings, which confirm the reality that you were hurt. That reality is simply easier for others to deny."

"Do you know how food and mother have gone together since the beginning of time?"

"Because mothers feed their young?"

"Yes. And milk and mothers go together even more. So when you reject both food and milk, you are really rejecting mother."

"I thought I reject milk because it gives me a stomachache. I used to really crave milk, though. I remember a baby-sitter getting angry with me when I drank too much milk at dinner after I arrived home dehydrated from the barn."

"Do you see how you were set up, even back then, to accept punishment for having a need? And now you punish yourself when you are needy. The baby-sitter should have sent you to the barn with a thermos of milk and should not have punished you for being thirsty at dinner."

"I have such a sense of loss about my childhood. I don't know what I missed, but once I hit sixth grade, my feeling was wait! stop! slow down, something is missing. Maybe what I missed was childhood nurturing of self-esteem. Then when I went to college, it was vividly clear that whatever I had missed was irretrievable. For a long time I sacrificed my self-development in attempts to get back my lost early years, so there was no self to take care of me. When I realized I couldn't recover what was missing, I chose death because I couldn't live without it."

"Jenny, you must give up your single-minded pursuit of a nurturing childhood you didn't have. You are grieving over its loss and that's natural. But you have to go on and find meaning in your life without it. Suicide is not an option for dealing with its loss."

"But how do I go on?"

"You need to develop ingredients for you to feel a *you* exists, develop self-esteem because you *are*, not because you survived abuse. You need to like, be liked, and have fun without a sense that the world will fall in."

"But how?"

"You have to quit nurturing the child. She's never coming back. Start nurturing the adult. You must create a self for yourself, a self you like and can be proud of."

"But how can I do that in a hospital?"

"We will help you begin the process."

"Are Mom and Dad meeting with Dr. Langley? I've only been allowed to talk to them on Mother's Day and Father's Day, and we didn't talk about my treatment at all."

"They stopped after several meetings. Your dad called. He said the sessions were going nowhere. Langley confirms that. Your dad says they can't work together because Dr. Langley looks too much like Tony. 'A dead ringer from the neck up' is what he said."

June 10. Dr. Weintraub says she and Dr. Langley think Mom may have hated me because I wasn't what Mom expected a child to be. Mom won't ever admit she hated me because she would be devastated by such an admission. I shouldn't condemn myself just because she doesn't like me in the way I have wanted. Nothing I do is going to change the fact that our relationship is not as good as those between her and my brothers and sisters. Whatever bad went on between us is over, and I need to say good-bye and quit investing so much energy in waiting for her to come around and like me. I have to quit punishing her with my illness. It's up to me to like me.

June 15. Results came back from chemical depression test. Negative. Today I start a grief group. Next week an anger group. That's what I am, my identity—a groupie!

June 19. I don't know how to help myself and staff doesn't either. I mean, help me BELIEVE I can beat this, help me BELIEVE I won't always be so consumed by self-hatred.

June 21. Another FUCKING disgusting awful day to live through.

June 23. GET AWAY FROM ME!!!

July 1. I hate life. I hate me, Mom, Dr. Weintraub, staff, my family, everyone. I feel like shit. I can't sleep. I don't want to eat. I hate my body, feel flabby, don't trust I will ever be normal. I can't stand to gain any more weight. I will rip myself apart. I can't stand how disgusted I feel, like I need to be beaten, hung up, dried out, and ripped apart.

"The anger you turn on yourself is your anger toward your family and others redirected."

"What you say sounds rational. Why can't I believe it?"

"You will. In time, you will."

"But the anger you say I'm supposed to have against my family doesn't seem real."

"What seems real, Jenny?"

"My disgustingness. My unworthiness. The fear that if I take it easy on myself, my body and I will be horribly worse. What's real for me today are my feelings that if I eat today, I will have to rip myself apart piece by piece, feelings that I cannot allow this body to become any grosser than it already is. If I eat I get fatter. If I get fatter I get flabbier. If I get flabbier I will lose my mind. I hate it! Even my hair and my face look fucking ugly to me."

"You will feel better as we work through your anger against others and your grief over the death of your relationship with Mom and other family members."

"So I have to keep working on feelings that don't seem real to me, while my real feelings run rampant and unattended? Why can't I go to a fat and flabby group?"

"Jenny, you know we don't have that kind of group. And staff is always available to talk to you about your delusional body image. All those terrible things you tell yourself—about how fat and flabby you are, how much you need to hurt yourself, how undeserving you are, what a failure you are—that's just Mom internalized."

"Intellectually I understand that, but emotionally I feel that I am bad. You used to tell me how bad I am."

"You're not bad, Jenny. Bad things were done to you. What I hold you accountable for is that you continue to reenact your misery. You're afraid to get better, so you don't."

"But when I tell myself I'm not bad, my inner voice says that's propaganda and if I believe it, I'll be even badder. That voice constantly says 'If people only knew.'"

"Jenny, do you agree that I know you?"

"Yes. You know me through and through."

"Well, I still like you, just for you."

July 12. *Today, after thirteen weeks, I get to go outside for the first time. YAHOO!!*

    July 15. *Today I get phone privileges—with others but not with family. Call Diane first. Weintraub is leaving.*

"I'm terrified about your leaving and going to Paris for a month. Same abandoned feeling I had when you were gone last month."

"Jenny, your anxiety is burning too many calories. You haven't gained weight in two weeks. You know Dr. Langley will work with you while I'm gone."

"Swell. Now I get to work with a doctor who has the face of a man who abused me."

"I thought we agreed that was just an excuse your parents used."

"At least they had a choice."

July 20. *Dr. Langley says I should write down what I want from my parents, then analyze if it's possible and if it's worth it. So here goes: MOM (1) Unprejudiced treatment. No setting up my brothers and sisters against me (talking about how rotten I am). No passing my problems around to neighbors and friends. When she does that I always come out looking crazy while she is the poor martyr who puts up with me. (2) Like me and be supportive—in some clear way. She verbally attests to both of these things, but for some reason I have never felt she was genuine. (3) Forgiveness for throwing up in her bathrooms, bingeing on her food, and doing whatever it is that has made her hate me so much; i.e., embarrassing her and being different. DAD (1) More belief in my abilities—scholastic, artistic, intellectual, self-supportive. I want to feel that Dad believes I could amount to something, do what I want to do and be successful. (2) Treat me like a woman. Compliment my looks, talk to me about* boyfriends, take an interest in my social growth. (3) Financial support until I am well established in that area.

IS MY FANTASY POSSIBLE? MOM—I feel like Mom hated me long before I became anorexic, but in becoming anorexic I gave her a concrete reason to hate me. So she will have to separate her anger at Jenny the anorexic from her anger at Jenny her daughter, a person. If she can do that, we could get rid of the anorexic anger and have a more clear picture of her real anger, at least get it out in the open. I don't know if Mom could do that because it might be too risky for her to admit she hated me before I caused her to. I'm not sure Mom will ever treat me humanely because she will have to let go of the old anger first. I don't think it's feasible that she can forgive me or treat me unprejudicially. I think someday Mom could like me. If I were to separate from her for a long time, live away, and develop a successful life for myself, maybe she could at least tolerate and respect me. Then there would be no reason for her to dismiss me as crazy. DAD—I feel that Dad could believe in me and treat me as pretty and womanly, but, I think, only after I have first proven myself. It will be nice to get that then, but, in a way, it'll be too late for him to help me achieve my individuality and self-worth. I'll have done it on my own. I know I can count on Dad's financial support.

IS IT WORTH IT? MOM—I honestly don't know. The only way it would be worth it would be if I wanted to be part of our family again. I am not and cannot become a member when the monarch cannot stand me. And I don't foresee needing to be part of the family unit. DAD—My relationship with my father is definitely worth it, because I think he loves me, despite his frustration with me.

Four months after Jenny's admission, Dr. Langley noted encouraging signs of progress:

- *Patient looks pretty good, has gained almost 10 pounds and now shows normal blood chemistry. She knows weight triggers discharge but doesn't know the magic number is 90 pounds.*
- *No longer mother-dependent on Dr. Weintraub.*

- *No longer abusive to herself or setting up situations for others to be abusive to her.*
- *Eating a regular diet and eating everything.*
- *Improved self-image with weight gain.*
- *Staff nurses are devoted to her.*
- *She is working hard on weaning from her image of her mother and grieving over her loss.*
- *She is beginning to acknowledge and accept responsibility for her contribution to the impaired mother/daughter relationship.*
- *Soon we need to shift program emphasis away from weight gain.*

August 2. Family going to the ranch for two weeks. First time without me. Feeling abandoned again. Weintraub gone, family gone. I haven't had any family contact in weeks. My grief group is supposed to help me overcome loss of family. It isn't.

August 3. Couldn't stand confinement. Ran away. Spent day riding around in the bus. Returned late. Dr. Langley stayed to talk to me. He's a nice man.

August 5. Can't stand being fat. Raged most of the day.

August 6. Raged.

August 7. Raged. Got locked in the quiet room again.

August 10. Raged in A.M. Family back. Langley said Dad called, wanted to know about my treatment plan. I'm not permitted to call Dad, so here's what I"m going to write to him. MOST IMPORTANT, I've been allowed more responsibility for my physical process: (1) I'm expected to gain 1 pound a week in order to retain the following privileges: unaccompanied ½ hour outside per shift, ½ hour outside exercise time four times a week. (2) Regardless of weight gain, I'm allowed two fifteen-minute walks per day—with staff. (3) I'm working with the hospital nutritionist to balance my caloric intake and output. She brings up menus, and I pick the foods I would like. Together we check for balance, nutritional value, and calories. She has been impressed with my ability to make good choices. (4) I am now weighed frontward so that I know my progress.

As I continue to gain weight, more privileges will be added: (1) More time outside. (2) Passes (for haircuts, movies, dancing). (3) Eating with others in the cafeteria downstairs.

On the therapeutic side, we have been discussing: (1) Self-esteem. Major emphasis. How it was lost and how to get it back. Also self-destructive impulses—why they occur and ways of dealing with them. (2) Expectations—what I want under control before I leave. Emptiness gone (feeling like I don't exist except physically). Self-destructive impulses gone. Normal weight, normal eating and exercise habits. (3) Plans for after discharge. When and where to return to college. Where I will live and work until I return to college. Some sort of vacation in a warm climate to make up for the summer I've missed.

As to my current treatment, no longer are decisions made for me. Using the advice of people I trust, I decide for myself what will be most beneficial for me to recover permanently. This is an essential difference between my current and past treatment. As my weight struggles are symptomatic of my greater emotional struggles, we reasonably assume my weight obsession will cease to be an issue as my psychological turmoil is alleviated. As I am at a weight we agree is beyond danger, no emphasis is given to weight issues.

The major treatment emphasis is on my learning to verbalize and cope with my emotions—the hopelessness, emptiness, sadness, existential terror—without acting them out either through starvation or other forms of self-destruction. This involves: (1) A lot of grieving, for not only am I losing my coping mechanism (anorexia), but I am also getting in touch with that awful emotional devastation that made me sick in the first place. (2) Not pushing myself to get out and about, get involved, reinvest, etc., because at this point I am not ready to do those things. Forcing myself to do them would only prolong my recovery by interrupting the grief process. (3) Feeling the loss, emptiness, and pain of twenty years of denial, which is necessary so that I can work through my grief instead of using up all my energy to avoid all that sadness. (4) My goal is to resolve my grief and be ready to take on life again—not because I was forced to, or weaned into it, or bribed into it, but because I want it. Hopefully there will come a time when I can truly set my past aside and reinvest myself in adulthood. At that time, life will be my choice, not my burden.

Here are the therapy parts of my day and week: (1) Community meeting and agenda groups daily—where I work on my experiences with people here on the unit and how I might learn to be involved with people in ways that would make me feel less lonely on the outside. (2) Staff time every shift—where I talk to my staff person about issues Weintraub and I are currently working on. (3) Staff conference every Friday—where we discuss my progress, what I still need to work on, and the best ways of doing that. Usually includes me, Dr. W., and two staff. (4) Dr. Weintraub (Langley in her absence, which is often, but at least he spends a full fifty minutes with me) every day but Tuesday. She is my biggest support and growth-producing experience. (5) Grief group five days a week. The anger group ended last week.

In between groups and other therapy-centered things, I've been walking, running some, reading, doing crossword puzzles, playing backgammon—like we used to do, riding the bus to bookstores, libraries, and shopping centers. And I have time to do a lot of thinking.

CHAPTER THIRTEEN
A Circle Ends
Only Where It Begins

August 31. *81 pounds. To discuss in my treatment conference today: MOVING UP TO FOURTH FLOOR THERAPEUTIC COMMUNITY UNIT!!! I want to go for it. I've been here twenty weeks, and locked up on third floor West has too many sick implications for me (suicide attempts, self-destructive rages, other sick people) whereas fourth floor TC has well implications. Last year a "well Jenny" came out from 4TC, so I associate that unit with feeling better about myself. 3W represents the "sick Jenny," and leaving 3W should help me leave the sick Jenny behind also.*

On 4TC I can have contact with my family again and associate with patients who aren't so sick, so wasted. I want frivolity in my life again. Laughter rarely occurs on 3W, and I am sick of sick people. You can stomach only so much of depressed, low-functioning, psychotic, manic-depressive people.

October 10. *78 pounds. Over five weeks on 4TC, and I've lost 3 pounds. Not good. Weintraub gone again. Dr. Langley and I talked about my RAGE when others want something from me—usually when they give me something or manipulate me to feel sorry for them. I feel like I am evil because my emotions are opposite what they should be. Rather than being grateful for gifts, I'm furious they were given and wonder what is now wanted from me. I feel obligated to care about the givers. When others tell me their problems and I perceive they want me to sympathize, I'm ANGRY that they want something from me when I am empty. Paradoxically, I can give abundantly to others, as long as they don't expect it of me. It's easy for me to be nice to people, but as soon as I sense they need me I run the other way.*

These angers are unacceptable; they indicate I am evil. To escape validation of my evilness, I avoid relationships where others give to me or depend on me—I avoid closeness like the plague. Langley says my believing my angers are evil is a way for me to keep myself in check. I agree, because I know my world would cave in if I changed that judgment of myself. I'm free of this anger only when I don't feel pulled or pushed—when I am accepted for myself. I feel accepted by very few people: Dr. Langley, some of the staff, Dr. Weintraub, one other patient, sometimes Diane.

October 11. What am I needing? (1) Prioritization. I don't like having to attack all my problems at once. Perhaps we could work on only one or two things per week. That way I don't get overwhelmed and can feel like I'm making progress. (2) Direction. I need a treatment plan with a specific goal and approach instead of this haphazard shit.

October 12. 79 pounds. The closer I get to life without anorexia, self-destruction, and interior rage, the more feelings of emptiness and hopelessness overcome me. Nothing has meaning. I don't know where to go emotionally. I'm overwhelmed with the idea of life, and I feel incapable of meeting life's expectations. This existential terror is so great when I start to let go that I feel I have to commit suicide or starve myself back down to a state of semiexistence where none of the realities of everyday life mean anything because once again I am obsessed with my weight. I'm sick of my cycle because I never go anywhere, never change. I step forward, get scared, and run for it. I am tired of running, yet the fear I experience at each step ahead makes me think my only choice out of the agony is death. But I don't want to choose death. I want to organize and understand my inner tumult so I can find a way out. But it's unorganizable. I don't understand what keeps me caught in the cycle and so certain my ultimate end must be suicide.

Weintraub says that once my grief over Mom and Dad and my past is resolved, I'll be able to face health and choose it without such awful terror. Health won't be something that hurts. But Langley says I just don't want to accept the discomfort and responsibility of health.

October 13. 79 pounds fully water loaded! I'm full of self-hatred this morning—disgusted with my water-loading deceit. I must pull myself together and gain back to a real 80.

I have to gain real weight, but that produces an overwhelming fear that something will go wrong if I do: I will be killed, molested, or abused, either by myself or, more terrifying, by someone else. When I am starving to death and isolated from the world, that fear goes away.

No one has ever understood what's really wrong with me. The only way I could be accepted in my family was to give them a plausible reason for my inability to cope with life. Then they could quit saying I was weird because I was inherently weird. Then they could say I was weird because I had this weird disease that made me weird.

October 14. 79¼ pounds. I'm trying to avoid reenactment of "the cycle"—lose weight get punished, gain weight, hit the wall, lose weight get punished. Staff wants to punish me, send me back to 3W, but I finally asserted myself, withstood staff anger, and said no. But I'm afraid that soon I will not have a choice. They won't ask, they will order.

When Weintraub leaves me, I feel abandoned. I can intellectualize and say she deserves a vacation and I'll do fine without her, but I feel she is telling me that I don't matter to her, that I am strong enough to go on without her. In a way that's a compliment; however, it also stirs up all the rage and terror and loneliness I felt as a child when my mother told me I was capable without her and abandoned me to child molesters. When W. leaves, I usually employ one of my self-destructive behaviors because I know it will ensure her reinvolvement with me. I regress in order to evoke her disappointment and anger. When Mom abandoned me, I did the same thing.

"Give it up, Jenny. Let her go. Quit making us all into your mommy. Yes, it was rotten and yes, I do believe those things happened to you, but you've got to learn to hate them and move away from them, instead of wallowing in them. You can learn to accept our care. You don't need to deny it. Just because you didn't get her care doesn't mean you can't have ours."

"When you tell me that, I believe it. You give my well side courage to step out of the cage. But then, when you are gone, my sick side takes over, and I feel hopeless again."

"Jenny, you hate your mother, yet you have bought into her 100 percent. Your whole self is defined as Mom defined you, and you cling to that, unwilling to let it go."

"I don't think I'm unwilling. I'm scared to let go, scared of the emptiness I'll feel without my self-punitive Mommy rage."

"Your fears are an extension of Mommy inside of you. Quit believing the interior voice that keeps saying you can't lead a productive, happy life because you are evil and incapable. That voice is wrong. That voice, its hopelessness, is Mom, not you. You can exist just fine if you will only allow yourself to believe it."

"That's a door out of the cage that I haven't tried to unlock yet."

"Try. It's not too late."

October 15. My meeting with Weintraub yesterday left me more peaceful than I've been in a long time. Why can't I stand up for my well side and say to my sick side, "I'm sick of you. I hate you. You've ripped me off and now I'm going to kill you. You are wrong. I am worthy. I am smart and I can be kind and I deserve some love in life. You are a shit, and I hate you for making me pay, for not caring what you did to me in your wild pursuit of Mommy, revenge, and God knows what. You are a bastard, and I don't deserve the pain you've given me. I'm gonna fight you tooth and nail." I wanna be whole! Dammit, I want to experience what I have with Dr. Weintraub with others. I want to take better care of me. I'm going to stop believing what is normal and attainable for others is not normal and attainable for me.

"Why can you sometimes let go of your angry nuclear furnace and be a likable, genuine person?"

"I'm not sure. When I'm with someone I trust? When I'm feeling safe with myself?"

"How do we get you to be more trusting? How do we help you feel safe with yourself?"

"I don't know. I know I still don't want to eat. I still want to hurt myself by not eating."

"Why?"

"I don't understand it. I'm pretty scared about it."

October 17. 80¼ pounds. I feel weak, almost sick. I am so sad. Sad that everything is such a major struggle. I can't even chew gum without my inner voice chastising me. I wonder if I'll ever be free enough from Mother so that I don't always feel a nagging voice saying you must do better, accompanied by the same voice saying no matter how much better you do, it's not good enough. What is wrong? Why am I so drained?

"It's amazing that you are still sane after everything that happened to you."

"Right now I don't feel so sane. I feel tired and sad. I also feel I should be better."

"That's Mom again, scolding you, saying you should be better. It's okay to feel tired and sad. That's just how you are today."

October 19. 80¾ pounds. I went home today to get some winter clothes. It felt weird, like I was an intruder in a stranger's house. I couldn't leave soon enough.

"I gained weight today. I'm terrified I'll lose control and start overeating again like I did three years ago."

"It all goes straight to Mom, Jenny. She ruled and controlled and threatened your household so much that the idea of losing control is terrifying to you. You have to figure out what is really her, and therefore part of the evil core and false, and what is really you."

"But how?"

"Sorry, we're out of time."

October 22. 78¾ pounds. I finally took the risk and allowed my real weight to show. No more water loading. I just can't carry that guilt anymore. Everyone says it's my anger that causes me to lose weight. They're as confused as I am. I think I lose weight because I'm anorexic. Today I lost weight because I didn't drink five glasses of water before weigh-in. I was angry, though—with my staffing last Friday. We didn't set any treatment goals for this week, even though I specifically asked for goals. I didn't get any guidance about how to separate what is Mom from what is Jenny. It pisses me off when Weintraub talks and talks, and I don't get to say what I need to say until the very end when there is no more time left.

What I needed to talk about was what happens every time I step away from anorexia—the fear and desperation I feel in facing life's decisions: how much do I want to exercise, do I want to chew gum, do I want to read now, write now, call a friend, keep a friendship, end a friendship, write a letter, go to church, worship God, listen to rock or classical music, go to college in Minnesota, Texas, or Florida, go to college when, study what, live where until I do, see the family how much, make my commitment to college with Dad's money which he won't 100 percent guarantee, what will I drive? This is a small sampling of the indecisions that seem to trigger my fears.

We should decide on something narrow and defined for me to work on each week, so that I don't build such a huge mountain looming above me and wind up immobilized by its spectacle. Maybe learning to look only at the slope directly in front of me and calculating a way to climb it will eventually bring me to the top. Why can't staff and Dr. Weintraub understand and help me with that? Help me with something practical—something more tangible? Why must they keep me focused on mind things—my anger, my grief, and separating from Mom? Why are they so paranoid about my weight, even though they say they're not?

October 23. 79¼ pounds. Well, the risk got me what I feared—punishment. I'm locked up on 3W again. I can't go back to 4TC until I weigh 85 pounds for a week, and there has to be a plan to gain beyond that. I worked out a diet plan with the dietician, and she was clear that a pound a week is all my body can handle. So that makes it seven weeks minimum before I can *return to 4TC. The punishment they have prescribed is too extreme. I'm going to confront my head nurse on 4TC. In fact I'm going to do that now.*

"Why are you doing this to me, Doris?"

"You know why, Jenny. You haven't been able to keep your weight above 80 pounds. You contracted to do that when you came up to 4TC."

"I know, but last week you all sat there smiling and agreed when Dr. Weintraub told me my weight didn't matter as long as my health wasn't endangered. Are you saying my health is endangered?"

"No."

"So, now you're disagreeing with the doctor, and what you agreed to last week was bullshit. My weight is all that matters."

"You must keep your weight up, and it's obvious you can't do that without going back to a more restricted environment."

"Did Weintraub order this?"

"No, you contracted with us. It's a 4TC staff decision."

"Weintraub wasn't even involved?"

"No."

"You know that forcing me to gain weight won't do any more for me than it ever has. I can't stand weighing much more than 80 pounds and 85 is like 100."

"We only want you to give up your anorexia."

"You can't force me to give it up."

"We know that."

"I can fight it better on 4TC than 3W."

"You haven't demonstrated that."

"I have to demonstrate by weight gain? Only by weight gain?"

"Yes. It's like an alcoholic having to give up his bottle."

"That's a stupid comparison. Gaining weight does not equal letting go of anorexia, it only equals avoiding punishment."

"Nevertheless, you will have to gain to come back to 4TC."

"Then the little things I've been able to change in me here on 4TC don't matter?"

"What little things?"

"Like playing the piano again, listening to classical music, not compulsively exercising, eating foods I haven't touched in years, experimenting with being less regimented about food and feeling okay about it, reading again, driving myself places, going to church. Little things that make me think I'm getting better. You're telling me they don't count in measuring progress?"

"Not if you can't maintain your weight."

October 24. Why can't I say to 4TC staff what I think? "Well, okay, fuck you. I don't need you. You rejected me because you perceived me as not trying, but you are wrong and I don't want you back." More fear—of making them madder?

I'm livid at Weintraub for avoiding involvement in this decision. She abandoned me to staff's whim and doesn't care what they decided. She'll be here soon, and I intend to confront her, but I'm sure she will renege on what she said last week and support the staff's decision. Last week we talked about the ways my mother set me up to be disliked by my siblings. I was either breaking my back playing the submissive child or I was standing up for myself and being hated. It feels like that's what's happened here.

"I hate you for avoiding involvement in this decision."

"Jenny, you made weight the issue, not me or the 4TC staff."

"You do not have the right to tell me I must gain beyond a safe weight. It's my decision whether I look skinny and childish or not."

"Is it your decision not to give up anorexia?"

"You're confusing me. I'm just saying I may always want to be too thin by most people's standards, but if I can be successful, responsible, and independent anyway, it shouldn't matter if I weigh 83 or 90."

"I hear you, and I know you are frustrated. But we have vowed, you and I, to beat this illness. I won't let you talk me into reversing the staff decision to send you back down to 3W."

October 25. *79½ pounds. I'm so confused and out of it and I don't know what the hell to do.*

"Why do you feel Mom will win and you will lose if you get well?"

"Well, I know Mom doesn't care for me. So, if I get well, it will free her from any obligation to me because of my dilapidated health. Then she can act on her true feelings and abandon me. The pathological aspect is that I have always thought I couldn't exist without her, therefore in health I die, while in illness I live. I knew she would abandon me, but I needed her, so I fixed it so she couldn't, at least not morally according to her strict convictions."

"You used the right word."

"What word?"

"Pathological. Also 'perverse' works. You're not a child anymore, and you don't need her anymore. Let her win, Jenny. You will win also. In health, there is just that. Health. A win for you. A loss for your confused, rage-filled, existential panic. A loss for your internalized Mom."

"But I can't get well on 3W."

"Why not?"

"You know what you're doing to me, don't you?"

"Yes, and it's different from what you think we're doing to you."

"You're denying me the chance to work on my major problem, that I still feel inadequate to face the world. The best way for me to get over my fear of inadequacy is to be exposed to the world in stages and learn how to deal with my emotions without starving myself. I can't do that locked up on 3W. I'm forced to do it on 4TC. More important, I want to do it on 4TC."

"Jenny, you were on 4TC for seven weeks, and you lost weight. Your words say you want 4TC, but your actions are more eloquent. They say that you want to go back to 3W."

"But I was still trying on 4TC. And you often say what I want isn't always best for me. Now you're enabling my give-up attitude. You're throwing failure in my face."

"Jenny, do you want to try a new program somewhere else? Do you want a new doctor?"

"You know I don't. Have you given up on me too, like the 4TC nurses?"

"I'll never give up on you, Jenny."

October 26. *Maybe I should leave, only I don't know where I'd go or what I'd do. I'm at the end of my rope. I'm close to giving up. My bones are my security blanket. When I can't feel them, I'm lost.*

A nurse just asked me why I was back on 3W. When I explained it to her, she just looked at me in disgust and said, "That's no big deal. Just gain the weight." Nobody but Weintraub seems to grasp how big a deal it really is: it is a fucking end-of-the-road kind of big deal. And maybe this is the end of the road. I'm trapped in a circle that can end only where it began.

CHAPTER FOURTEEN

The Beast Within

October 25. 79¼ pounds. Dr. Weintraub is afraid the insurance company will throw me out. I'm afraid too, but like she said, I'm the one in control.

Last night my shift nurse said my real problems just begin to get close enough to the surface to work on and then, boom, food and weight become the issues again. Others only get so close to me and then that is lost in the control struggle over my weight. God, am I fucked up.

October 27. 79½ pounds. Last night Lorie binged out and threw up. She probably thinks I will judge her. But I won't because I love Lorie, and her bulimia isn't going to erase all the wonderful things about her which make me care. After barfing, Lorie said she was feeling suicidal again. By holding out against the "impulse," at least I have hope.

October 29. 80½ pounds. Lorie didn't return from her pass last night, and I was afraid she'd committed suicide. At the same time a part of me almost hoped she had. Isn't that awful! I think the only way I can separate from her is if she died. It's hard for me to change, or to see her change, and not feel exactly like she does. We shared so much this summer, and we are so very alike, yet now I am beginning to see how we are different, and it scares me to be different from someone I love. To me it means she will not love me anymore. Rather than experience the loss of her love, the sick part of me would rather she just die.

November 10. 80½ pounds. When my weight is left up to me, I become lethargic, terrified, and confused. When someone else controls me, I feel like I'm not going to binge out and do something destructive. Similarly, when others control my time off the unit, I know how to use it. When it's up to me, I'm overwhelmed trying to decide what to do.

"For you, Jenny, control is good, lack of control is bad. Like with Mom. Mom liked you when you sat quietly in church or waited patiently for her to buy her antiques or for Nancy to take a piano lesson. If you stepped out of Mom's strict behavior codes, you were punished. Similarly, you have set up strict behavior codes, and whenever you step outside them you think you need to be punished. When you follow your codes, you give yourself permission to leave yourself alone."

"But they don't seem to be mine. Why do I need an authority figure to establish codes?"

"That's the sick dependency on Mom we're trying to wean you from."

"But how can I be weaned if you're still controlling me?"

"We want to release control to you gradually, as you become better able to deal with it."

November 13. *80¼ pounds. I've finished my application essays to Rice. I wanted to return to Carleton, until I realized how cold and bleak it is there. I need warmth and sunshine in my life. My essays are focused on the future, but I've never believed there could be a future, and part of me says it's a joke—I'll never go, I'll never be well, I'll always struggle with this fucking disease.*

I'm very depressed, and I'm not able explain why to staff. I had pecan pie for lunch, and now I feel like: HOW DARE I?

"It means nothing, Jenny—to control every last crumb of food that goes in your mouth."

"But I'm afraid I'll get fat."

"Trust yourself, Jenny. Let *yourself* be."

"But what self?"

"The real Jenny, the one who is independent and vital, competitive and capable, who is vivacious and now lost."

"It's like I've been on a search, sailing across this vast ocean, not bothering to chart a course because I was sure thatI'd hit my island without having to turn around. Well, I've suddenly found I need to turn around and am sailing back through uncharted waters trying to find the real me."

"You found your way here. We can help you find your way back. The real Jenny is not that far from your reach."

November 16. 80½ pounds. Last night was my worst night yet. I haven't experienced such intense panic and hatred since before I became anorexic. It was like being possessed. I didn't talk to a nurse because I didn't want anyone to know my degree of rage. I thought if I acknowledged it to someone, I would be giving it power to exist. I thought I could conquer it alone, but I couldn't. It was alive and powerful and devastating, and by trying to deny it, I acknowledged it. It was like when I was little and had "devil dreams" and woke up believing the devil was in my room and going to get me. Last night the devil was inside my body and going to KILL me. It was AWFUL.

" . . . and then the dreams after I finally fell asleep."

"What did you dream?"

"Incredible molestation dreams. I was living on a farm, which was really our neighbor's backyard. It was in ruin, and a man came and assaulted me . . . in front of people. I liked it, but I also hated it."

"When you awoke, did you remember anything?"

"No. I've been in this down spiral all day. All I do is cry and feel isolated."

"Jenny, what did you do yesterday?"

"I went home and organized my horse equipment. I'm going to try and sell some of it."

"Don't you see how your awful night was related to the abuse feelings that were stirred up when you went home and the messages you fed yourself about those feelings?"

"You're disappointed with me."

"I'm not disappointed. I just want you to see that your crazy dreams are not mysterious events. They relate to what happens in your day. And they can be taken care of here, with us, before they become so monstrous that they feel like a devil who comes to get you in the night."

November 17. 80 pounds. Today I feel so much better, it is incredible.

"Do you know why you feel better?"

"Because I lost weight? I don't think that's all the reason."

"Maybe you learned something yesterday . . . about how to cope."

November 21. 81 pounds. Yesterday Janis came home for Thanksgiving, Lorie slashed her wrists, and I gained a pound without trying. I haven't been able to stop crying all morning. I feel as if I hate Lorie. I don't trust her, I'm scared of her, and I'm afraid she's gonna kill herself. What can I do for her? I can't make her not hurt. At least the weather is nice today.

November 23. 80 pounds. Weintraub read an article in Life *about sexually abused children, and got worked up about my "fitting" the symptoms. I told her about my flashbacks of Tony being on top of me and some fears I've had that something could have happened between me and Dad when I was very young. She's sure Tony is the key to my sexual abuse.*

November 24. 80 pounds. Everyone says I'm doing so well, and I am better, but I am not well yet.

November 26. 80 pounds. Why can't Dad stand up to the rest of my family and make them accept and face their part in my illness? Why does he let the fantasy that I am crazy continue to go on and on and on, when it has cost me so much? It's cost me them all! It's cost me Thanksgiving, will cost me Christmas, a vacation this winter, a home.

November 29. 80½ pounds. I want to starve myself today. Push IT out, be empty of IT. No weight gain in weeks. Is that good or bad? Today we're supposed to talk about family abuse.

"You have to change your fondling attitude toward the abuse your family heaps on you."

"Fondling?"

"Yes. Rather than accepting that they treat you like shit, you keep getting astonished and shocked when it happens again and again. Instead of saying, 'Well, fuck you too, family,' you allow yourself to be surprised, which only brings you more abuse."

"But, what should I do?"

"Let them go. Acknowledge and accept that they hate you and will set you up for abuse as often as they can. Then you won't be so badly beaten by how they treat you."

"I don't seem able to do that."

"That's because you haven't decided to get well yet. I'll believe you have decided to get well only when you eat and gain weight, and show you are overcoming the mother inside of you."

"It's never that simple for me. Even now, I feel like I'm fading into nonexistence. I'm caught up in that transference stuff. Like, oh God, now you hate me too, and I'm going to die."

"I don't hate you, and you are not going to die on me."

November 30. 80¼ pounds. Diane gets home today and wants to do something tonight. I'd like to go dancing, but I can't afford it, and I wonder about the men. I'd also like to see a movie, but I definitely can't afford that. Big uncertainties today about abuse.

"I don't truly believe anything bad ever happened to me."

"Of course it did, Jenny."

"But when I look in the mirror, there's this fundamental underlying knowledge that it did not happen. Whenever I talk about being abused, I feel split in half. Half of me says it's true. The other half of me sits back in this chair shaking her finger at the first half saying 'You liar. Tsk, tsk. You know it isn't true.'"

"You're experiencing extinction burst, Jenny. The closer you come to giving up an old thought process or belief about yourself, the harder those feelings fight for survival. So, the closer you come to believing you were abused as a child, the louder a voice is going to scream that you are a liar. You committed no sin worthy of the treatment first Mom and then the rest of your family gave you. Your abuse is true. You are not a liar. Your defenses are just meaner to you."

"But why would Mom hurt me?"

"She hurt you and allowed you to be hurt by others because something about you reminded her of something she hated and wanted to deny in herself."

"Like her abuse of Uncle Bret?"

"Precisely. That was the reminder she couldn't tolerate."

"I've been worried I may have inherited her sadistic quirk, and that's why she chose me to hate. She punished me for exhibiting a quality she hated in herself. But that makes me deserving of punishment, validates my inherited evilness as the cause of her hatred, and repudiates the premise that my feelings of being bad are a result of her hating me."

"No, Jenny. You've not inherited her meanness. And sadistic isn't the right term. We don't know yet, may never know what triggered her abuse response. Once she began abusing you, she resented that you had been allowed to see the meanness in her, and she was unable to break the pattern: abuse feeding resentment feeding more abuse."

"Sometimes I think I have no business examining all this stuff. It seems such a farce."

"It's very real, Jenny. You just have to accept it. Then you can go on."

December 3. *79¾ pounds. I remember years of feeling fat and hating my body before I connected those feelings with food. I know I am not fat, but fat FEELINGS continue and extend beyond my body—BODY is the exterior representation of my tortured inside. Weintraub and staff want me to say, AND BELIEVE, "Jenny, you know it was abuse and not food that causes those feelings." The problem is I don't totally buy that I was abused, despite their insistence I was.*

It would give me a great sense of relief if Dad could read the Life article and say to me, "Yes, I remember you behaving that way. I believe you were abused by Mom when you were little, and I'm sorry." If he could validate what everyone here believes, maybe I could finally accept it and let it go. It is hard to let go of something when you are not convinced there is anything to let go.

December 4. 80½ pounds. Today I'm as close to suicide as I've ever been. I even wrote a suicide note to Mom and Dad and a letter to Dr. Weintraub. Staff just tells me to take my Librium, but other than making me tired it doesn't do a damn thing. I called Weintraub, but she hasn't called back.

December 8. 80 pounds. I HATE my body, my life, my existence, my soul, all parts of me. And I know it is a sin to feel that way, but I do.

December 10. 79½ pounds. Last night I had my first lesbian memory. I was with someone I loved and trusted. This woman did things that astonished and terrified me. Was this an early lesson that I cannot let myself care for another because it will turn into a lie, cannot let myself trust because it will result in betrayal? I always feel pressured to sabotage relationships that become important and nurturing to me, and I've never understood why I want to push away the people I love. Maybe my flashback explains why. I couldn't see a face in my flashback. Was the woman Maria? Maria of the horses, whom I trusted and loved so much. She was so entangled in food, I can see why I would choose food as my weapon against her.

December 11. 79½ pounds. I feel better today. Dad asked me to go to see Meme with him, but my gut feeling is that I wouldn't enjoy it. I'd rather have the money for a new wardrobe when I get out of here—for when I start school again. But I'm worried about rejecting a loving gift from him.

"He left you a long time ago, Jenny, just like the rest of your family, and he is never coming back. His gift of the trip you thought you wanted is not a symbolic love offering, only something he offered you because he thought you might enjoy it."

December 12. 79½ pounds. I'm stuck between the old autopilot and the new well Jenny. Supposedly I have these angers and anorexic behaviors dictated by repressed memories of abuse which will go away as my memories surface. Now my memories are surfacing, but I don't want to believe them. When I allow myself to believe them and be nurtured by Weintraub and staff who support my belief, I become terrified my nurturers are

going to get me, exploit all I've invested in their trust and care, just like
Maria. Do they invest me with their delusion? Or I them with mine?

"Nancy and Janis are home for Christmas. Dad invited me to go out with the three of them, maybe as soon as this weekend."

"Do you want to go?"

"I'm undecided. I think I can be the well Jenny, go with them and put on a happy face, and then do the same thing at Christmas. No one wants to listen to the cringing, terrified child anymore, but I'm afraid I'll act her out. She is still there inside me, still strong, still needing to be expressed, and I don't know if the well Jenny can override her."

"The real Jenny is the happy face. It's time to show it. Show all your family the well Jenny at Christmas. That will destroy their power over you, break their spell."

December 13. *79½ pounds. I ate a brownie today. How am I gonna deal with feeling fat?*

"Still undecided about spending Christmas at home?"

"Yes. I know I can do it if I try hard enough, but I'm not sure I want to."

"Why not?"

"Part of me says they don't deserve the well Jenny—they've always hated me well or sick."

"Jenny, you have a way of exaggerating about family relationships. You fabricate tales so you can justify your feelings that they have been unloving to you."

"I know you're right. There have been many instances where interaction with a family member was okay, but I took some minor, innocent remark, twisted it, and used it to hurt myself."

"Do you know why you do that?"

"I don't know. It makes me wonder if I fabricate my memories of abuse. Do I make up that CORE awful, grotesque, scary, rageful experience I think I had with Mom to justify my obsessions, my fear of her? Do I fabricate all my flashbacks?"

"Jenny, your memories are real. But you can't find external validation of the past, so you seek external validation in the present."

December 15. 79½ pounds. The beast inside me is still very ALIVE and saying, "Watch out, you'll be fat tomorrow!" I must not eat and feed the beast, or if I do I MUST exercise. The beast says I'm fat today, but the scale says I'm not any fatter than yesterday.

"How was lunch with Dad and your sisters?"

"Part was fine, part not so fine."

"Tell me about the fine part."

"I ate normally, interacted with them as the well Jenny, and was basically myself. The real me was more flowing than ever with my sisters."

"But?"

"I had to try so hard not to let them stir me up. I put so much energy into being the me you think I am, but that me didn't flow as naturally as it does with Diane or you or staff. No one asked me anything at all, and I felt like it just isn't to be found in them—whatever 'it' is."

"Is 'it' compassion?"

"Probably."

"Were you expecting too much from your family again?"

"Probably."

December 17. 79 pounds. What do I want? I want peace and no more battles with myself. I want to know I am safe. Most of all I WANT to kill the BEAST! Not the fictional voice inside my intellect, but the BEAST I feel in my intestines—the beast that is as real to me as writing this paragraph. I need to focus on not being alone with the BEAST after I challenge it.

"Jenny, you've raged and raged and raged. You have to put rage behind and get on with sad. You won't stick with the grieving. That's what's holding you back. The only time we make progress is when you confront your sadness."

December 19. *79½ pounds. Today I again write "sad." I'm sad because the rest of my family designed a Christmas card over the weekend. Dad called and said it was a playful letter poking fun at all those Christmas letters where people bombard their friends with grand but boring family travel and achievements. Brian will add cartoon illustrations. My grief turns to rage and self-deprecation when I imagine what they wrote and drew about me.*

"Jenny, the basic problem is we are on the wrong track. The more that someone loves you, the more the well Jenny loves back, the more self-destructive you become."

"What should we do?"

"You have to make yourself change and trust. Above all you have to believe that you will not be abused if you love and are loved again."

"But how?"

"I don't know. You have your own internal agenda. You understand our psychotherapy, but like Dad, you don't trust or believe it. You treat it like 85 percent bullshit and continue to self-destruct."

"85 percent bullshit. That's what Dad says it is. But he's always been hopeful I could get something out of the other 15 percent."

"You're not. After four years of working with you, I still feel no connection with you. You are leaving me, and your ultimate goal is to go home and commit suicide on Mom's lap. If you lose any more weight, you will force my hand."

December 21. *77¾ pounds. Weintraub is wrong again. My internal agenda is the voice that speaks louder than any other, the voice that says I am not worthy of food, love, happiness, care, freedom, success. Why can she never understand that, help me destroy that voice, kill the beast inside me?*

I went to the hospital Christmas party last night. After taking some Librium, I was able to relax. And then, as often happens after an intense day, I became almost manic. We played some Police and danced our asses off. This morning I feel like suicide is an inch away. My life is a fraudulent joke. One minute I'm dancing, the next I'm suicidal. Dancing lasts a moment—I last until I die and I don't know where "I" is. If I could only dance forever.

"You need to forgive. Take off your glasses lensed with transference and allow yourself to enjoy life. Yes, you were abused. You have every right to feel sad, mad, hurt, and scared. But you must not allow this to consume you any more, because you are dying. You need to forgive those who hurt you and quit transferring your anger to the world and yourself."

"But how?"

"Look for and create good experiences for yourself. As hard as you work on how much you hurt, work harder on having relaxing, positive, nurturing interactions with others. Allow the good encounters to slowly but surely become more real, more dominant than your pain."

December 22. *77¼ pounds. I felt attacked by the staffing confrontation this morning, like I was being told I was bad because I feel bad. From now on I'm going to try this: After I experience, think about, or talk about painful things, I am going to do or feel something good—cook, listen to music, play backgammon, joke around. The same here in my journal. I need to write about good things, too. The more intense the negative encounter, the more intense I need to make the positive response.*

So here's a bad thing—part of me wants to punish me because of the pecan pie I ate yesterday. And here's a NEW (good) TAPE: My body isn't bad because of what I put into it. Even NEWER (better) TAPE: My body isn't bad, PERIOD.

I had a good time with Diane yesterday. We saw Beverly Hills Cop. It had wonderfully foul language, and I laughed with more abandonment than I have in months. Today I plan to make Christmas presents, and I will feel good if people like them. Even better, I will feel good making them.

December 25. *77¼ pounds. Yesterday Nancy, Janis, and Brian came down. They brought some great gifts: a Walkman and a new purse were both things I've really wanted but didn't expect.*

Last night Dad came to see me while Mom and everyone else went to church services. I asked Dad why he didn't hate me when everyone else did— BEFORE I was anorexic. He said, "Well, that is where we differ in perception, Jenny. I believe the underlying hostility came after your childhood, after you got sick." Our conversation upset me and negated a lot of my belief that

I have an alliance with him. He obviously disagrees again with Weintraub's conclusions about cause. Could she be wrong again?

December 26. 77¼ pounds. I'm glad I didn't go home yesterday. Today is MY Christmas break. Diane is picking me up, and we're going to have lunch and hang out downtown. Should be a fun day. But why am I afraid something might happen to me if I go?

"I've prepared a summary for today's staffing."

"We have only one thing to talk about today, Jenny, and that's your indecision. You've lost weight steadily over the holidays, and you have to make a decision: Are you going to become a perpetual anorexic or are you going to get well?"

"What I want is help figuring out how I can get the vacation I need so badly."

"No, Jenny. No vacation. You have to decide if you want to get well."

"I'm exhausted. I need to relax."

"First you have to make a decision."

"You don't understand. I've made that decision. I've rejected anorexia. I will not be like other anorexics, floating in and out of the hospital, or worse, living here permanently. My decision now is not between perpetual anorexia and health. It's between health and suicide."

"You're just avoiding the issue. What prevents you from giving up anorexia in the same way you gave up thumb sucking, throwing up, and abusing laxatives?"

"Why do you always assume it's my choice to be sick?"

"Because it is, and it's time for you to make a final choice."

December 28. 76½ pounds. My staffing today stank. Weintraub wouldn't even read my summary. It was just BANG—make a decision and NOW. I feel like she told me: Henceforth you are not allowed to grieve anymore; you have to decide NOW who you are. She was in a hurry, so we didn't pursue what keeps me from giving up anorexia.

December 29. 77¼ pounds. Today I learned about coping. I must stop seeing starvation and suicide as options, otherwise I will develop no new skills. When I finally believe starvation and suicide are not options, I will HAVE to develop a new coping route, and it will be good for me.

Here is how I can survive my panics without being self-destructive: Librium, talking with staff, naps, focus on the immediate terrain—what can I do today. Also games like Ping-Pong and backgammon. Movies. Shopping and time with Diane.

December 30. 78¾ pounds. Hatred is within me and projected from me and that is why I hold on to anorexia. Somehow it abates the hatred. Pure and simple.

December 31. 78¼ pounds. Here is my New Year's resolution. I am going to eat 2,000 calories a day until I'm back to 80 and maybe that much every day thereafter.

Now I am at breakfast facing the war between my emotions and my intellect. I don't want the fucking food—but I know I have to eat it. I wish I could slice my emotions away from my intellect. I should talk to someone, but my assigned nurse is too busy to talk to me, and if she wasn't too busy, I'm not sure what I would talk to her about.

I've been on the wrong path for many years and now not only must I turn around and return to where I diverged, I also must catch up for all the time I lost traveling the wrong path. My journey is more complicated because the path behind me has become overgrown with brambles, making it hard for me to return to the true path. I turn around, take a long look at the treacherous journey back, and say, "It's impossible." Maybe I should analyze what the brambles are: (1) Loss of family relationships. (2) Existential fear and emptiness—the biggest, thickest bramble. (3) Low self-esteem. I need to remove the brambles, focus and build on my strengths, what's good about me: my eyes, my intelligence, my humor, my empathy, my honesty.

"Jenny, the obstacle in bramble number one is your fixation on Dad, your hope that he will come and rescue you and whisk you away from all of this. You must let go of your notion that if you can't have your ideal family, you can at least have him."

"But why would he do that? Where would he take me?"

"You are going nowhere. If you don't show more improvement, he will have to step in and send you to some other program, probably Johns Hopkins in Baltimore."

"Even if I don't want to leave you?"

"Yes. He would perceive it as his fatherly duty."

"I suppose my fantasy is that he would take me away, reject the family, devote himself to nurturing me and making me feel loved until I was ready to go out and face the world on my own."

"But don't you see what would happen in reality? Dad would deposit you in Baltimore and then return to your dysfunctional family no more supportive than before."

"Part of me still says there's a chance my fantasy could come true if I pushed him to the limit and he had to rescue me."

"There is zero chance."

"My emotions want to disagree, but my intellect says you are right."

"Maybe you need to experience the reality of Dad abandoning you elsewhere to face and accept your loss of him, of your whole family."

"But then what would I do?"

"I won't abandon you, Jenny. I would wait for you to return."

"Then I should bypass all the pain, hassle, and humiliation of changing to a new program, stay here, and face my loss with you to help me."

"Precisely. Dad is not going to rescue you. He might change your geography, but he will not save you. You get so caught up in your worship of him that you forget he was involved in evil things. He didn't perpetrate these things and he didn't know of them, but he took the hear no evil, see no evil, speak no evil approach to the evil going on right under his nose. Mom was hurting you, your uncle and others were sexually assaulting you. Isn't it clear he chose to protect himself by enshrouding himself with innocence? Is that a quality to worship in a person? Is Dad really as admirable as you've fantasized him to be?"

January 1. 76⁵/₈ pounds. When I woke up this morning I thought it was a year later and I should graduate from college this year. Somewhere between sleep and consciousness, I was aware of praying that in the new year I could accept and forgive and return to a normal life. I think I have the capacity to accomplish this, but I'm not sure I have the will. I'm so tied up in what I've lost that I want to halt time, my life, everything, until I recover my loss.

One of the reasons I plead for more time is I never experienced the "in-betweens." First I'm a child and suddenly I'm an adult. I never went through adolescence. I was born and fed until I could feed myself, and then Mom always expected me to know what and how to feed myself and make my own lunch for school every day. I was dressed until I could dress myself, and then Mom expected me to know exactly how to dress. I was given a horse and some lessons and then was not expected to need protection at the barn. No one helped me find a safe path from total dependence to total independence. And that applies today: I don't let go of anorexia for fear I won't know how to deal with the in-betweens.

January 2. 76¾ pounds. Yesterday my roommate and her boyfriend took me to see Stop Making Sense, the Talking Heads movie. There in the theater, I discovered a part of me that is uniquely me. I've always known I enjoyed dancing and music, but I thought everyone did. Yesterday I had to make a conscious effort to keep myself from flying down the aisles and dancing with the same abandon as the movie's lead singer. I noticed that no one else in the audience was nearly as plugged into the music as I was. My observing ego said, "Remember this, Jenny. This is a you that others don't have, an ability to submerge completely in music and move with it naturally." Music magnetism is something there inside of me—and that's what I've been groping for, a part of me which is intrinsically good and sub-stantial and has nothing to do with my body, eating, or exercising.

January 3. 78¾ pounds. I gained 2 pounds, and I am eating nothing except breakfast today. I want to kill myself. I cannot stand the inner feel-ings. I want to claw and tear and rip and reach down inside my gut and pull the food out of me. I want to tear my intestines open and spill them on the floor. I WANT TO BE DEAD DEAD DEAD DEAD. I hate! I hate this goddam fucking world. NO GODDAM FOOD for today. I hate my fucking body and I hate life, and the only way I don't commit suicide is by totally avoiding everything. 2 pounds. What a fucking pig. I hate this life, I hate it. I didn't eat very much yesterday, barely what my diet calls for, but my body is punishing me: how dare you talk or eat like a normal person. HOW DARE YOU you fucking sickening faggot pig loser. HOW AM I EVER GOING TO GET BEYOND THIS? I cannot stand these feelings. Stay away from me, rage STAY THE FUCK AWAY from me or I will kill you. I will lose my mind and end up in the quiet room, and then I'll use that to give me a heart attack, and then finally I'll die. Please God why did you make me? I don't like it here I feel so scared and unresolved. I still want to hurt and claw my body. I slap my face, please let me die, please? PLEASE! What is the point of my existence? I have accomplished nothing, and I am so engulfed in my rage I will go nowhere until I kill it. Help!! I wanna kill myself. I don't know how to handle this. I don't want to listen to music, and I don't want to pretend things are fine. They aren't fine no matter what anyone says whether or not I control this rage inside me or not, it is there BURNING away. Today I'm going to be how I am—goddam fucking mad. I'm gonna kill myself if I can think well enough to decide if it is worth what it will do to Weintraub. I am only one person and no way do I have the power to ruin her career, unless she chooses to let my death ruin her. That would be her choice. If I killed myself, it is clear who the failure is: me, and I am so who gives a fuck.

January 4. 77¾ pounds. The major obstacle to my recovery is the rage and self-hatred I feel on days like today. Amazingly, at these times when I need them most, staff won't come near me. If they do, I don't seem able to explain my feelings. I just chant about how gross my body is. We don't connect, and I scare them off.

I have nothing new or worthwhile to report to my staffing today, except that I gained a pound this week. Weintraub will be ecstatic. Her pleasure at my weight gain nauseates me, scares me. I feel she is applauding and coaxing something evil to occur within me.

Well, they wouldn't let me into my staffing. Weintraub had that old "you've been a bad girl, Jenny" look and you don't deserve to be treated like other patients. I felt like she was punishing me so I split, and here I sit in Bagel Nosh waiting to see Beverly Hills Cop again.

I called in to say I was okay. Weintraub refused to tell me what they had decided. "Come home and I'll tell you," she said. I told her, "No fucking way." There is no worse feeling than being locked out of a room where others are making decisions about you. Good old Bertha is banking on my reason to bring me back. So what do I do after the movie? Go back, commit suicide, go home (real home, not the hospital), call Diane, do nothing and just sit in this miserable mall until they kick me out?

I called staff, and they won't talk to me on the phone either, which means they've decided something I won't like. Should I call Dad? I can't just sit here the rest of my life.

January 5. 75¼ pounds. I called Bertha and came back after she promised me nothing had been changed. I have to change so that I become alive and quit playing this silly game of existence—like some endurance contest.

I called home last night to tell Dad I was safe, but he was still out looking for me, so I told Mom I was back at Willowcrest. She asked if I was okay. I said, "Physically yes, but emotionally no—obviously." I was too exhausted and strung out to lie and protect her anymore. She said, "You know your pain hurts us, too." I said I could sometimes feel that from Dad but that I didn't really feel that from her at all. She said, "Well it does and we would do anything we could do to help alleviate it." And then I lost it and said, "Come get involved in therapy, then." And she said, "We were and it didn't work and we didn't think it made sense to see the doctor without you there, too." I told her, "I WILL be there." And she said, "I never understood that would be the case ever." I tried to say very calmly, "Well, I guess we just misunderstood each other, then." But she RAGED out at me, "EVEN IF WE DID COME, THERE IS NO WAY YOUR FATHER AND I CAN TAKE AWAY YOUR FEELINGS OF HATE TOWARD US." Observing ego says, you're right, you can't, but observing ego also says what I then said to her: "No, Mother, it can't, but maybe it could help me feel better about me, by your explaining your feelings of hate toward me." She said, "Well I don't and didn't, and I am not getting involved in therapy to prove it." I responded, "That's what's so hard: You and Dad can't see what I see, what you did to me, yet I'm expected to forgive you anyway." Then, in an attempt to reach out beyond I said, "Mom, I offer you forgiveness now for that and for this phone call," and she raged again, "Well, I offered you forgiveness eons ago, and you threw it in my face." I could take no more and said I was too emotional, the conversation was doing me no good, and please tell Dad I was safe and good-bye. She always has to win, and she always does.

After getting off the phone, I tried to analyze: Why didn't she understand that family therapy includes me? Why did she reject that? Why does she say she offered me forgiveness, and I threw it in her face? That implies I did something wrong first and discredits the abuse. A part of me says I have thrown her attempts in her face. Don't I do that by staying anorexic?

My therapists tell me: Do your best, BELIEVE your gut reaction to a difficult phone call, forgive her, leave it behind so you can enjoy today. BELIEVE your flashbacks and do your best to accept others' inability to believe them. Go have a good life anyway.

January 13. *77 pounds.* I just read a letter from Nancy, and I am crying. I was expecting her to scold me for not coming home at Christmas. It was, instead, a very nice thank-you note, and she caught me up on what is going on with her. So, why do I cry? I'm ashamed of prejudging her—wrongly. I'm sad that we don't talk. I'm sad because her letter is a subtle apology for not coming to see me on Christmas day—even though we both know it would have been impossible. She needed to be at home. Coming to see me could have destroyed some of her closeness with Mom.

Reality is Christmas is over and today I got a lovely letter from my big sister. I will respond soon and perhaps we can begin to rebuild our relationship.

CHAPTER FIFTEEN

I Quit

Jenny began to mend—gradually but steadily. A transfer back to the Therapeutic Community Unit helped. So did more activity off the unit, including a part-time job. As focus on a life outside her illness increased, her journalizing decreased. Six weeks passed.

February 27. 85¼ pounds. Get car, church 8:45, call Diane, run, case conference 11:00. Work 2:00 to 6:00. I bet you thought I'd never write in you again. I wasn't sure I would. Writing in you helps but can also be nonproductive because I dwell on the negative aspects of my life and get so caught in a spiral of unending analysis and hopelessness that I don't come out of it easily.

Someday I might like to write a book chronicling my long journey.

March 2. 85½ pounds. Got bike and papers for car, got raise and extra hours on Saturdays, ran, met Diane for shopping and movie after, Janis home next week. I don't water load anymore. I don't lie anymore. I don't cry over my weight anymore. Sometimes I cry over my fear about what will become of me in my new role.

March 28. 86¼ pounds. Payday! Breakfast with Marybeth. Call Diane about Saturday. Bring pizza to work. See doctor about bad hip. Hello again. Although I'm still at Willowcrest, my life is moving, and I think I'll be discharged soon. I'm now working as hostess in a Harvest Restaurant full time. I'm also dating someone. CRUSH CITY. But I'm afraid he'll dump me—maybe already has. I hurt my hip and can't work out for at least two weeks.

There is still a lot of anorexia left in me. I'm scared of some foods. I feel self-destructive and can only bear those feelings through exercise.

Gaining weight and satisfying my hunger are still perceived by me as bad. What is better is that anorexia doesn't dominate my life, and I do things despite my scary feelings. I'm beginning to confront life on my own two feet.

I am very pressured by Weintraub to give up anorexia right now. She threatens that I must choose between her and it. She still thinks I can choose. I'm still not convinced.

Who's more irrationally stubborn?

When Jenny discharged from Willowcrest in May, she weighed 85 pounds, 10 pounds short of her goal weight. During fifty-seven weeks of hospitalization, she gained 11 pounds. This time neither her weight gain nor her therapeutic program was successful. Her discharge fantasy was that she would be able to function outside a psychiatric hospital, eat healthily, work full time, have a normal social life, and return to college.

Her long search for the cause of her illness had provided more questions than answers. Was Jenny abused as a child, or was her abuse another phantom diagnosis? And her memories? Were they events that happened? Or were they childhood fears, converted to false reality by the awesome power of suggestion? In response to therapeutic pressure, did Jenny twist unpleasant but benign experiences into malignancies in order to satisfy a demand that she find plausible cause for illness in her childhood? Did her mind distort images from the past as well as from the mirror?

After five years of psychotherapy, Jenny's anorexia was as unchangeable as the resolve of a fanatic, as enigmatic as the Sphinx. Her illness denied all theories and defied all treatments.

Dr. Weintraub badgered her patient to give up anorexia, as if such a decision still lay within Jenny's power to choose or the doctor's power to dictate. "Give it up, Jenny," became the doctor's weekly insistence, as if its repetition alone could force a change.

Jenny attempted to live her discharge fantasy. She moved in with Sally Dorsey, a friend of her parents, the widow of her father's best friend, and mother of five grown children. This change in living environment was endorsed enthusiastically by Jenny's parents, Dr. Weintraub, and

Dr. Corbin, who remained a concerned advisor on Jenny's case. A gentle, cheerful, and compassionate woman in her midfifties, Sally welcomed her new boarder. Jenny welcomed a chance to function from a home where she could be independent, wouldn't feel prejudged, and could be free from conflict with her mother.

Jenny developed a new, close friendship. Rachel Foster, a caring and compassionate young woman, was a medical student whom Jenny knew well from a decade of church Sundays and youth group activities. They became confidants—up to a point. Some things Jenny just didn't talk about outside the safety net of a therapy session. The black cloud from her past, too dark to share even with her most intimate friends, remained a taboo topic.

By July, Jenny again struggled with exhaustion and malnutrition, yet she continued to push her fragile body to maintain a full schedule of work and social activities. Alarmed at Jenny's decline, Dr. Weintraub weighed her patient weekly. Nothing could halt Jenny's cycling into another downward spiral, and Dr. Weintraub's consternation and impatience grew as the needle on the scale slipped lower each week. Something had to give.

With a disapproving look on her face, Dr. Weintraub steered Jenny from the bathroom weight scale back to her office. "You've been losing weight all summer, Jenny," she scolded.

Jenny's appearance was forlorn. "I know. I've been frightened and depressed since June, and I don't seem able to pull myself out of it. I don't understand why I can't. I feel comfortable living with Mrs. Dorsey, and I'm able to talk to you more as an outpatient than when I saw you only for a few minutes most days in the hospital."

"Without a change in attitude, a change in geography and more time with me are useless."

"My fault. I know." Jenny was genuinely apologetic. "I should have stayed at Willowcrest longer. I want to go back."

Dr. Weintraub shook her head. Her voice was emphatic. "I won't readmit you to Willowcrest. There's no point repeating all that anger and grief counseling. You're past that now. You have to stop losing weight, show some indication you are willing to give up anorexia. If you don't, I'll urge your parents to commit you to the state psychiatric hospital at Fort Logan."

Surprised by her doctor's reaction and its intensity, Jenny's tremulous voice resurfaced. "You . . . you know how terrified I am of being committed."

"Maybe you need that kind of fear for motivation."

"That's punishing me. You know Fort Logan can't do any more for me than Willowcrest."

"No one can help you if you won't let them."

"I'll die if you send me there."

"Probably."

"Is that what you want me to do?"

"No, Jenny. I want you to get well, but I don't think you want to. I can't help you if you don't want to get well, and I'm fed up with trying. I take you home with me at night, and that's something I've never done before. We have an appointment scheduled with Mom and Dad for a week from now. If your weight is down, I'm resigning, and I will not see you again."

"You . . . you mean, after . . . after four years, you'll quit . . . just give up on me and walk away?"

"That's precisely what I mean. As I've said to you many times, I will not stand by and watch you die."

Hysterical with fear, Jenny called Rachel after she left her doctor's office. "I'm going to lose her!" she sobbed.

"Weintraub?"

"Yes. I'm losing weight . . . unless I can stop . . . she's going to resign."

"Aren't you eating?"

"I can't make myself eat . . . I just can't . . . I'm too hurt and upset. She's throwing away everything . . . the four years we've been together

. . . everything . . . like I'm some kind of trash cluttering up her life. I trusted her . . . and . . . and now she's going to abandon me, like everyone else."

"Jenny, slow down. Think for a minute. What has Dr. Weintraub ever done for you?"

"She's been my . . . my . . . my best friend. I even dream about her. She's the only one who really knows me . . . the only one who listens and tries to understand."

"Jenny, you talk like you're breaking up with a lover. What has she accomplished to justify so much devotion? You're not improved."

"It's my fault. Dr. Weintraub was right. I'm a terrible patient."

"Don't you see what I mean, the way she puts you down, how she batters your self- esteem? She's hurt you far more than she's helped you."

"No. She was right. I didn't let her help me."

A funereal mood pervaded Dr. Weintraub's office as she addressed Jenny's parents. "Jenny told you about our discussion last week?"

"Yes," Jenny's mother answered for both.

"I can tell what's happened by all the long looks." Dr. Weintraub shifted her gaze to Jenny, giving full visual force to her disapproval. "You've lost weight again."

Jenny dropped her eyes, unable to meet the piercing accusation in her doctor's glare. "Yes," was her muffled response.

"Do I need to weigh you?"

"No," was the feeble reply.

Dr. Weintraub folded her hands in front of her as her eyes returned to Jenny's parents. "I'm afraid your daughter's case is hopeless. She's determined to starve herself to death, and no one can stop her. I've done everything I can to keep her alive, and I'm resigning effective today."

She's talking as if I'm not here, Jenny thought. *I'm already a nonperson to her.* Jenny's eyes remained riveted to the floor. *Should I beg . . . in front of my parents . . . for a second chance? Why bother . . . Dad doesn't have any*

confidence in her and Mom hates her now, so they won't support my plea . . . and
I know she'll say no. I'll never see her again.

"What sh-should we do?" Jenny's mother stammered. "Surely there's something."

"You should commit her to the state hospital at Fort Logan."

"We discussed that, and her father told her we would never commit her."

"He's letting Jenny manipulate him again. What do you think?"

"I don't see how we can deal with Jenny, particularly if she moves back home."

"That's understandable," Dr. Weintraub commiserated. "No one can deal with her."

"What about a different private care facility or another doctor for her?"

"She's untreatable, Mrs. Hendricks. I can't recommend any other hospital or doctor to you. She belongs in Fort Logan. You should commit her immediately."

"Stop it . . . STOP IT," Jenny shrieked. "You're all talking like I don't exist anymore. I'm the one at risk. This is all pointless. I won't go to the state hospital."

Dr. Weintraub frowned her patient into silence and added harshly, "Jenny, when you decide to starve yourself to death, you forfeit your rights to self-determination even if you are twenty-one."

Jenny's father spoke for the first time. "How do we get her to Fort Logan when she refuses to go? Handcuff her and transport her by bodily force?"

"Don't be difficult, Mr. Hendricks," Dr. Weintraub scolded.

"I thought I was being practical. I also need to understand what happens if we get her there and she refuses to admit?"

"The doctors will put a hold and treat on her."

"I've heard of the term. An against-her-will admission. But isn't that temporary?"

"Yes."

"And then how will they keep her there?"

"By a court order."

"Who gets the court order?"

"As parents, you and Mrs. Hendricks could."

"Sounds like legal turf to me. So, now we have to bring in the lawyers?"

"Not necessarily. Fort Logan's doctors can petition for an order."

"Which Jenny or I or both could fight?"

"A fight is your choice, but you won't win."

"At least I wouldn't have abandoned my daughter without a fight."

"Her tie to you needs to be severed, so you quit enabling her illness."

"That sounds familiar. While we're fighting Fort Logan's doctors and after we lose, how do they keep Jenny there physically? Restraints?"

"If necessary. More likely confine her to her room or a locked ward."

"I see. And what in your judgment will happen to Jenny at Fort Logan?"

"I'm sure she will die there." Jenny's mother gasped at the doctor's bluntness and stifled a sob. Jenny grimaced as if in physical pain. Dr. Weintraub plunged on. "By committing her, the two of you will at least alleviate your own guilt feelings."

Jenny thought her father looked confused when he responded. "But . . . how does committing her to Fort Logan alleviate our guilt feelings?"

"You will know you have done all you can do for her."

He shook his head in disbelief. "Sending her someplace where you are sure she will die and I am sure I have abandoned her will only make me feel guiltier. I will always wonder if I gave up on Jenny too soon."

"You misunderstand me. Giving up isn't the issue. Jenny is terminal. She is going to die wherever she goes. You must quit denying that reality. You—"

"Stop it, STOP it, STOP IT," Jenny shrieked, finally reduced to tears. "I can't stand listening to you fight about me like this. C'mon, Mom. C'mon, Dad. Let's leave . . . now. We're not accomplishing anything here."

PART TWO

Searching for a Cure

CHAPTER SIXTEEN
God's Child

September 16. It's been a long time since I've written in here. Weintraub said it's unhealthy for me. Too much intellectualizing, too little action. It's painful to chronicle the past few months. Suffice it to say I lost all the weight I gained in the hospital, plus I lost Weintraub. "Mental health care discards," Dad calls all of us, "wounded by the process."

The day Weintraub resigned, the three of us stood in the parking lot with our arms locked around each other for a long time, like we were a family again. We vowed we would continue to fight my illness TOGETHER. "I still believe in you," Dad told me. "There's still time left for you." He was convinced that we could convert Weintraub's resignation into a positive turning point, that we could quit wasting time searching for cause and find a cure. Now I hate myself because I couldn't turn and go forward even though I wanted to. I've gone nowhere but backward.

After I moved back home from the Dorseys, I started seeing Haley, a Christian counselor who approached me at the Harvest Restaurant. She recovered from anorexia after an endless struggle similar to mine. She did it by turning to God, and I am trying to figure out how to do that for myself. If I can bring the presence of God inside me, that should provide some defense against my consuming death drive.

I weigh less than I've ever documented (66), and I must be very ill right now. I'm weak and probably a little insane from starvation. This means I won't think clearly about what's good for me until I gain enough to provide energy to do so. Meanwhile I continue to act destructively. I must break this cycle. Tomorrow I will see if I can force myself to eat enough to gain

161

strength. I am very scared and pray to God to get me through this crisis. I know God has a plan for me, otherwise I would be dead.

September 28. I now weigh 64. Today I don't feel much of anything, not even hunger, except I am obsessed with thoughts of food.

October 2. I am writing this partly for Haley and partly just to get it out. I started bingeing and purging last Saturday. When I didn't die and nothing earth-shattering happened, I did it again and again, every day since. I am SO VERY hungry I can't stand it. But I'm afraid to let myself gain weight. So I solve my dilemma the cop-out way, by eating and emptying it all out again. My weight is 63 and I'm dehydrated.

I started with a new psychiatrist, Dr. Carillo, yesterday and tried to explain to him what was going on. He was nice, but I don't think he realized how DESPERATE I am NOW. I am terrified I'm going to kill myself—especially when I give in and eat. My body is in a state of horrible shock, and I don't know how I can control myself and stop self-destructing.

According to Haley's tapes, I am God's child. He loves me, and I deserve to eat for him. Why can't I apply this? I think it is because of the RAGE I still feel at gaining weight. I'm so terrified of the horrible things I may do to myself should I gain, that I would rather deny myself and go against God's will than experience that rage. Clearly I have lost it real bad this time. I know I need to get healthy, I just lack the conviction I can do it. I'm consumed with guilt. How am I going to WORK? I'm too weak to stand up.

October 8. I'm in the hospital tonight, Presbyterian/St. Lukes, because I couldn't take it any more. Mom and Dad brought me in, and the emergency room sent me to intensive care for cardiac evaluation. I don't think anything can help me. I'm beyond caring—so lonely and hopeless. I feel guilty at eating one-half an orange and bran and some lettuce for dinner. I want to get it out of me. I AM DEAD INSIDE. God, I am so scared. I don't want to kill myself because of what it may do to my family. But I want to die because I cannot face any more of this charade called life.

October 9. Today I'm under observation, meaning the hospital doesn't know what to do with me. I'll save them their indecision, refuse treatment, and leave. Dr. Carillo wants to see me three times a week. Maybe that'll help.

Fighting to remain functional, Jenny resumed work part-time and struggled to find a coping mechanism in the expanded schedule with her new
doctor. "Why is it so hard for me to grab on to something that will make
me want to get well?" she asked Dr. Carillo, trying to focus her mind on
their discussion. "Why can I think about returning to college and starting
a real life, and then let that glimmer of hope drown in a puddle of mud?"

"Jenny, you've just finished a long counterproductive relationship with
Dr. Weintraub. Your illness sucked her into the wrong treatment. You
and she focused entirely too much on your weight and why you got
sick. She didn't work with you enough on the more important goals,
rebuilding and helping you find an identity for yourself."

"But why can't I get motivated? Why does my anorexia mean more
to me than anything?"

"Because Dr. Weintraub wouldn't focus on a new identity for you
and became obsessed with ending the old one, your anorexia. How
could you be expected to give up your anorexic identity when you had
nothing to replace it with? The more attention you paid to your
anorexia, the less prospect you had of finding any other significance
to your existence."

"I have to acknowledge Dr. Weintraub didn't help me. But I was so
devoted to her. I still mourn her loss. Nancy, Rachel, and Diane all told
me she was bad for me, but I didn't listen to them, and I was too
attached to Weintraub to see for myself. So many years I wasted with
her! Years when I was still strong enough that I could have easily looked
for other answers. Now it's so difficult. Is it too late?"

"It is never too late to try."

But it was too late. Too depleted to respond to her new therapist,
Jenny again faced an emergency hospitalization, this time with chest
pains and atrial arrhythmia. A shuffling skeleton at 58 pounds, she
was barely recognizable, her face a fleshless death mask. Her skin
appeared parchment thin and brittle, as if painted to her bones. Outlines
of her teeth showed through where her skin stretched tautly over her
cheeks. Haunted eyes stared from hollow sockets.

October 19. Now I'm at Rose Medical Center with a new doctor, a gastroenterologist. I'm seeing a gut doctor for something wrong in my head that head doctors can't do anything about. His approach—NO FOOD! Only Ensure, gross, water-added Ensure. Like drinking chalk. I'm trying to force one down now, but mostly I want to kill myself. I brought some Tylenol just in case. Like most hospitals I've been in, I could easily do it right here. I don't have much hope. The rage is starting again—it has been VERY intense this week. I don't give a damn about what all these fucking doctors say about getting well. What do they know about a pulsating self-hatred so deep and intense and physically present that the only way I can avoid it is to move move move or starve myself to the point I can't feel the evil.

October 21. Today was the absolute worst. I starved myself yesterday only to get up this morning and find my fucking body has still gained half a pound. I'm going to refuse food again today. They say get to 75 pounds and I can be discharged. Discharged into what? Hatred of my body and a neurotic need to PUNISH it? Oblivion?

Part of me prays God will help me feel differently this time. How I wish I could allow myself the rest and nourishment my body and soul need so badly, rather than the compulsive pacing up and down the halls which consumes my day. If I could just let myself watch TV, sleep, eat, read, write, draw, and needlepoint until I find something worth caring about in me.

October 23. Yesterday I was crazy with bulimia. When I was admitted I vowed I would do everything they said, but I'm freaked out with weight gain and loneliness. My guilt is terrible, but I can't seem to cope with eating. My doctor will only give me two more days on my own before he puts me on a feeding tube. Maybe I should go on a tube now, get over this initial hump and get my body used to food. Then maybe I'd have more emotional strength to deal with eating.

October 25. I want to kill myself. I woke up depressed, and sure enough I've gained half a pound. I cannot seem to accept weight. I want to binge and barf and hurt myself till I die. I hate myself. HELP me, God! I am so scared! HELP help help!!! I want to end it. Carillo is coming to see me, but he doesn't understand how I feel.

"Think about the way you manipulate, Jenny. How you don't care about others when you are in pain and ignore their attempts to help."

"My fault, Dr. Carillo. I know."

"Think about how you try to prove to others how hopeless you are and then become hysterical when they are convinced. Quit the bullshit and rely on your strengths to get through the hard moments, and quit telling yourself you can't do it."

"But how?"

"Ask yourself, is this really how it is?"

October 29. I'm still at Rose—10 days now. My doctors delayed my feeding tube for three days. I guess my behavior scared and manipulated them into waiting. Carillo only gets half of it. He doesn't understand that I don't love myself when I'm not hurting or dying. I want to punish myself for having more energy than yesterday. I want to punish myself when others say I look or sound better. Part of me wants only to be sick, weak, totally depleted, and finally dead. Taking that away from me only enrages me because then I don't know how to accept myself. In Carillo's view, this is bullshit. In my view, it is unfortunate reality.

I'm mad at Carillo because he confronts me with things I only halfway comprehend (because of my physical state?), and when he doesn't know how else to come down on me, he says stupid things like "bullshit." Weintraub did the same thing when she used to tell me to consign it to the manure pile. I think he's mad at me, and I don't like that Mom adores him so.

October 30. Today I lost it. I couldn't handle a tube down my nose, so I pulled it out and discharged myself against medical advice. They didn't have the guts to put a hold and treat on me. Dad refused to come and get me, though, so Karen Johns drove me home. I met her in the hospital. She came down with Haley to see me. Like Haley, she recovered from bulimia through faith, and she's sure God can help me, too. She wants to give me some scripture references to study. I like her a lot. She seems to really care about me, not judgmental and condemning like my doctors. But Carillo and Karen and Haley and God are all too late.

October 31. Halloween and I'm out of tricks. Mom and Dad didn't make me go back to Rose. I'm an untouchable now, even by God or his disciples. Today I told Mom and Dad I wanted to die—at home, where I could be safe and at peace. Over six years of intolerable suffering is enough—for me and for them. They agreed and held me for a long time, trying to comfort me. Mom promised to make me as comfortable as possible, and Dad said he'd try not to intervene. I don't think they've told my brothers and sisters. But Brian is still at home. I'm sure he knows.

When a neighbor asked how painful my illness was for my parents, Dad said the burning pain that seared his heart was to my pain as a candle to a bonfire. Time to cut off fuel supplies and let the bonfire extinguish itself.

Too distraught to rest, Jenny paced by day, and at night lay staring at the ceiling. She waited for death. And waited. Three days later when her chest pains returned, family resolve wilted and Jenny's parents rushed her to University Hospital, on a Saturday.

The emergency room couldn't decide whether to admit Jenny as a medical or psychiatric patient. Indecision was infectious, and while she waited, Jenny became anxious about another hospitalization. She sat silently, staring straight ahead, squeezing her clasped hands rhythmically every few seconds. Conversation was impossible. Finally a psychiatric resident appeared and guided her and her parents through a maze of corridors into a small, windowless conference room with a table, four straight-backed wooden chairs, a single overhead light, and a long mirror on one wall. They talked for an hour as the resident tried to understand his new patient's case and evaluate her current condition. He asked Jenny a number of cognizance questions, like who was president, governor, mayor. Then he had her count backward from twenty. Despite her physical weakness, she remained mentally alert and answered everything correctly. The resident left looking confused, indicating he needed to consult with someone else.

The family sat quietly for a moment. But the oppressive, cell-like nature of the room and Jenny's omnipresent fear engulfed her. Tears erupted from her tormented eyes. "I hate this place already," she sobbed. "I can't stay here. Take me home, Mom. Please."

"Jenny, you agreed to come."

"I can't go through with it," Jenny screamed.

"You have to."

"I'm terrified, Mom. I want to go home. Please."

"We can't do anything for you at—"

"Let me die at home, Mom. Please. I know I'll die here . . . abandoned just like Dr. Weintraub said. You promised me I could die at home."

"We tried, Jenny. We just couldn't sit there night after night, waiting for you to starve to death."

"I can't believe this is happening to me. I can't go through it again. They did nothing for me at Willowcrest, nothing at Presbyterian, nothing at Rose, and—"

"Jenny, you wouldn't let them."

"And . . . they won't do anything for me here. Do I have to go through every fucking doctor in every fucking hospital in the whole fucking city to prove they can't help me?"

Her father tried to reason with her. "Jenny, we haven't tried a medical hospital that also has a psych ward. Here they can treat both your medical and mental condition."

"But you know they won't, Dad. You just want to get rid of me."

The door opened as the resident returned with two orderlies. "We've seen enough," he said. The two orderlies approached Jenny.

She cowered in her chair. "Bastards," she screamed. "You spied on us through the mirror." Like a wild creature fighting capture, her eyes dilated. She pleaded with her father. "Don't let them take me, Dad. Please. I'll be good. I can't stand being locked up again. I'll be good."

"I can't stop them, honey," her father said. He reached for her hand.

She shrank from his touch. "You knew they would do this to me."

He buried his head in his hands. "I didn't know, Jenny. I didn't know. I'm sorry."

The orderlies carried her away—she was an easy burden for them, like transporting a small bundle of sticks. In their arms she shook and sobbed uncontrollably. "I can't believe you're letting them do this to me," she shrieked. "I'll never forgive you—never. I hate you." Then a small child's primordial scream of anguish and betrayal wailed behind her and filled the tiny room. "No . . . no . . . oh, no . . . please, Daddy . . . no."

The resident stayed and waited for Jenny's parents to regain their composure. His voice was strained but gentle. "We'll sedate her so she can sleep and take her to intensive care for cardiac monitoring and evaluation. We've ordered a seventy-two-hour hold and treat. Are you familiar with the process?"

"Yes," Jenny's mother said listlessly. "And a court order after that?"

"If we have to."

"We won't oppose it."

"But she might?"

"If she's still alive."

The walls of the intensive care waiting room were barren except for an old clock. Every sixty seconds, its minute hand marched forward a fraction of an inch with a loud click, as if sounding out an ebbing life. Twice each hour, Jenny's parents shuffled the few dozen steps to their daughter's bed. She slept surrounded by a forest of medical electronics squeezed into a narrow wedge-shaped cubicle, one of a dozen similar units separated by partitions radiating from a central control station like spokes in a wheel. The digital readout from a monitor showed a slow-beating heart and confirmed a continued presence of life; whether in decline or recovery was indeterminable.

The hours crept by. Other visitors came to see other patients, stayed briefly, and left. Daylight faded. Darkness fell. Night closed in. Jenny slept on. Her father looked at the clock and nudged her mother. "Look, Anne, five hours we've been here, and they haven't done anything."

"They're watching her as closely as they can."

"That's what I mean. They're just monitoring her."

"What else should they do?"

"Get some nutrition into her. They don't even have her on an IV. She's dying of starvation, and all they're doing is monitoring her?"

"Maybe sleep is the best thing for her. Talk to one of the nurs   if it will make you feel better."

He approached the nursing station on unsteady legs. "Excuse 1   is there someone I could talk to about my daughter?"

"Perhaps I can help," a voice answered.

"My daughter is anorexic."

"We know that."

"She's . . . she's starving. Isn't there something you can do besides watch her monitors? Some way to get her some nutrition . . . now?"

"Not without a doctor's orders."

"Could I talk to her doctor, the young resident who sent her up here?"

"He's a psychiatric resident and has no authority while your daughter is under medical jurisdiction."

"So who has authority?"

"Dr. Evans, our ICU resident. Until shift change at seven."

"Which is in a few minutes. Can I talk to Dr. Evans now?"

The nurse looked around the unit. "I'm sorry. Dr. Evans is with a patient now. He checks on your daughter every thirty minutes."

"Like we do?"

The nurse looked at him quizzically.

"I mean he just looks at her? Does nothing?"

"He will take care of any emergency."

"Isn't dying an emergency?"

"Your daughter isn't dying. She's sleeping and her vital signs are stable."

"So you will watch and wait until they're unstable, then do something?"

"We're doing all we can."

"Then why don't you feed her, for God's sake!"

"Jennifer will go on a regular meal schedule when she wakens."

"If she wakens."

"She will when the sedative wears off."

"You don't understand. She rejects food and needs special attention."

"She will be assigned to a staff physician on Monday, and, if necessary, a special diet and treatment plan will be developed for her then."

"That's another whole day lost. Does she have to wait until Monday?"

"I'm afraid so."

"If she can survive that long. I'd forgotten how useless weekend admissions are."

He turned his back on a frown of disapproval and retreated to Jenny's mother who was still sitting placidly. "Take me home, Anne," he said, anger turning to resignation. "I need to leave before I go berserk and they have to lock me up, too."

By Monday Jenny was out of intensive care, rehydrated by an IV, and eating—a little. However, she was still an unresolved jurisdictional problem. The hospital concluded she was too sick mentally for medical doctors to treat and also concluded she was too sick physiologically for psychiatrists to treat. The experts rushed around in circles avoiding responsibility. No one took charge and no treatment plan was devised. Perplexed doctors and hospital staff conferred, tested, evaluated, observed, filled out forms, scratched their heads, and debated. Jenny languished. Finally, the hospital's psychiatric unit agreed to take her when she could demonstrate she didn't need to be there by eating a meal without psychiatric support.

On Tuesday Jenny accepted temporary admission to a medical wing for a week of medical rehabilitation. The seventy-two-hour hold and treat expired without conversion to a court order. Jenny was in no condition to fight a forced confinement. The system had taken over. A week later she transferred to the hospital's psych ward.

As Dr. Carillo was not on the hospital's psychiatric staff, he could not assume responsibility for Jenny's care. Another turf problem. He remained on her case as an informal consultant who visited weekly to provide advice and continuity.

During rehab, Jenny became a celebrity. The hospital teemed with medical students, and Jenny consented to be an academic model for classes studying eating disorders. Embarrassed at first by so much attention, Jenny soon welcomed the fresh, inquiring faces that thronged into her room. "I don't want to make this a career," she told them.

Jenny reconnected with Karen Johns, her friend from her Rose Hospital days. An attractive fortyish mother of two teenagers, Karen saw Jenny daily. In contrast to the quickie power sessions with Dr. Weintraub at Willowcrest, which usually kept her on edge, Jenny was able to relax, sit calmly with Karen, and talk quietly for at least an hour. Karen was a patient and sympathetic listener, with a genuinely compassionate approach, unlike the abrupt and confrontive style of psychotherapy Jenny had grown accustomed to. Jenny felt like she was finally important to someone else.

She was able to patch into a modest spiritual strength she had not experienced before. She looked forward to discussing Bible passages with Karen. Loyalty and an unselfish, unflagging effort characterized Karen's devotion to Jenny's welfare. Jenny responded with her trust, began to eat again, and gradually gained physical strength. Preoccupation with the weight scale was less fanatic than at Willowcrest, but weight gain continued to be the measure of progress. She gained 14 pounds in seven weeks and was discharged in time for Christmas.

Jenny wrote her grandmother from home.

Dear Meme,

Merry Christmas and Happy New Year!

I got out of the hospital yesterday, and of all my hospitalizations, this one has been the hardest, by far. I suppose that is because I have finally decided to give up anorexia and when I no longer have that escape mechanism, I have to face a lot of emptiness and sadness in its place. Tonight I am trying to deal with my uncomfortable feelings by writing to you instead of starving myself. I am trying to get stronger, coping with things in healthier rather than self-destructive ways. My doctor is very supportive and makes me feel like I can and will survive and overcome this stupid disease. I hate my problem with a passion, I am just uncertain what to put in its place; all I know is I am ready to find something else no matter how desperate and uncomfortable I might feel while I am looking.

Do you like my card? I drew it while just goofing around one day—I like it a lot. I think drawing will be something I'll fill my time with in this period of transition.

I plan to go back to work after the holidays, and then, provided all goes well in my recovery, I will go to Rice this fall. Say some prayers for me, that I will be able to come to a true recovery and pursue my goal to go to college. Thanks so much, Meme.

I'll write again soon. Love always,

Jenny

Despite a comfortable Christmas with her family and her determination to maintain a positive attitude, depression stalked Jenny like a bounty hunter. Like rising internal floodwaters, her fears of weight gain breached her resolve to recover. Binge and purge impulses again overwhelmed her. Biweekly sessions with Dr. Carillo didn't help. Panic-stricken by her loss of control, Jenny called Karen, whom she hadn't seen since her discharge. "I'm so depressed," she told her confidant. "And I'm bulimic worse than ever. It's a terrible habit I can't seem to break."

"Come to the house, Jenny, after lunch," Karen suggested.

Karen's accommodation calmed Jenny. Her urge to binge subsided. She busied herself with lunch—vegetable soup, tuna fish salad on a plain bagel, an apple with cottage cheese, and a Diet Coke.

After listening thoughtfully to Jenny for several minutes, Karen asked, "Have you thought about a different church, to help with a new start?"

"Some. I'm more comfortable at St. Matthews now, thanks to your help. And I've tried Father Thornley's church, which seems nice. My godparents go there."

"Come to our church, Jenny . . . come tomorrow with Phil and me."

"Happy Church? It's charismatic, isn't it?"

"Some call it that. We'd so like to show it to you, help you experience our joy."

"I think my parents would disapprove. Mom's church is critical of charismatics."

"Aren't you free to choose?"

"Yes, it's my decision."

"Well, think about it tonight and call us. Now I'd like to try something which I'm sure will help you. Phil will join us."

Karen led Jenny into a small dining room, darkened by blackout shades over the windows and furnished with a single straight-backed chair before a rectangular table covered with a fine linen cloth. In the center of the table rested a garland of red roses, an open Bible, a silver chalice filled with wine, a small silver cross, and a larger cross with matching chain, flanked on both sides by silver candelabras, each containing seven candles. "Take the chair and the small cross please, Jenny, while I light the candles," Karen instructed. Karen's husband entered the room, wearing a white ministerial robe and carrying a small booklet in one hand and in the other a third silver cross, this one entwined with the suffering figure of Christ. He stood on the other side of the table and smiled reassuringly at Jenny.

The odor of burning incense filled the room. "Wh-what are you going to do?" Jenny asked, her voice tremulous. "Some kind of ritual service?"

Karen picked up the remaining cross and slipped the chain over her head. "Next to baptism, it's the oldest sacrament of the Christian faith and the only one unchanged in nearly two thousand years."

Jenny felt her heart race and her cheeks suffuse with blood. "My God," she gasped. "It's an exorcism. You're going to exorcise me?"

"Don't be frightened. Phil and I are both ordained for this. We've been doing exorcisms for years."

Jenny watched with horror as Phil opened his booklet to a book-marked page. "B-but," Jenny protested, "we've never talked about this. I'm not possessed."

"Your anorexia, the evil presence you feel when you eat—that's Satan inside you. We've got to drive him out." Karen moved toward Jenny. Her eyes flamed with fierce, antidemoniacal ardor.

Jenny rose abruptly from her chair with her hands pushing in front of her, fingers and palms spread wide in the classic defensive pose against menace. "N-no way," she hissed in a desperate whisper, straining to get words out.

"We only want to help you, Jenny."

Jenny shrank further from Karen's outreaching arms. "Stay away from me," she shrieked. "I can't believe I trusted you, and now you want to do this to me."

"But we love you, Jenny. We want you to love God as we do and come to him in purity and health." Karen's beatific smile sought to recapture Jenny's trust.

"No . . . no, not this way," Jenny cried instinctively. She mustered her strength, turned, and fled unsteadily from the room, then ran sobbing through the front door and toward the street, digging frantically for the car keys in her jeans pocket.

CHAPTER SEVENTEEN

Full Throttle Back Pedal

Dr. Carillo's counseling avoided two pressing immediacies: Jenny's binge/purge compulsion and her pervasive depression. Therapy detoured around food and mood issues and bogged down in a swamp of analytical introspection. More thought-provoking conversation was added to a case already overburdened with provocative conversation. Long-term contemplative approaches were applied to a problem that couldn't stay unresolved long-term—like fighting a raging fire by first taking two months to develop a plan of containment.

Desperate for more focused help, Jenny sought counsel from yet another expert. Dr. Gale, a psychologist who specialized in behavioral treatment of bulimia, agreed to supplement her sessions with Dr. Carillo. Dr. Gale would work only with Jenny's urge to overeat and throw up. He first provided Jenny with a copy of his treatise on treatment of bulimia. "Read it with your parents," he prescribed, as if it were a designated family text. "We'll follow the approach discussed, expose you to foods you like to binge on, and help you develop ways to prevent purging. You need to be with others while you eat and then afterward," he instructed, "so you don't obsess so much about food and can give your purge impulses time to subside. Ask your parents to help."

Although the approach seemed simple and sensible, Jenny had reservations she didn't voice. "I'll try," she said.

A week later Dr. Gale asked, "Did you talk to your parents about our plan?" He was oblivious to the frown his question induced.

"Yes," she said. "Dad will sit with me for dinners and after. But I'm alone at lunch, and I've been on my own at breakfast for a long time."

"What about your mother?"

Jenny answered abruptly, "Mom won't help with my meals."

"Why not?"

Jenny shrugged her shoulders and remained silent.

"She's lost patience with you?"

"Probably. I'm sure she still thinks I'm sick just to torment her."

"So you avoid meals with each other?"

"Not always, but mostly. It's easier for both of us that way."

"Hhhmmm. I gather your relationship with your mother is strained?"

"Yes, it improved after someone I thought was a friend tried to exorcise me. But we can't seem to maintain a good relationship for long."

"Should we get into that?"

"No. I talk to Dr. Carillo about it when I need to."

Thwarted by practical problems, Dr. Gale's eating program was unable to translate from textbook to reality. His in-office attempts to modify Jenny's eating habits succumbed to the immutability of her illness.

In the third week Dr. Gale shifted into full throttle back pedal. Jenny's case had advanced far beyond his capabilities, which he painfully realized in a family session. When Jenny erupted into a hysterical fit of anger and despair—"WHAT CAN I DO . . . NOTHING WORKS . . . NOTHING . . . I WANNA BE DEAD"—fear grew in his belly like a consuming virus. He didn't know how to react. He was terrified Jenny might actually hurt herself while in his care. "I'm s-sorry, but our t-time is up," he stammered, as he struggled to end the session, return responsibility for Jenny to someone else, anyone, and beat a hasty retreat from his patient's histrionics. "I really can't help you with your feelings. They're so extreme. You should take them up with Dr. Carillo."

"I HAVE," Jenny shrieked at him, as he physically guided Jenny and her stunned parents from his office. "HE CAN'T HELP ME, AND YOU WON'T EVEN TRY."

Dr. Gale waited apprehensively for one more week to pass and resigned.

Rehospitalization loomed on the horizon as Jenny's condition continued to deteriorate. But she agreed with her parents and Dr. Carillo that she was too weak emotionally and physically to live independently outside the home. Her efforts to find part-time employment were unsuccessful. She became too depressed and distraught to read. She felt like a zombie. Jenny knew she had to change but felt powerless to accomplish anything without help. What to do? She couldn't go back to Willowcrest. She hated the idea of eventually being forced back into University Hospital. Commitment to the state system was unthinkable.

Maybe she should try hospitalization in an EDU, one of the specialized eating disorder units she had read about. EDUs were springing up like mushrooms after a long rain, fertilized by an epidemic increase in eating disorder cases. More and more people with eating disorders were emerging from the closet and seeking professional care. Medical doctors couldn't help. Psychiatrists and psychologists welcomed the opened closets—and pocketbooks—as they rushed to meet the challenge.

Dr. Carillo had no EDU recommendations for Jenny. Adding to her frustration, he balked at Jenny's suggestion of a new program. "Jenny, you bounce back and forth between doctors looking for magic solutions. There aren't any. You keep seeking an existence free of frustration. There is none. It can neither be expected nor achieved."

"But I can't function anymore on my own, even with your help."

"Your 'I can't do it anymore' is not a safe refuge for you. You have to take responsibility for yourself. It's a part of the human condition that can't be abdicated. You've never given an outpatient program a chance to work."

"That's not fair. I would have stayed with Dr. Corbin, but he wouldn't let me."

"And why?"

"Because I couldn't keep my weight above 80 pounds."

"Because you *wouldn't* keep your weight up. My point precisely."

"And Dr. Weintraub resigned."

"Because?"

"Maybe because she was convinced I was going to die? I'm still confused why. I guess because I couldn't give up anorexia."

"Because you *wouldn't* give up anorexia."

Jenny raged. "That's not fair either. I go to doctors for help in solving my eating problems. Then they refuse to work with me if I don't solve the problems myself. If I could keep my weight above 80 pounds on my own, why would I go to Dr. Corbin? If I could give up anorexia on my own, why would I ever see Dr. Weintraub? You're all alike. None of you takes responsibility for your own failure. You all say it's my fault, put it back on me. No wonder I can't improve."

"Time's up for today, Jenny. I'll talk to your father about my EDU reservations."

"NO. TALK TO ME."

"Very good, Jenny," Dr. Carillo clinically observed, as he ushered his distraught patient from his office. "You're standing up for yourself and getting some real therapeutic value from your rage outbreaks."

Convinced she needed a change, Jenny and her parents reviewed alternatives. Johns Hopkins was ruled out—Dr. Weintraub had tried that approach. None of the EDUs in Colorado had a track record. But what about Perretons in Missouri, the preeminent name in mental health care nationwide—very expensive, but the best? And, yes, they had an eating disorder unit. Why not try the best? Perretons's literature promoted a "five-week regimen" providing a "comprehensive diagnostic evaluation and nutritional rehabilitation program as a starting point for a return to a normal life. Patients thirteen years and older are involved in intensive educational and experiential sessions focusing on the underlying psychological disturbances often masked by ongoing symptoms." Despite Dr. Carillo's opposition, Jenny and her parents decided on a change of venue. Perretons seemed to offer precisely what Jenny needed. The insurance company readily endorsed the change.

Jenny admitted to Perretons in late February at 70 pounds, her discharge weight from University Hospital. Compulsive personality disorder was added to her obvious diagnosis of anorexia with major depression. Post-traumatic stress disorder was considered and ruled out. She reentered a regimented system with renewed determination, as she resumed her search for an island of hope in an ocean of knowledge barren of understanding.

CHAPTER EIGHTEEN

Angry

February 28. *Somehow I have survived a year of crisis, and today I'm better in a few ways. I'm able to hope a little, eat a little, and feel okay about it, even do some crafts. I want to assume responsibility for my well-being; discover what makes me acceptable to myself; resolve my remaining feelings about the abuse and abandonment by Dr. Weintraub; figure out the rage, if it is rage—and let it out; talk about why I perceive opposition as a physical threat (this was Dr. Carillo's interpretation of the cause of a lot of my rage); get my self-destructive tendencies under control. I HAVE to.*

March 1. *The patients here are all very nice—and intelligent, too. But I feel the need to compete with them. Idiotic, I know, but it's as if I want to be the thinnest. In a lot of ways I am except for Carol, but she is so screwed up in this cage of a disease that she nauseates even me.*

Another patient, Rebecca, reminds me of me when I was leaving Willowcrest last year—so snobbish, not interested in anyone—so sure I was so much more recovered than the others that they could offer me nothing. I'm sure she's a neat person underneath it all. I know now if I get better, more self-confident again, I will always make time for others.

March 2. *I'm feeling skeptical about Perretons. All the little doubts— other patients talking about relapse, Dr. Carillo telling me Perretons would not help me solve my underlying problems. I fear he may be right. I'm to see the psychiatric resident, Dr. Bellows, weekly for thirty minutes. How can he help me in that short a period? I gather all we will talk about is the weight gain program. Dr. Stormeier, director of the EDU, seems capable. I like him, but I'll only see him occasionally, sort of like in passing.*

March 3. I tried to talk to Dr. Bellows about my confusion over the validity of my childhood abuse. He said in a few weeks, once my medical records arrive and they get to know me better, they will work out the best treatment approach for me.

Carol continues to get on my nerves. She is beautiful but tries to make herself ugly. It scares me to see so much of myself in her: the hopelessness and despair, the competitive desire to be thinnest, the inability to laugh or smile or enjoy anything, the consumption by a disease that means absolutely nothing, yet not being able to let it go.

March 5. We videotaped today's group session. I was disgusted by the way I looked—like a pixie. I should speak more to the group and the camera rather than look into my lap like I did.

March 6. I feel sorry for Carol. In wrap-up she talked about her feelings of being hopeless, lost, and attacked. When you feel that bad, there is no reality beyond the pain of the moment, and you cannot process feedback from others at all.

March 8. I wrote Weintraub today to ask her to call Dr. Bellows about me. I miss her support so much, the security of her belief in me. I hate her for giving up on me, and I fear she will only tell Dr. Bellows of my negative qualities—of my insane desire to hang on to anorexia. I remember all the times she yelled at me and insisted I would never get well. So many thoughts I have about her—loving her, hating her, missing and needing her.

March 9. I woke up fat again. They never help me with this fat feeling. Maybe when they assign me a therapist—if they ever do.

Rebecca is driving me crazy with her plain yogurt. She has it two out of three meals and breaks a bunch of eating rules despite having been ordered not to. I don't know how she gets away with it and no one else can. She also bosses the nurses around; they do exactly what she wants.

I worked on essays for Dr. Bellows. He wants me to describe Mom, Dad, and one other significant person. None of the essays turned out. I didn't want to make them too long, but you can't write something like that in one paragraph. Next I have to write one on me.

March 11. I just got back from an educational session on coping strategies. Paula Jacobs, my social worker, had me talk about my negative and positive qualities. Then she lectured me for a long time about how out of balance my list was. She talked about choosing not to believe the negative and seeking out the positive, even on days I'm feeling awful. This all made perfect sense, but it pushed a button in me, and I cried and cried and couldn't stop. I've heard all that before and tried to live on positive feelings, but those feelings never last. They die the minute I leave the hospital. Why don't they understand that? I felt as if Paula was scolding me, like some of my sessions with Dr. Weintraub, telling me I was bad for feeling bad.

March 12. I had a good talk with Paula about Mom and Tony and the men at the cabin. Next week she wants to talk more about Meme and Mom.

I'm plagued with fear about what happens when I get on the outside. While I'm in the hospital I can sit and think, write in my journal, draw, crochet, or make a collage, but the minute I'm on the outside, those activities have no meaning for me. Why is that?

March 13. I've gained another ¾ pound. They have me on too many calories. That makes 3 pounds in two weeks. Disgusting. They don't make Carla gain that fast. I'm angry, out of control, and mistrustful. Nobody has mentioned a goal weight. Meanwhile I'm blowing up like a balloon.

March 15. After lunch we watched an educational film on the eight stages of personal development. Then I worked on the questionnaire Dr. Bellows gave me. One question asked what I would choose to be if I wasn't human. I chose to be the classical music score, Pachelbel's Canon.

March 17. I asked to see my weight every day, but the nurses said no. I also requested cafeteria privileges. Another no. I don't get what the big deal is, why they treat me like a baby.

May 18. Everyone else has cafeteria privileges, and I'm the only one still eating on the unit. I feel like I'm being punished. It hurts my pride. I'm angry at being stuck here like the baby of the unit, the patient least trusted. Everyone else can say, well, at least I'm better than Jenny.

March 19. I just got back from Paula's lecture on family issues. The lecture reminded me of the anger my eating disorder has generated in my family. Paula talked about how you get recognition for being sick, and I think that was once true in my family, although not anymore.

We had to draw our families in art therapy, and my anger at my family erupted. I'm so confused. I don't know what's reality and what's my perception. I've believed forever that my family leaves me out, but is that real? Maybe I don't try hard enough.

March 21. Rebecca is making discharge plans. I wonder if she is as improved as she thinks she is. I don't know if I'll ever be able to leave. I still feel unsafe. It terrifies me to think of going home again—to that cold house and my bedroom, empty and lonely. I think there is no way I can ever lead a normal life. Then I think of what Dr. Carillo told me, how I'm just hiding, and things will never get better until I face up to my responsibilities. The nurses say I should make a list of my positive qualities and read them to myself every day and when I feel bad.

March 22. Dr. Stormeier told Carol that Rebecca didn't utilize the hospital, which sets up Rebecca as the cause if she regresses. I wonder if that would pertain to me also. The nurses say I'm in worse shape than Carol, but when I look at her I'm sure she is thinner than I am, and I question why I must gain weight and she is permitted just to maintain.

March 26. Mom and Dad called last night. Dad said he knew I would need more than five weeks to recover. Now I'm fighting feelings of despair: Who am I trying to fool about finding a cure for my disease? Recovery is a joke. I'm safe today, but the minute I get out I'll lose it.

March 27. I gained a pound and I want to cut myself. My body is my enemy. It is determined to make me pay. I'm feeling fragmented. Part of me wants to destroy me, and part wants to care for me. Should I be nice, should I be mean, should I cut on my wrist, should I joke around? I feel crazy, not sure how to treat myself.

March 30. Carol wakes up in a good mood and is really talkative with staff, but I wake up angry and self-destructive. The more Carol talks, the more I feel like a disgusting loser because I can't seem to communicate. This morning Carol was permitted to eat only half her cream cheese, but I had to eat all of mine. That's so unfair.

April 1. Paula called Mom and Dad last night, and they assured her they understand I may be here a long time. That is such a relief because I was worried they wanted me to leave.

April 3. *Today I had gained ¼ pound from last time I saw my weight. Dr. Bellows said, "We wondered how you lost weight today." I told him I had gained since two days ago, and he said I had lost since yesterday and wanted to know how. I stared at him blankly and said I didn't know how. Then I finally got it. He was accusing me of purging or cheating on my food. That infuriated me, and I told him I felt unfairly attacked. He wouldn't meet my eyes, so I know he didn't believe me.*

Sometimes Perretons makes me feel like my problems are secondary to others.' This afternoon, without explaining why, Paula canceled our appointment. Then I saw that Renee had taken my time with Paula. When I asked my primary nurse, Gerta, if she had time to talk to me, she said no, yet I saw her talking later with Renee. Also, Carol told me she talked to Paula and Dr. Bellows today, and they promised her a therapist next week because she has problems that need immediate attention. As if I don't. I'm here five weeks now without a therapist and none in sight.

April 5. *This morning my night nurse weighed me. For the first time ever, someone talked to me and tried to calm me both before and after my weighing. It really helped. The day nurses know how intense my destructive feelings get when I am weighed, so why do they avoid helping me with that? Why am I always on my own at my most difficult times, weighing and eating?*

April 7. *My weight is down again, and I'm worried Dr. Bellows will accuse me of doing something wrong again, or worse yet, assume I have and take away some of my meager privileges. Like the time Dr. Weintraub assumed I was bingeing and purging at Willowcrest—when I wasn't—and punished me by putting me in isolation with that psychotic woman.*

Today Dr. Stormeier lectured me on body image. He talked about the two reasons a woman would keep her body asexual: (1) because she wants to be a boy, and (2) because she is afraid to face the responsibilities and discomforts of being a grown-up. I asked the doctor HOW I stop being afraid of growing up. He said you work on it. So, how do I work on it?

April 8. *Today Paula talked about the messages I feed myself: gaining weight is bad, gaining weight is out of control, gaining weight means I am a pig. My body is gross. I hate my body. I want to destroy my body. She said I devised this system of beliefs a long time ago, and to* dispose of them I need to look at what was going on at that time—what made me devise such a crazy system to deal with my emotions? I ended up thinking about those deep dark memories which hide from my consciousness and which others deny. Even as I write I'm cringing because I hear Dr. Carillo telling me, "Lots of people have been raped. You certainly weren't the first, that is if you did experience it. And it's not important now. The only thing that's important is for you to grow up and face your responsibilities."

April 12. Today I wanted to rip myself apart, so I clawed my stomach some. Nurse Trina told me I need to practice biofeedback and get my well side in control. She said I feel bad because I let myself feel bad. Like everyone else, she assumes I can control bad feelings. I wanted to scream at her, "You don't understand." Trina also scolded me for not adding more combination foods to my meal plan. She's uninformed about nutrition and insists that calories in combination foods are equal to their exchange counterparts. She said cheese has the same calories per ounce as tuna or turkey. She's wrong, of course, and I tried to explain it to her, but she wouldn't listen. If the nurses won't let me discuss my food fears, how do I get over them?

April 18. They increased my calories again yesterday because they don't think I'm gaining quickly enough. I HATE THEM. Carol walks around more emaciated than I am but is allowed to maintain because of her fear of gain. I have the same fear, but they keep raising my calories. It's so unfair. I feel like my identity is being stolen and given to someone else.

My head is throbbing because I gave in and slapped my head again and again. I'm afraid if I tell Gerta, they will punish me.

April 20. Tomorrow I have my doctor consultation. Will he think I'm crazy?

April 25. Dad said he wouldn't make me leave. He doesn't see any alternatives, even though he's disappointed with the program, and he's frightened by the length of time. He's not upset with me, and he said he would be supportive if I were willing to keep trying.

April 26. I'm empty and bad, without character, personality, or talent, worthless, disgusting, void of thought or worth. I took an Ativan.

April 29. *Gerta is limiting the number of times she will allow me to talk to her each week. It made me feel abandoned and unworthy, like at Willow-crest, when Dr. Weintraub limited her time with me and would watch the clock to be sure she left after twenty minutes. I had this picture of me wander-ing aimlessly around the campus, crazy as a loon with no one to talk to.*

Sometimes I want to run up and down the halls, screaming my head off, bashing my head against the walls, clawing myself until I fall down dead and bloody. When I get these impulses my observing ego reminds me what happened when I acted them out at Willowcrest. I usually ended up in the quiet room more ashamed than I could bear. I get to feeling suicidal because there is no resolution to these impulses. Acting them out doesn't make them go away and only brings me punishment. Sitting them out doesn't make them go away either. Every road leads to despair. Now they're restricting my staff time, and nobody will know how hard I'm struggling if all they see is a calm exterior. INSIDE I AM EXPLODING. MY HEART IS BREAKING. I AM SO DESPERATELY SAD.

April 30. *I HATE THIS PLACE. I HATE THE STAFF. I HATE MY BODY. I HATE DR. BELLOWS. I gained over a pound in a week. Dr. Bellows won't tell me my goal weight, because he knows it will freak me out. I WILL NOT weigh 100 pounds. If he tries to make me gain to that I am leaving.*

Staff says I can talk to someone only once a day. When I need sup-port the most, I get a gag order. They deny me any way of expressing how I feel. I'm not allowed to show my anxiety. I can't cut on myself, starve myself, throw up, or overexercise. I don't have a therapist, and now I can't talk to staff. HOW THEN AM I SUPPOSED TO DEAL WITH MY FEELINGS?

NO ONE would talk to me today, so already the first day THEY'VE VIOLATED THEIR OWN RULE. They say if I can't control my feelings by myself they will punish me, take away my privileges, make me eat from trays. I keep telling them that won't work.

May 1. *I'm missing Mom and Dad a lot after talking to them today. Dad said I'm old enough to make major decisions about my life, and I should decide about staying here. That felt kinda bad because I don't feel any more respon-sible for myself now at twenty-two than I did at fourteen. His statement* scared me because he is growing older, and what happens when he is gone? What do I do then?

May 3. Seeing Carol's thirteen-year-old daughter reminds me of Janis when she was younger, and I would try to help her like herself. Now we are both grown up. Only I don't feel grown up.

May 4. I haven't accepted that I have to gain weight. Occasionally having doctors to talk to briefly doesn't help. They nod their heads and say uh-huh, uh-huh, we know, that's why you are here, we know you have an eating disorder, and that's why we have to control your weight. Then they walk out and leave me more outraged and frustrated than when they walked in.

May 5. A friend of Mom's wrote that her son who is my age is only a few weeks away from graduation and is already interviewing for jobs. I get so scared when I hear things like that and consider how far behind I am. Dad says there's still time left for me, but I don't think so.

May 7. I HATE THE STAFF FOR MAKING ME DO THIS ALL BY MYSELF. IF I COULD DO IT BY MYSELF I WOULDN'T BE HERE. I HATE LIFE.

May 8. Today in art class I drew what I felt. As ugly as it is. My drawing frightened the art teacher, and she insisted we come back to the unit and talk to staff about it.

May 9. Dr. Bellows is taking me off the antidepressant because it isn't helping. I'm scared I will get more depressed and commit suicide.

May 24. Next week I finally get a therapist, a Dr. Breen. They wanted to wait until my nutrition improved and my nervous system recuperated. I guess my nutrition is better, but my nervous system feels worse. How did they expect that to recuperate when they won't help me with my feelings when I gain weight? I'm kinda bemused that I am attempting this again. Who am I trying to fool, anyway? Is it possible to get well after all this time?

May 28. I saw Dr. Breen today and cried the whole time. We talked about my depression and my feeling that I drove Dr. Weintraub away in order to force myself into suicide. Then he observed, like Dr. Carillo, that even good things—the fact that my parents still love me despite everything I've done—don't feel good to me. That really shook me up because he sounded like Dr. Carillo, accusing me of twisting positives into negatives. Unlike Dr. Weintraub, who was so sure my memories confirmed childhood abuse, Dr. Carillo thought the events I remembered might not be abusive at all but were everyday, ordinary things that I made negative and chose to believe were abusive. I feel extremely confused and scared about seeing a new therapist.

June 5. Today I weighed 79⅜. What a pig. The doctors assured me I can stop at 80 and maintain, but they won't decrease my calories, just increase my exercise. I'm gaining 2 pounds a week, and that means in order to maintain I will have to burn off 7,000 calories per week, and that seems impossible. How can I trust their assurance when it makes no sense?

June 6. My rage comes in waves like nausea. I'm crazy with rage today, feeling like there is a wildcat stuck inside me, clawing, ravaging, making me want to pull myself apart.

June 15. I'm insecure with relationships now. Carol has far surpassed me, and I'm only held in medium esteem. I don't know why I'm so plugged in to her, but it seems like she has stolen my identity. This is nothing new. I've done it with others. I wonder if it has to do with when the Landers at the horse barn dumped me for Libby. She came along cuter, smaller, sweeter.

June 20. Carol feels manipulated and watched by me. Gerta says Carol is trying to draw me into her problems. Now I have to avoid Carol so I don't stir her up. What a mess.

June 23. I talked to Dr. Breen about my rage when I perceive a need that someone else is not meeting. Dr. Breen expressed it more eloquently. He didn't make me feel defensive like Dr. Carillo used to. I wish I could remember his exact words. They went something like this: I realize I have an incredible need from someone (Mom to love me), but this person is not fulfilling my need. I become enraged, first at this person then at myself for (1) needing so much and (2) being angry that the need wasn't met. We talked about my ambivalence: Part of me is rational and able to see the other person's limitations, part of me is immersed in the rage I feel over being denied. A lot of my sadness results from not knowing how to rectify this discord within myself. How can you love your mother and want to protect her and still be caught up in this crazy illness, part of the purpose of which must be to punish her? I asked him, "What am I punishing her for?" He didn't have an answer, except to ask me what I thought I might be punishing her for. Despite all the hospitalizations and therapy I do not understand even minutely what I am so enraged about.

June 24. I want to take some classes at the local college. I believe I should do something outside the hospital, like I did at Willowcrest. Outside involvement could help me develop new coping mechanisms and accomplish something. Dr. Bellows is reluctant. He doesn't think I should enroll, especially with classes available to me only in the mornings. He thinks I only want to prove to my dad that I am still accomplishing—that therapy isn't the only thing in my life. I explained that this is my third long-term hospitalization, and I wasted a lot of time in the other two. He said outside classes might be appropriate once I really commit to the therapy process. He says I'm still uncommitted. How else should I be after all my experiences thus far?

June 25. I talked to Paula today about school. She thinks it's too early. I'm really confused. Dr. Weintraub pushed me to get involved with school or work while I was still at Willowcrest, and I know it helped. Now I have the courage to initiate a similar effort on my own and Perretons discourages me because they think I'm not ready. I believe I am ready. I cannot fathom continuing to waste so much time sitting here.

June 27. Mom and Dad came for a workshop and left tonight. Our visit together was the most carefree and relaxed we've had in a long long long time. They really spoiled me: some new clothes, new shoes, hair shampoo and lotion, and also some new music. Mostly it was nice just being with them. Dad was more physically attentive than he has ever been. He held my hand in one workshop, and he hugged me a couple of times and also held my hand walking to and from the cafeteria. It was a very nice, loved feeling. Mom was also very close and loving and trying oh so very hard. I feel guilty about the pain and turmoil I've caused them, though I know initially I must have liked it that way. In the early stages, part of me wanted to punish them, especially Mom. I really don't want that anymore.

July 1. Today I felt confronted about giving up anorexia. I know I don't want to weigh more than 80 pounds, so maybe that means I can't give up anorexia.

Why didn't I commit suicide last year when everyone was prepared for me to die? I kept that bottle of pills safely hidden in University Hospital. But I was afraid I wouldn't die, that I'd just end up a vegetable. Then I was so entranced with Karen Johns and all her religious promises that I actually thought I might be okay after all. I got out and within two days I was puking wildly again.

July 2. I'm not doing well with Dr. Breen. Trina said I deserve to know his plan for helping me. So I asked him what his "plan of attack" was for me, which was a bad choice of words because he brought that phrase up again when we discussed my fear of men. We got into the abuse issue some but not in any real detail. I still don't have a clue of how he intends to help me. While we were talking, I got these vivid mental pictures of killing myself, of quietly and purposefully going back to the unit and methodically slitting my wrists, lying down on my bed, and bleeding to death. Such a pacifying fantasy—to be able to succumb to my death wish.

July 14. Today I hit the wall again, became hysterical and out of control. Dr. Bellows reneged on his commitment to let me maintain at 80 pounds and raised the limit to 81. He wants to see what happens to my body over the next several days and then reevaluate. I think he wants to fatten me up for a period. I told him that I don't want a period, don't care if I never have one again, don't perceive that as part of my goals here. He said maybe I was refusing treatment, and I said maybe I was and maybe I should go. He said maybe I should. And then he said if I couldn't deal with gaining a pound, I certainly could not deal with school. Well that is untrue, and he had no right to say that. Then he left, and I didn't have a chance to tell him it was my hope that I would be allowed to maintain at 80 pounds, start to reinvest in school, and continue with therapy. I thought this routine would slowly bring me to the point where I was ready to gain more weight AFTER I began to feel better about myself through school and therapy accomplishments. Obviously Perretons's priorities for me are reversed. I thought they would do things differently here. But it is the same stupid approach—force me to gain weight and lose my anorexic sense of safety before I begin the search to find something healthier to replace it with. Also,

Dr. Breen is still hung up on his favorite topic—the anger I feel for having needs not met. This discussion never goes anywhere.

July 26. I'm afraid Dr. Bellows will raise my calories. He says trust him, he won't make me fat, and then I see his other patients with their pooched-out bellies and gargantuan thighs. I cannot deal with looking like that.

I question whether this is the right place for me. The program isn't set up to benefit a long-term patient, and I've been shocked by how little information or thought-provoking material is provided in the educationals. I fantasize about writing Dr. Pruitt who practices at Willowcrest and asking him if he would take me as a patient, perhaps rehospitalize me there. He helped Tina Martin so much at Willowcrest, while I languished with Weintraub.

July 27. Everyone else is fantasizing about leaving, too. Carol thinks she'll leave in August. She doesn't want to gain any more weight either. Dr. Stormeier told her she must gain weight or forget about him writing to renew her medical leave. They just never get it. Our feelings about weight gain can't respond to their threats.

July 28. They increased my calories today and accused me of not eating the food I'm supposed to. They're wrong, but they're making me go back to eating on the unit from supervised trays. Now everyone else will think I've been cheating on my food, too.

July 31. I thought Brian's birthday was today so when Mom and Dad called I said I was sad missing his birthday. Mom said it was yesterday, and I felt like such a fool. She asked how things were going. I said awful, I want to come home to Willowcrest.

August 1. I got a letter from Janis today. She is doing so much with her life while I sit here bored doing nothing and feeling incapable.

August 5. Today I feel fat as a cow. My family is at the ranch, and I woke up remembering what it is like to be there: all the excitement of the trail rides and new friends. I wanna go home bad. I see no good coming from this hospitalization, and I'm becoming an Ativan junkie. Dr. Bellows talked about a new antipsychotic drug, Trilafon. He's not familiar with the cortisol inhibitor drugs being tested in California or other drugs being tried in Boston. He says Trilafon helps control negative thinking. I wonder if I could get better if I didn't have such pervasive pessimism.

August 6. My relationships with other patients continue to be rough. Renee vacillates between being angry and rejecting and sweet and inviting. I've exposed my irrational and crazy side to her, and she says she feels helpless to stop my negative thinking. She thinks I'm focusing too much on weight issues—but that's all she'll ask me about, and that's what Perretons forces me to think about. She asks how things are going with Carol, then turns around and tells me I'm too focused on Carol. Carol says I get away with stuff—cheating on food—she wouldn't be able to get away with. Which is exactly my observation of her. I'm sick of having to live with sick people.

My best nurse, Gerta, is leaving. All week I've been questioning whether this is the right place for me, whether Breen is the right therapist for me, and now the one person I know helps me is leaving. I think I should leave, too. The EDU rides on Perretons's general reputation and has none of its own. I haven't met one patient who's been cured of uncontrollable binge and purge impulses. Those who come here with an eating disorder all keep it when they leave.

August 8. I've been seeing Dr. Breen for two months now, and his approach seems pointless and not goal oriented. I'd like to request a different therapist, but it could take Perretons six months to act on my request. So I wrote Dr. Pruitt asking if he would treat me at Willowcrest. At least Willowcrest had group interaction and support. Here there is none. I hate it. I am so lonely.

August 10. This place is a joke. I sit in my room, cry, and contemplate cutting myself. They make rounds but never say a word. They don't care what kind of pain I'm experiencing as long as I don't break structure. So I laid it on the line with Dr. Bellows. I told him I will leave if Dr. Pruitt accepts me. I do not understand how Dr. Breen can help me. We do not click, and I don't have any sense of accomplishment after seeing him. Perretons is outstanding at structure, but forget it when it comes to support. Dr. Bellows said it would be a mistake to leave. He thinks some of my negative feelings about Perretons result from my not grieving the loss of Dr. Weintraub. I told him I wasn't getting any help with that either, and he asked why I don't bring it up. I told him everything I bring up gets redirected to therapy, and all Dr. Breen wants to discuss is my excessive need.

I'm angry—angry they increased my calories, angry they don't care, angry there's so much emphasis on structure, FUCK STRUCTURE, angry Gerta is going, angry Dr. Breen is back and not worth shit. My mood is so BLACK. I HATE EVERYTHING TODAY, and I can't imagine ever feeling any better. Better doesn't exist for me.

After breakfast the next morning, Jenny opened her purse and counted her money. Confident she had enough, she stuffed a change of clothes, Pooh, a hairbrush, toothpaste, and a toothbrush into her backpack, walked off campus to a gas station, and called a cab that took her to the Greyhound bus terminal where she purchased a ticket to Denver. An hour later she was dozing in her seat, oblivious to the Missouri landscape rapidly disappearing behind her.

After six months at Perretons, Jenny's accomplishments were weight gain 10½ pounds, therapeutic gain zero. With ostrichlike mentality, Perretons remained steadfast in its denial of the care Jenny needed most urgently—help in relieving her intense feelings when she ate and when she was weighed. Coping with the mental consequences of weight gain was left to the patient, as Perretons pursued the myth that psychological work had to wait until a patient had successfully dealt with the emotional devastation of weight gain on her own.

CHAPTER NINETEEN
Pine Grove

September 2. I'm home now and have spent the past few weeks trying to organize a totally disorganized life. First I called Dr. Pruitt, but he refused to see me. So I'm seeing Dr. Corbin again, which seems the right thing for me now—and he's not weighing me this time. I had to get on with my life. I couldn't do that at Perretons. I couldn't take the stagnation and go-nowhere feelings that time would pass me by, I wouldn't be able to change, and I would come out even more emotionally crippled.

Today I start a part-time job bagging groceries, and tomorrow I begin a trigonometry class at Aurora Community College. Next week a new eating disorder support group starts meeting at the YWCA. I swim for thirty minutes every day at the health club and make time for my friends, Diane, Melinda and Jim, Mrs. Dorsey, and the MacGregors. You might say I'm too busy to be sick. At least I have my own car now, if you can call an old Dodge Omni a car.

Jack called from Perretons tonight. He really made me feel good. He came just before I left, and I didn't think he cared about me beyond playing backgammon occasionally. Already it feels as though my time at Perretons was a figment of my imagination—just a bad dream.

Jenny's strength gradually failed and with it her resolve. Depression reasserted its stranglehold on her emotions. Positive thoughts couldn't establish any holding ground in her mind. Feelings of hopelessness overwhelmed her, and suicidal impulses grew more difficult to restrain. Reviewing her journal before Thanksgiving, Jenny realized she had written nothing since September. On the journal cover she wrote in bold capital letters, SHIT YEAR. Then, turning to the first blank page, she made what she thought would be her last journal entry for the year:

November 27. *Time to die.*

"You're calling from where?" Jenny's mother had rushed inside to answer the phone, leaving several bags of Thanksgiving groceries still in the station wagon, wondering why Jenny's Omni was parked in front of the house.

"From the pharmacy at King Soopers."

"Yes? I just left King Soopers."

"We're calling all the names in our customer files which sound like Hinders."

"Yes? What about?"

"About fifteen minutes ago we received a call from a person who identified herself as Jan Hinders. She didn't sound upset, but her speech was slurred and she wanted to know how much Tylenol would be considered lethal."

"DEAR GOD! That's my daughter! She's supposed to be in class."

"We told her a lethal dose varies with age and weight, but then she hung up before—"

"Thanks, but I have to go now—sorry.

"JENNNEE!" Jenny's mother screamed as she raced up the stairs and down the hallway. She glanced through the open bathroom door where two uncapped pill bottles lay empty on the countertop. Heart pounding, she rushed to Jenny's still figure where it sprawled diagonally across the bed. Her piercing cries filled the room. "JENNNEE . . . OH NO . . . DEAR GOD . . . JENNNEE . . . PLEASE NO."

Still conscious but unable to respond, Jenny listened groggily to her mother's screams and felt hands shaking her roughly. Go away and let me die, she wanted to say but couldn't. Despite her drug-induced stupor, her brain registered her mother's departure and calls from a hall phone outside her door, three in rapid succession. She identified the calls—first 911, then Father Potter, then her father's office. She's sure I'm going to die, Jenny thought. *But there weren't enough pills left in the two bottles; otherwise I'd be gone already. Shit, I can't even do this right. I was sure she'd be at church all afternoon. Why did she come home so early?*

Stiffly and slowly, Jenny turned on her back, drew up her knees, clasped them with her hands, and turned on her side into a fetal position. She waited without emotion—for oblivion or paramedics, whichever might come first. Unconsciousness finally claimed her.

Waking briefly, aware that she still lived but feeling detached from life, Jenny watched a flutter of white-robed figures working methodically over her, their blurred movements shimmering in slow motion. A gag reflex shook her as she felt a tube slide down the back of her throat. *Pumping my stomach*, she thought. Fragments of conversation penetrated the cold, damp fog that she felt envelop her.

". . . bloodstream already."

". . . transport her to Porters . . . Dr. Calvin's waiting . . . leading expert in the country on . . . "

". . . going to OD on Tylenol, Denver is the place to do it."

"She's very lucky."

No, Jenny thought, as unconsciousness claimed her again, *I'm very unlucky.*

Tube-feeding Jenny with doses of charcoal, it took Dr. Calvin several hours to neutralize the acetaminophen and flush it from her system. Late that night he declared Jenny out of danger and released her from intensive care.

Paradoxically, Jenny's failed suicide attempt dissipated the black cloud of depression that had enveloped her. She wakened with fresh resolve to maintain a positive attitude. That a suicide attempt could drain her despair and eliminate the risk of a repeated attempt was incomprehensible to physician and parent alike. Dr. Corbin insisted she obtain psychiatric hospital care immediately upon discharge from Porters. "She should not spend even one night at home," he advised Jenny's parents. "Too big a risk she'll hurt herself again." They readily agreed.

Struggling to maintain some control over her own destiny, Jenny sought temporary sanctuary at Willowcrest, despite Dr. Corbin's and her parents' urgings she look to a different program in a different place, somewhere untainted with the past. "I want to admit only for stabilization," she pleaded with Dr. Pruitt. "I'm not looking for a cure, just a place to stay over the holidays. Staff knows me well, and I think they can help me."

"I'm sorry, Jennifer, but I won't take you as a patient," Dr. Pruitt repeated his earlier refusal. "I can't help you."

He's afraid to try and won't take the risk, Jenny thought. "Dr. Weintraub has poisoned you against me," she said.

"Now, Jennifer. No one's against you. You know that."

"I know. I'm sorry. Is there someone else I could call?" *Someone else who's not infected*.

"Umm . . . Langley's on vacation. You might try Dr. Prince, he sees a few patients here."

"I'll call Dr. Prince."

Dr. Prince admitted Jenny to Willowcrest upon her discharge from Porters. Although Dr. Corbin couldn't see Jenny at Willowcrest, he encouraged her to remain in touch by phone. He did not give up on her, nor did she lose trust in him. She called him five days after admission.

"It's not working," she said.

"Why not, Jenny?"

"It's not the same. Lots of the staff I knew are gone. I've seen Weintraub on the unit every day, and that freaks me out. She gives me this weird look, but we don't speak. Today she was talking with two nurses as I walked by. I heard her mention my name, and then they clammed up and looked guilty. She's gossiping with staff about me. It's not fair."

"It's also unprofessional."

"Dad wrote the hospital asking them to instruct the staff not to talk to Dr. Weintraub about me without Dr. Prince's consent. But I don't think that'll do any good. I have all these eyes following me, staff and patients staring at me, as if saying, "What's she doing back here?"

"Have you thought more about Pine Grove in Colorado? I've talked to my colleague there, Dr. Borger. He could help you make a fresh start."

"You're sure he's willing to work with me . . . after all my history?"

"Yes. You need a hospital structure, Jenny, and we're running out of options."

"Didn't you tell me Dr. Borger does drug therapy?"

"Yes, when he concludes it's appropriate."

"You know how I feel about drugs."

"And I generally feel the same. But conversation therapy doesn't seem to work with you. I think you should give Dr. Borger's program a try."

"What does Dad think?"

"Your dad and mom are both convinced you need a change."

"How soon can Dr. Borger take me?"

"Immediately. We can arrange a hospital transfer, and your parents can drive you to Pine Grove tomorrow. You can still back out if you don't feel comfortable there."

Desperately unhappy with her current condition and fully aware her fragile emotional strength could soon fail again, Jenny grasped the straw. "Allright, I'll go. At least it's closer to home than Perretons."

Tall and athletic, young and darkly handsome, nonconfrontational, articulate, and a considerate listener, Dr. Borger quickly gained Jenny's trust and confidence, dispelling apprehension she had felt on the long drive down from Denver. "We like him too, Jenny," her parents confirmed. The campuslike setting of Pine Grove reminded Jenny of Perretons but was much smaller and more naturally pleasing, with its surrounding forest of ponderosa pine trees providing a cloistered, restful feeling of sanctuary.

Maybe I can get well here, Jenny thought as she unpacked. *There's no eating disorder unit, so at least I'm not surrounded by other anorexics I'm likely to compete with!*

"You're off the scale with depression," Dr. Borger advised after his initial evaluation.

"I know." Jenny sat passively, trying to focus her tired mind on the conversation. She spoke slowly, in a monotone. "I have so few days depression free."

"I believe your depression is an underlying cause, not just a symptom of your anorexia."

"I've been tested before for chemical depression. The results were negative."

"Science doesn't have a handle on all chemical imbalances. Have you ever tried lithium?"

"No. Isn't lithium for manic-depressives?"

"It's used for severe depression also."

After further discussion with Dr. Borger about its side effects, Jenny consented to take lithium. Anything to bring her some peace.

December 16. *We're having weekly family sessions with a social worker, Dr. Conlon, and Mirriam, my head nurse. Dr. Borger doesn't participate, but he said the purpose of family sessions is to emancipate me from my family on a gradual and gentle basis. I don't think Dr. Conlon got the message, though. Like Weintraub, he's obsessed with finding the cause of my illness in family relationships. Although he's nice to me, he's confrontational with Dad and Mom and attacked them right off yesterday. I talked to them last night, and Mom said she was in tears for the entire ride home. Weintraub never did that. They like Mirriam but can't stand Dr. Conlon. "The man has the sensitivity of a hungry python," Dad said. I guess Dr. Conlon made it clear to him that I couldn't improve if he and Mom didn't come down for family sessions. Emotional blackmail, Dad called it. I told them I think they should stay involved too.*

My brothers and sisters are home for Christmas, and Dr. Conlon wants the whole family to come down next week. Dad asked if he should bring our dogs, too, and I don't think Dr. Conlon appreciated that remark. I'm scared about everyone talking about me in front of me.

After forty minutes of analyzing family interactions with all the Hendrickses present, Dr. Conlon leaned back in his chair and summarized his findings. He trotted out a favorite textbook hypothesis. "You have two opposing factions in your family," he announced with great solemnity. "It's a classic male versus female conflict, except that Janis sides with the men."

Confused by Dr. Conlon's evaluation, Jenny remained silent, mind racing. *I'm the one in conflict with Mom and sometimes my sisters, not Janis. Nancy and Janis get along great. They're even closer since I've been sick. Janis and Brian are like twins, but that's not a faction. And I'm closer to Dad than anyone else in the family.*

Jenny's mother showed distress at Dr. Conlon's assault on family unity but remained silent, lips quivering with unvoiced anger.

"But how does that connect to Jenny's emancipation?" her father asked skeptically.

David preempted the doctor's response. "You see factions after only forty minutes with us! That's ridiculous."

"It's apparent by the way you react to each other."

David responded under his breath with "Bullshit."

Nancy leaned over and hissed at Janis, "Traitor!"

Suppressing laughter, Janis raised her right fist and waved it at Nancy. "You're just jealous because I've got the swing vote," she hissed back.

Dr. Conlon scowled.

"Are factions bad?" Brian asked.

"Yes. They're destructive. It's part of your family's dysfunction. You're not together." Dr. Conlon struggled to maintain dignity.

"Does that mean Fri and Frida have to be on opposite sides, too?"

Dr. Conlon looked confused. "Fri and Frida?"

"Our pet alligator puppets."

"Young man, are you making fun of me?"

"No, sir."

"I'm sure no one could make you into fun," Janis added with mock seriousness.

"I apologize for my sister," Nancy said, trying to frown at Janis. "She's undisciplined."

"I am not undisciplined."

"You are, too."

"I am not."

Dr. Conlon looked at Jenny's parents, as if appealing for disciplinary intervention.

Jenny's father smiled and shrugged his shoulders. "It's your show," he said. "They're too incorrigible for me."

The session disintegrated into laughter. Jenny felt embarrassed by her family's reaction to Dr. Conlon and disappointed that a family meeting failed to accomplish something she wistfully hoped for—a better understanding, particularly by her siblings, of her condition.

Unfortunately, Jenny's strain of depression remained impervious to lithium, and as Jenny's "shit year" ended and a new year began, Dr. Borger suggested a more aggressive antidepressant program. He prescribed shock treatments, an old approach with a new, less menacing label: electroconvulsive therapy, or ECT.

Jenny was more curious than apprehensive. "What about side effects?" she asked.

"ECT is less hazardous than drugs, actually," Dr. Borger explained. "And it's no longer the inhumane procedure that lingers in popular view. California has even lifted its ban on ECT."

"What results can I expect?"

"ECT has been used successfully with anorexia as well as depression. I still think you have some kind of chemical imbalance of long standing which causes your depression."

"Which then causes my anorexia?"

"That's my belief. But I acknowledge it could be a classic chicken or egg situation."

"But if lithium didn't help, what are my chances of a good response to ECT?"

"About 85 percent of depressions respond to drugs. Unfortunately, you appear to be in the 15 percent that don't, but 85 percent to 90 percent of depressions not responding to drugs do respond to ECT. For women, ECT is more effective than tricyclic antidepressant drugs."

"Any side effects from ECT?"

"You may experience mild disorientation and short-term amnesia, both temporary."

"Like I'll be so zapped, I'll forget how I feel about eating and won't think not to eat?"

"Something like that. If ECT can keep you depression free long enough for you to improve nutritionally, then drug therapy might become more effective in controlling your depression on a long-term basis."

"My sisters are gonna freak out about my having shock treatments."

"How do you feel about it?"

"I'd like to try ECT. I'm not afraid of it."

Ten times in February technicians administered anesthesia and then strapped cold, metallic electrodes to Jenny. Ten times her frail body convulsed for the doctors, as if, while unconscious, she literally could shake herself free of the depressions and obsessions that tormented her. ECT treatments and subsequent drug therapy moderated her depression. The long, dark tunnel of hopelessness that had encased her for so long now showed a glimmer of light. But from the end of the tunnel? Or merely from some short-lived incandescence along the way?

Depression retreated. Food obsession did not. Anorexic thoughts maintained supremacy in Jenny's mind. Unlike previous doctors, Dr. Borger was open to using alternative therapy programs. With the urging of Jenny's father, Dr. Borger researched a cortisol-suppressing drug regimen, which was widely publicized as successful in anorexia patients treated by the Parsons Clinic in Florida. Although experts generally agreed there was a correlation between eating disorders and elevated levels of cortisol, they disagreed about which was cause and which was effect. Many psychiatrists were reluctant to abandon or modify their beliefs that psychological and social causes were preeminent. Dr. Weintraub had dismissed the use of cortisol inhibitors with Jenny and refused to counsel with the Parsons Clinic. None of Jenny's previous doctors had shown any knowledge of the cortisol connection or willingness to pursue information about it.

Dr. Borger prescribed two cortisol inhibitors, Dilantin and Periactin. Jenny responded. Her food fears subsided. She began to gain weight without overwhelming anxiety. The light in her tunnel grew brighter. Pine Grove relaxed its restrictions on her freedoms, and she planned an August reentry into college. Her therapy finally seemed headed in a positive direction.

Family therapy, however, headed nowhere and was characterized by skirmishes between Dr. Conlon and Jenny's parents, with Jenny a spectator. Still exploring family problems, Dr. Conlon probed for something dysfunctional in the love relationships. Who was loved? Who wasn't loved? Who felt loved or unloved by whom? Who felt who was able or unable to love? Who had loved? Who should have loved? *Like we're conjugating a verb*, Jenny thought.

Then Dr. Conlon's exploration ranged further afield. "Now, Mr. and Mrs. Hendricks, we need to discuss your sexual relationship."

Jenny's mother gasped, and Jenny squirmed with discomfort, looking aghast.

"You're serious?" her mother asked.

"Yes."

"You want Gordon and me to talk about our sex life right here in front of our daughter?"

"Yes."

Jenny wondered how Dr. Conlon planned to connect the sex life of her middle-aged parents to either her illness or her emancipation. Her parents looked at each other in disbelief, and her mother's lips formed the word no, accompanied by a vehement side-to-side headshake.

"No way," her father said angrily. "There will be no conversations with you about our sex life. Even if we excuse Jenny, that subject is off limits to you."

"Mr. Hendricks, I'm tired of fighting with you. You're the most difficult man I've ever worked with."

"Surely you know why."

"It's something I've been trying to analyze."

"Let me help you. It's my bad attitude, which the experts would say has been transferred to you. I was frank with you when we started. I told you that Jenny's experience with mental health care has converted me from thankful believer to hardened skeptic. I think confrontational therapy sucks, and my opinion of you sinks lower each week. I don't like you. I don't respect you. And I don't trust you. I don't think you have the slightest idea what you are doing, and I'm here submitting to your blackmail only because Mirriam gives me hope that something positive for Jenny can come from our sessions, despite your negative influence."

"You realize my resignation from your daughter's case is not an option?" Dr. Conlon smiled nastily.

"Unfortunately."

"So we'll have to continue to work together."

"Unfortunately. I think we've all played this game before . . . where you are the designated asshole, purposely provided to sponge up our anger?"

"If you must put it that way."

Dr. Borger abruptly terminated family sessions after one more meeting. Jenny was disappointed. Her parents were relieved. Dr. Conlon moved on to other cases.

In July, Jenny's tunnel light waned, flickered, and finally extinguished. All therapies—ECT, drug, and conversation—had once again failed, after initial benefit. For the first time, her physical condition actually worsened while she was still hospitalized.

August 8. *After many months, I have decided to start writing in a journal again because so much is going on with me that I don't understand. I thought this might help me sort it out. I am leaving here August 25 and moving into the dorms at Loretto Heights College. Once again my anorexia has become all-consuming. My weight has dropped to 60 pounds, and Pine Grove has severely restricted me in a last-ditch effort to make me gain weight.*

I seem compelled to starve myself regardless of the price. This time I stand to lose my return to school and all my rights by being committed to the state hospital. I must risk gaining weight fast and becoming self-destructive. It's time I said, "Stop it, it's okay not to be empty. Being full of food is not the same thing as being sexually abused." You see, I've never truly believed I was sexually abused, and that makes it harder to accept this explanation of my disorder. But, like Dr. Borger says, it does not matter one iota what my starvation means to me, it matters only that I give it up.

CHAPTER TWENTY

What Went Wrong?

August 9. *For me to believe I need to gain weight, I have to experience the excruciating pain of starvation. Because of the wonderful medicine I'm on, I feel good, don't feel pain, and don't experience the usual ketosis that accompanies starvation. How ironic. The drugs I'm taking block the trigger mechanism that gets me eating again. Intellectually I'm aware that it doesn't matter if I don't feel the pain of starvation; what matters is I have to gain weight regardless of how good I feel. The problem is I can't get my intellect to override my true feeling that I don't deserve to eat.*

I know I'm not strong enough to go to school. At the same time I wanna continue on a starvation diet. I've had bulimic impulses today, too, but I will not allow myself to hide in that again. I'm also feeling guilty because I ate less yesterday than the day before. I took a big risk at lunch and added 130 calories and, sure enough, by dinner I was so freaked out that I tried to make up for my excess, only eating ¾ of my candy bar, no salad, half of my butter, etc.

August 10. *I have an assignment today. Fight illness with reason.*

Positive assertion: I deserve to eat properly today and every day.

Negative response: Bullshit, you have a low metabolism, and you know you will gain like a pig. You are so dirty and ugly and nonproductive, how can you deserve to eat when you sit on your butt all day? Just think if you gave in what a cow you would become, and you know you couldn't cope, you would want to hurt yourself. You know what eating does to you, and you know, even if you are painfully hungry, that hunger pain is more bearable than the psychic pain of feeling food inside. It's safer to be empty. Empty is pretty. Empty is pure. Empty is deserving.

Rebuttal: *(1) You know you might gain at a scary rate initially, but then you would be allowed to exercise again and raise your metabolism. It may not be as easy for you to gain as you fear—remember when you were at University Hospital and only gained 2 to 3 pounds per week without exercise. (2) Remember, a lot of initial gain is only temporary water weight. (3) You are in control and will not allow yourself to get fat. (4) You are not ugly and dirty, you just feel that way from being abused. You are productive, you help others, you read, you cross-stitch. You do your best to accomplish things given the hospital limitations. (5) Emptiness and hunger hurt, and you are tired of hurting. Empty to the point of starvation is not pretty. You know that food will not kill you.*

August 12. *The experts say unhealthy behavior occurs because it allows expression of the child within. My child within is sad, depressed, and scared. Anorexia permits me to express that. If I'm eating I have to deny my inner child.*

I'm so hungry that I'm afraid giving in and eating will lead to bulimia. That's what happened last night. Today I have to be careful to eat enough but not get carried away. I find it's not food I want, it's hunger I don't want. I have only two weeks left until discharge, and I am weaker now than I've been since University Hospital. I need to eat, gain weight, and get stronger. I CAN DO THAT! I've done it before, and I must do it again.

August 13. *I'm freezing. The air conditioner is on full blast, but the sun isn't shining and it's cold outside. It's such a ridiculous waste of energy, keeping the temperature at 65 or less.*

"Jenny, the nurses think you've been purging again."

Ashamed, Jenny responded truthfully. "Just once, Dr. Borger. Last Tuesday. But I'm terrified it will happen again, if I let myself eat at the level you want me to."

"Without restrictions, you lost weight for six weeks. Even with increased calories the last two weeks you haven't gained, and that's unacceptable. You force us to impose full restrictions on you again. No relaxing them until you bring your weight above 62 pounds."

"I know. I have to show you that I can regain my weight."

"Have you thought any more about Karris House?"

"I don't want to go to a halfway house. I want to live in a college dorm."

"It's too much of a change to go from here to a college dorm. You're too weak. You need structure, Jenny, while you try to restart a college program. Karris House will provide that."

Jenny thought, *He won't tell me I shouldn't go back to college because that means I'd have to stay at Pine Grove, and he doesn't want me here.* She said, "Karris House scares me. It's where the crazy repeaters from University Hospital live. If Pine Grove and all the other places I've been can't help me live with this fucking disorder, what makes you think Karris House can?"

"They only work with tough cases."

"That's what Perretons told me."

"And you will have your classwork to keep your mind away from anorexic thoughts."

"Which I will also have in the dorms. Maybe structure is doing more damage than good."

"I don't think so. We just don't seem able to help you at Pine Grove."

"What went wrong?"

"I don't know. I wish I did."

August 19. Yesterday I only ate 1,670 cals instead of the 2,200 cals I'm supposed to. I'm still not gaining weight, and I'm completely exhausted. If I had to pack today, I wouldn't make it. Just organizing my cosmetics box seems like too much. And I'm not sleeping well; I wake up frequently during the night feeling bloated and constipated and scared and fat. Then I'm awake permanently about 4:30 every morning, just lying there obsessing about food and anxious about being weighed. I can't relax. I'm terrified Dr. Borger will force me to stay at Karris House.

August 26. A lot has happened in the week since I last wrote. My bulimia got worse, and I finally faced the reality that I was too sick to go back to school. Pine Grove threw me out, and I didn't think a schizo halfway house

would help me either. That left going to a medical hospital for tube feed-
ing. I racked my brain and then remembered Perretons. All the doctors said
I should have stayed there, gotten my weight up, and maintained it for a
couple of years in the safety of the hospital. I think Pine Grove cured my
depression, and maybe Perretons can cure my self-destructive impulses.
So here I am. Perretons took me back and is reducing most of the drugs I
was on at Pine Grove. I feel fat and bloated and probably ketotic.

"Please, Dr. Stormeier. My blood work showed all normal. And I feel like I need to exercise when you increase my calories."

"No, Jennifer. No exercise until I see an upward trend in your weight."

"Can I have something to help with constipation?"

"No. We want to cut back your dependence on drugs. I'm afraid Pine Grove was too aggressive with your meds program."

"But I feel so bloated."

"It may take five to seven days to get your system functioning naturally again."

"I'm afraid of my self-destructive feelings when I gain weight and don't get to exercise."

"The nurses will help you with that."

If they're not too busy, Jenny thought. "Will you assign me a doctor to talk to?"

"Not until you're able to improve your nutrition and eat normally. Then we can start to work again on your underlying psychological issues."

"Sometimes I think my feelings about eating are the underlying psychological issues."

"No, Jennifer. They're just symptoms."

"That's what everyone keeps telling me."

August 27. *There's a girl here named Lacy, and she's very nice but*
also very sick and makes a big investment in staying that way. She cuts
herself and flaunts it. She's a total pity pot and spends most of the
day crying to whoever will listen about how awful her situation is.

Aware of nurse Trina's eyes following her and uncomfortable with Lacy's presence, Jenny began slowly slicing a fresh pear onto her luncheon plate.

"Jennifer!" Trina's reprimand was harsh and scolding.

Jenny cringed and responded hesitantly. "What?"

"Stop being ritualistic with your food."

"I was just slicing my pear."

"You can cut it into small pieces for cereal or yogurt but not for lunch."

Feeling humiliated, Jenny quickly consumed the pear remainder and used her napkin to mop up the juice dribbling down her chin.

"My roll is cold," Lacy complained.

"I'll heat it in the microwave for you." Trina excused herself and returned a minute later.

Jenny watched Lacy worry the roll with a fork, turning it over several times and finally cutting it into small pieces without reprimand. No longer able to restrain herself, Jenny voiced her resentment to Trina. "What's the difference between my being ritualistic with a pear and Lacy being ritualistic with a roll?"

"Lacy's roll was hot."

"Like yesterday when bit by bit she pulled the crust away from her quiche? You didn't object to that ritual either."

"I didn't notice anything yesterday."

"You're so used to it with her, you don't notice anymore. I still think it's okay to slice my pear. Lacy does it every day with her apple which is nowhere as juicy as a ripe pear."

"I do not," Lacy retorted angrily.

"She doesn't do it ritualistically, like you," Trina said.

"That's so damned unfair," Jenny said. "Lacy's slices are even smaller than mine are."

August 29. We had goals group today, and the nurses scolded me about badgering them and not trusting them. I'm really humiliated. It's like I've regressed since I came here. I feel so insecure and needy. I need to talk, but the nurses ignore me. I asked Carmen for some time this morning, and she said she would talk to me this afternoon. Well, Lacy grabbed Carmen right after lunch and kept her until break time. Now it's time for Carmen to leave, so I asked Trina to talk, but Trina said she couldn't because she has to watch Lacy. Lacy, Lacy, Lacy. The entire unit revolves around her, and it makes me sick, sick, sick.

August 31. *Two new patients start today, and I'm scared they'll be thinner than me. Dr. Stormeier says I'm gaining right on track. He hasn't a clue how self-destructive that makes me feel. Lacy has been throwing a fit all day long, slamming her door, crying hysterically. I see so much of myself in her.*

September 2. *They wouldn't let me have bran this morning and said I must take it at night. Then Trina wouldn't let me have bran tonight because the kitchen didn't send anything appropriate to have it in. I'm so scared of being constipated I freaked out, screamed, and cried, and worked myself into a frenzy. The more desperate I became the more Trina got meaner. When I was here before I sensed that she gets a macabre pleasure out of causing someone else distress.*

September 5. *Today I almost had heart failure. The nurses said my calories had been increased again—by 400. Thank God it was a typographical error. It drove home how obsessed I am. I've been pacing in my room this week; it's the only thing that makes me feel clean.*

Lacy woke me up at 11:00 last night. She screamed NONSTOP for fifty minutes. She has no shame and blames everything on her illness as if she has no control of it. She refuses to take any responsibility for her behavior, and that makes me really frustrated with her.

September 13. *Today I can't stop crying, I feel so unsafe. Something terrible is going to happen tomorrow. To escape the pain I took an Ativan, but it didn't work. I am so AFRAID and sad. When is life going to start mattering to me? Help.*

September 23. *I'm out of control and the nurses are hard as rocks, except Carmen and Bev. But I can't blame my unhappiness on staff. I think I'm just crazy because I have to eat, and when I can't avoid my feelings by starving I go nutso bonkers with anxiety and a need to self-destruct.*

CHAPTER TWENTY-ONE
Red Blood on
White Sheets in Sunshine

*S*till in her pink sweats, Jenny lay on her hospital bed, waiting. Fixed in her mind was an image of red blood on white sheets in sunshine. She watched as light streaming in from her west window advanced slowly toward her. She looked at a shaded speck on the floor until it illuminated, then moved her focus to a new shaded speck and repeated the process. She sighed, picked up her journal from beside her, propped it on her knees, and began writing.

May 30. *It's been so long, I had to find this in the storage box and dust it off. I have a lot to cover—eight months—and not much time.*

I'm not sure what went wrong at Perretons last fall. I tried to go back with a good attitude. After a few weeks they brought in their resident expert on post-traumatic stress disorder, Dr. Horton, to evaluate me for PSD. I liked her, and we seemed to connect.

"A classic case," she told me. "Your childhood sexual abuse causes recurrent distressing dreams and terrifying flashbacks." When I told her how unsure I am if I was ever abused, she seemed surprised and asked, "Isn't that where your therapy centers?" Then she was really surprised when I explained, "Not really. We always bog down in food issues, and Perretons waits forever before assigning me a therapist. It's like everyone assumes I was abused, but we don't talk about it anymore."

She said I should go to Perretons's group sessions for sexual abuse, and I explained that Dr. Stormeier wanted me to, but I had to go on a waiting list first. Then I asked Dr. Horton if I could do therapy with her on PSD while I was waiting to move up the list, and she said, "I'm sorry, but my practice is full. I can't take another patient just now." I felt rejected again, and Dad was furious when I told him Dr. Horton wouldn't see me. "I can't believe it," he said. "They bring in their expert on post-traumatic stress disorder, who obviously will diagnose you positive, and then she refuses to treat you. That's outrageous." He told me PSD was ruled out in my first Perretons evaluation.

Dad talked to Paula Jacobs, and I think he wrote a nasty letter to Perretons, but nothing ever happened.

Then Dr. Stormeier wanted me to do individual therapy with Dr. Breen again. Unbelievable. "But we tried that last year," I objected. "We don't work well together." But Dr. Stormeier insisted. Again Dr. Breen and I didn't connect. So we terminated after a few sessions, and Perretons delayed assigning a replacement. Perretons wasn't crowded, but I sure was spending a lot of time on waiting lists.

Even though they wouldn't assign me a new therapist, Perretons made me go through a month of daily lecture programs, mostly the same stuff I'd had the year before. I sponged up lectures on the digestive system, human sexuality—twice, Erikson and Freud theories about consequences of early childhood deprivations, strategies for coping with distorted thinking, spiritual needs, food myths, value systems, medical complications, personal well-being, problem solving, body image, cultural and family issues, and other subjects I can't remember anymore.

While I was waiting for therapy, I took instruction in the Catholic faith—thirty-four lessons, but I haven't been confirmed yet. I was worried Mom would be upset about my leaving the Episcopalian Church, but she was really nice about it. I just can't take all the Anglican holier-than-thou attitudes at St. Matthews.

One good thing happened at Perretons. I finally got approved by Social Security for disability payments. It took over a year because my application went to the wrong department, and they didn't tell me about their mistake when they denied my application. Dad finally straightened things out, and they paid me a bunch of back benefits. So now I have my own mea-

ger financial resources and Medicare in case Dad's insurance gives up on me. I have some money saved, about $4,000, which I obviously won't be using. I need to leave a note asking Mom and Dad to divide it among my brothers and sisters.

Perretons weaned me from all the drugs Pine Grove pushed into me, and then Dr. Stormeier wanted me to take Thorazine, but I refused. Maybe I should have tried it, but I decided to run away instead. After three months, I hadn't accomplished anything, so I split and came home again.

Feeling chilled, Jenny put down her journal and visually measured the distance to sunlight. About 2 feet remained—plus the bed's vertical. She rose and padded unsteadily on stockinged feet to the window where she knelt in sunshine and felt its warmth suffuse her. Drowsily, she rested her arms on the windowsill and looked out. *Mountain View Sanatorium . . . it's well named,* she thought. *The nicest room I've ever had. I've seen autumn end and winter change to spring from here, watched snow advance toward me lower and lower on the mountainsides, like creeping glaciers threatening to engulf the city . . . and then melt back as if by magic. Now summer's almost come. I enjoy evening best, when mountains turn purple in backlight from the setting sun, like in the words from "America the Beautiful." Days seem to be their prettiest when they die. I wonder, will I?*

A bird's nest nestled in an elm tree fork opposite Jenny's window. She could hear a noisy chorus of juvenile chirping as a mother robin flew in with her beak full of worms. Jenny smiled. *I remember when I was a little girl how upset I got seeing fat robins in spring. At least that doesn't bother me anymore. Everything outside is so full of life, and everything in here . . .* Jenny placed a hand on her chest . . . *is so dead inside.*

Her back hurting from its twisted position, Jenny scooted on her haunches back to sunlight beside her bed, braced up against the bed frame, and reclaimed her journal.

Mountain View seemed like such a good choice—at first. I liked Dr. Hanes. So did Mom and Dad. And I've always admired Dr. Reynolds—her beauty and intelligence. Mountain View's patients didn't seem as spaced out as patients in other psych hospitals. When Pine Grove refused to take me back, I got pretty desperate. Then Mom and Dad found Dr. Hanes. He was highly recommended, and we all thought a psychologist who specialized in eating disorders might be better for me than a psychiatrist who specialized in confrontation. But psychologists can't prescribe, so Dr. Hanes brought in Dr. Reynolds to assist him, mostly for meds, but for psychotherapy also.

I was badly depressed, and Mountain View recommended another round of ECT. Shock treatments helped me at Pine Grove, at least for a while, so I consented. Mom and Dad were worried I'd become a juice junkie. Like before, the treatments only helped for a short time. Then, even though I talked to Dr. Hanes and Dr. Reynolds regularly, I had a string of bad days in March. I got really low, realizing I'd tried so hard for five years and hadn't even had a vacation. So I ran away from Mountain View and flew to Florida. I had this crazy idea of seeing Meme and asking her to help me find a sunny beach where I played with my brothers and sisters when I was a little girl. I remembered dolphins rolling in the swells beyond the surf, like they were beckoning to me, and the urge to swim out and play with them was so strong Mom and Dad had to restrain me.

But I just hung out at the Orlando airport, afraid to call Meme, reading magazines and trying to think. I finally realized I can never go back, that I'll never restore my past the way I want to remember it.

I made some decisions on my own and returned to Denver the next day, determined to make it outside the hospital. Dr. Hanes agreed to keep seeing me as an outpatient as long as I kept my weight above 67½ pounds. I got lucky and found a good job at Pennington Drugs, moved into a small but sunny apartment, and started exercising again, to keep depression at bay.

Dad suggested laughter therapy, like that guy—I forget his name—who wrote the book about watching funny movies to cope with serious illness. Why not, I thought, we've tried everything else. Dad made a deal with a video store so I could get six videos every Monday afternoon. A new video to watch every night, and then Mom and Dad took me to a movie on Sunday night. Like my other therapies, this one didn't work either. But I sure laughed a lot and saw some great films—and a few turkeys.

I spent most of Easter with Katy and her two kids. Such sweet kids. Katy's a good mom. I wonder why her marriage broke up—she didn't say. So many things have happened to my friends and family while I've stalled out of life. Diane is in Japan. Rachel is in medical residency, Courtney is married. David is still in Sydney—I don't think he'll ever move back. Nancy is working for a law firm in Portland and running the women's crisis hot line on Friday nights. Janis is going to stay and work in San Antonio. Even my baby brother is halfway through college. Dad's talking about an early retirement. Me, I'm nobody going nowhere. I'm nothing doing nothing.

The bad days started again after Easter. I was depressed all the time, and my weight dropped. My electrolytes went crazy, and I had to go back to Rose Hospital. They put me on Declomycin, and I readmitted to Mountain View. A failure. Again. Always. Last week I still couldn't work. Cut off from my best therapy, depression overwhelmed me again, like a blanket suffocating me. I didn't want to get zapped again, and Dr. Reynolds was on vacation, so I didn't have anyone to prescribe new drugs for me. Maybe it's just as well. I don't want chemicals messing with this decision. Good thing Mountain View forgot to recontract me. At least I don't have to wait through another rainy day.

I couldn't end my life at home yesterday, after I ran away from here. Sitting alone all Sunday in that cold, dark house, listening to rain falling outside and only silence inside. I just couldn't do it. I practiced though. To see how it would feel, I nicked my wrist a tiny bit. It didn't hurt at all. Only a drop of blood oozed out, not enough to make a mess.

I'm glad Mom and Dad brought me back to Mountain View last night after they returned from Janis's college graduation. Now they don't have to find me dead at home. I didn't fight with them about returning. Not like last Christmas when I got hysterical about coming back, and Dad and my uncle had to subdue me physically, carry me out of the house, and force me into the car. I was screaming my head off, and Mom and my sisters were crying almost as hysterically. But none of our neighbors came out. I'm sure they all thought it's just that crazy Jenny again.

I wonder if I should leave a note. But what would I say? I don't have anything to say I haven't said before. Nothing that everyone isn't sick of *hearing. I'm tired of trying to say in different words what it feels like to be depressed and hopeless so much of the time. I know I'll never get better, let alone get well. These past four years I've spent more time locked up in hospitals than Janis spent getting her college degree. I'll never be free.*

Jenny looked up and watched sunlight envelop her bed. "At last," she whispered. *Sunlight makes me feel less like prey trapped in a giant, dark spider web.* She rose and wrote a short message on her desk notepad, "Please divide my money between my brothers and sisters." She signed it, then entered the bathroom, removed a new razor blade from beneath the flap in her cosmetics kit, walked slowly back to her bed, and lay down. She looked at her watch—4:15 P.M. How long to the next room check? About an hour. *I'll probably bleed faster if I sit up,* she thought. Elevating to a sitting position, she maneuvered her pillow between the headboard and the small of her back, removed her watch, and placed it on the bedside table.

Fascinated by the lethal appearance but benign touch of a shiny metal edge, Jenny very softly grazed a forefinger along the length of the blade. Uncertain about which wrist to cut first, she carefully transferred the blade back and forth between the thumb and forefinger of each hand. *My right hand is stronger,* she reasoned, *so I'll start with my left wrist.* Her muscles tensed. Resolve shifted her reflexes into automatic, and her mind detached from her body's preoccupation. As if she observed someone else perform slow-motion surgery on a stranger, Jenny watched as her fingers slowly guided the blade's first incision and a thin reddish stream escaped over the side of her wrist onto her bedclothes.

CHAPTER TWENTY-TWO
Flight Without Escape

*N*urses discovered Jenny as she began her ultimate act of despair. They restrained her before she could inflict more than a superficial wound. She was placed on suicide watch and confined to the quiet room. When her father came to see her the next day, she felt a sudden rush of shame as she was escorted out to meet him. Instinctively she hid her left hand behind her back.

She could see the concern in his eyes as he asked, "What's happened, Jenny? Why the quiet room only two days after your return?"

She dropped her eyes and extended her left arm, slowly rotating it until he could see the bandaged wrist.

He grimaced. "I'm sorry, honey. I didn't know. The hospital didn't call."

"They found me too soon, Dad. I'm so sorry."

Father and daughter embraced, and Jenny felt him stiffen. She looked up and saw a flash of disapproval cross his face as he looked over her head into the darkened interior of the quiet room. "Wh-why?" he stammered, sadness, not anger, in his voice. "Why must they always punish you when you hurt the most?"

"They don't know any different. And it's just for three days. They'll accept my contract after that." Jenny grew wistful. "Will I ever get out of here, Dad? Will I ever be free again?"

"I'm sure you will, Jenny. Please don't give up."

"I feel so like a captive."

"You are." He barely mouthed the words. "Captive to the system. And there's little we can do about it." After an awkward silence, he added, "Did they take you to Metro General for medical attention?"

Poor Dad, Jenny thought. *When he's feeling sad, he talks about logistics . . . a safer subject than feelings.* She brightened at what she had to tell him. "No. Dr. Steiner came here and stitched me up."

"Dr. Steiner?"

"An M.D. from Metro General who takes care of Mountain View patients when they have medical problems."

He smiled. "Like a house call!" He shook his head in mock disbelief.

Jenny became animated. "I like him, Dad. He's kind and patient, and he doesn't judge me or make me feel guilty. I think he understands. I've not felt that with a doctor since Dr. Corbin."

"He sounds like an unusual man. Maybe your suicide attempt has actually connected you to an oasis of humanity . . . surrounded by all this . . ." He gestured toward the lounge where a cluster of patients sat quietly with vacant faces. Then he finished bitterly, ". . . this terrible desert of lost souls where nothing flourishes."

Jenny spent the summer and early fall in a staged emancipation from Mountain View. The plan was a sensible one: gradually increase her outside activities but continue an inpatient therapy and support base while she resided in the hospital. The goal was also sensible: discharge Jenny and return her to independence when she was ready—no deadline. Jenny, however, chafed at her meager input into execution of the plan. She could make requests, but she couldn't participate in weekly staff conferences where decisions were made.

Arriving early for her October 26 meeting with Dr. Hanes, Jenny waited impatiently. She sat erect at the front of her chair, back straight, hands folded in her lap, nervously fingering a tiny ruby ring that slid easily between her finger's knuckle and its first joint, wrapped with adhesive tape to prevent the ring from slipping off. Her eyes darted around the small, drab conference room. *So many meetings here,* she thought. *Over 200 already. Sometimes I feel like a Ping-Pong ball bouncing back and forth between Dr. Hanes and Dr. Reynolds . . . no direction to my life except where they choose to send me.*

"I'd like to walk outside again . . . alone," she requested when Dr. Hanes arrived.

"You know we're concerned about patients being outside alone," Dr. Hanes said. "It's not safe walking through the poor neighborhoods around Mountain View."

"But I know which areas to avoid, and staff is always too busy to come with me. Please."

"Your walks are important to you, aren't they?" Jenny nodded her head up and down, her eyes pleading. "Well then, I think we can restore them." Dr. Hanes's manner was reassuring.

"And I'd like more work hours. Work is my best therapy."

"Anything to escape confinement here?" Dr. Hanes chuckled.

"It's the control. I'm sick of it."

"We have to exercise control as long as we're responsible for your care."

"I know. I'm just sick of it."

"I'll talk with staff about more work hours for you."

Work demanded that Jenny focus outside herself for three afternoons, Tuesday, Thursday, and Saturday. That left Jenny with three weekdays of introspection, its insidious preoccupation with her illness, and her obsessive need to remain physically empty. Physical emptiness brought no relief, just a perversely different emptiness—of spirit and purpose—which tormented her with needs for mental filling. Introspective days exacerbated her depression. On those days she depended on endorphins released by her walks to keep melancholy at bay.

Jenny's care plan required that she continue participation in Friday group meetings where patients reviewed their goals and achievements— and their frustrations. Group sessions seemed trivial to her. "I've spent too many years attending too many group sessions in too many hospital settings," she had complained to Dr. Hanes. "They have nothing to offer me. They're pointless, repetitive, and tedious."

"I know," was Dr. Hanes's consolation. "But you still must go."

So she did, suppressing her resentment. Some sessions helped, most didn't. She'd spent too many years listening to the same petty concerns, including her own. *Society's misfits . . . all of us*, Jenny thought each session. *No place for us to go except to the company of each other, no place for us to talk except in ritual Friday gatherings.*

Then there were Sundays. Why hadn't God left Sunday out of the week! Sundays were Jenny's worst days. Her calendar logged Sunday after Sunday as "ANOTHER BAD DAY." Her father visited regularly during the week but never on Sundays. "I need weekends free from your illness," he told her. Her mother came on Sundays after church, looking fresh and pretty, and talked animatedly about parishioners, neighbors, family, and friends. Her mother's cheerful renditions of current events in the lives of others depressed Jenny. They were testaments to a normalcy she felt incapable of achieving. After her mother left, boredom and exhaustion fought with gloom and anxiety for domination of her remaining unstructured hours. The conversion to Catholicism she had pursued a year before no longer interested her. Sundays no longer had religious meaning for Jenny. God was in danger of losing her childlike faith and trust.

On Halloween Jenny felt too sick to walk. An infected finger throbbed with pain, and images of an amputated digit terrorized her mind. Another black Sunday. She set her clock and watch back an hour to mark the end of daylight savings time. *Another six months down the drain*, she wrote on her calendar.

The following week Jenny sought to numb her senses with heightened activity. She joined a YWCA and began attending its weekly abuse support group and lecture series. On Friday, a longtime family friend, automobile salesman Jim Berger, called to say he'd found a new car for her. "It's an old Somerset," he said. "High mileage but in good condition. And the price is right."

"What's a Somerset?"

"It's a little Buick. And very pretty—sky blue, with silver trim."

Excitement fought through Jenny's despondency. "Can I come see it?"

"Anytime. Your mom and dad have already seen it."

"I know Mom will be negative."

"I've told her the car you're driving now is unsafe."

"She doesn't think I should drive at all."

"Well darlin', I'll not get in the middle of that. Come see the car this afternoon if you can."

New car expectations sandwiched a difficult weekend. Saturday morning Jenny was too tired to get up and slept all morning, an unusual pattern for her even when depressed. After a drop in weight on Sunday, she became apprehensive Mountain View would force her to increase calories or reduce activities, or both. On Monday, Jenny shared her enthusiasm about a new car with both her doctors, first Dr. Reynolds at 7:30 A.M., then Dr. Hanes at 2:00 P.M. They didn't sense her discontent, nor did Jenny discuss her unrest with them. *Dr. Reynolds doesn't do anything for me,* Jenny thought, *except order pills. The pill doctor! And all Dr. Hanes wants to do is stuff me with more calories.*

Also on Monday, Jenny arranged to pick up her new car on Wednesday. She hesitated when she realized she was draining her college funds, but her father assured her, "When you are ready to return to college, the money will be there." She hadn't thought about school for a while. She pulled her college file that evening and confirmed that her acceptance to Rice University in Houston was still open. An idea flashed into her mind.

Tuesday, November 9, was Election Day. In the morning Jenny drove to vote at her old elementary school. *Six years I was here,* she thought as she entered the familiar front doors. *Some of the happiest years of my life. With Courtney and Katy. They were worse brats than I was, but they turned out okay. I left my childhood here. But I never found adolescence . . . only anorexia, that big black hole in my life. It has sucked everything from me and left me with nothing.*

Jenny waited briefly and filled out her information slip. She handed it to a poll worker behind the registration desk who copied her name into the voting log. "How nice to see you, Jenny," the woman said.

Jenny recognized the poll worker as a neighbor she liked, but whose name she couldn't recall. "Nice to see you, too," Jenny said.

Jenny struggled to move a big red-handled lever that closed the booth curtain behind her. It took both hands and most of her strength to execute the simple maneuver. Then she quickly pulled tiny position levers opposite her chosen candidates.

Jenny felt tired and anxious when she returned to Mountain View. A walk around the adjacent park didn't help. She called in sick to work and spent the afternoon alternately dozing and worrying about her next day's staffing, which she knew Dr. Hanes would be unable to attend.

On Wednesday morning, her primary nurse confirmed Jenny's apprehensions. "We're increasing you 300 calories per day and switching you to a low-fiber diet."

"I can't handle it," Jenny said.

"Of course you can. We'll help."

"At least let me stay on a high-fiber diet," Jenny pleaded.

"We can't. Dr. Hanes ordered this change because you're losing weight again."

"Can you . . . can I talk to Dr. Hanes?"

"Not until this evening. You know he's unavailable until then."

Same as Pine Grove, Jenny thought. *After I'm institutionalized for a long time, I start losing weight and my doctors panic. Pine Grove threw me out. What will they do here? If they force me to eat more, I'll need to exercise more or purge again. Then I'll be back to bathroom supervision and have other privileges withdrawn. It's like starting over again. I won't do it.*

At lunch, Jenny dutifully ate all the food put before her. Then she returned to her room, entered the bathroom, stuck her finger down her throat, and consigned her first meal under the new diet plan to the toilet. Relieved of her caloric burden, she brushed her teeth, transferred her toothbrush and toothpaste to her purse, stuffed clean underwear and socks into her jacket pockets, and left Mountain View on her afternoon pass. Stopping briefly at her bank, she picked up a cashier's check for the Somerset and withdrew $1,000 in cash, flinching when she saw her new bank balance drop below $400. She closed the car purchase and drove to a nearby Holiday Inn parking lot, where she locked her car and placed the keys under the right rear tire. From the motel lobby she called a taxi. Thirty minutes later, she stood in a ticket line at the airport. An hour later she boarded a Continental Airlines flight to Houston.

When she arrived in Houston, Jenny called to inform Mountain View she was safe. "No, I won't tell you where I am," she responded to their first question. "No, I have no intention of returning . . . unless there are some changes made," she responded to the second. Checking into an airport hotel, she dined without fear on a small chef salad, grilled chicken breast, carrots, and mashed potatoes, no gravy. She looked longingly at a dessert menu featuring home-baked pies. Feeling no impulse to binge and wondering why, she ordered a piece of apple pie and ate it slowly, without guilt. She returned to her room free of any purge impulse. Feeling proud of her success at dealing with a few hours of freedom and independence, she was also feeling a little ashamed that her need to escape had caused her to flee so far.

Jenny watched television for an hour, her churning mind unable to concentrate on the programming as she debated about making more phone calls. She was reluctant to call home. She thought, *The hospital will inform my parents that I'm okay, so I'll wait and call Dad in the morning. I'll call Dr. Hanes tonight and then Dr. Reynolds.* First pressing the mute button on the television remote control and then deciding to turn off the set entirely, Jenny retrieved a small address book and two notepad pages filled with carefully organized notes.

She reached Dr. Hanes on her first attempt. "Please don't worry about me, Dr. Hanes. I'm doing fine on my own."

"I'm pleased to hear that, Jenny."

He doesn't sound angry, Jenny thought, *and he didn't ask why I left or where I am. It's nice to have a doctor . . . well, psychologist anyway . . . who doesn't judge me or try to make me feel guilty, someone who's always friendly and . . . well . . . just plain courteous.* "I had to get away. To someplace neutral where I could think, figure some things out."

"I think I understand. Have you figured anything out?"

"Some, but first I need to know if you've called the police."

"No, I haven't done that."

"I'm worried you or Dr. Reynolds will call the police and have them search for me."

"I can't promise you we won't call them, if we think you're too much at risk. You've left against medical advice, and it's important that you keep a dialogue open. Will you agree to stay in touch with us while you're figuring things out? Perhaps we can help."

"Yes, I'll agree to that."

"Will you consider coming in so we can sit down together and talk about your concerns?"

"I won't come in if there's any chance you will rehospitalize me against my will."

"That's a decision we can't make until we can evaluate how distraught you are."

"Actually, I'm not distraught. And I'm willing to return to Mountain View voluntarily if you are willing to give me more involvement in my treatment plan."

"The old control issue. You know we can't do that when your weight slips to a dangerously low level."

"Like it is now?"

"Precisely."

"Isn't it obvious then that my treatment doesn't work when I don't have involvement?"

"Nevertheless, we are responsible for your care while you are in the hospital."

I'm so sick of hearing that, Jenny thought. "Then why don't you act more responsibly and consider my feelings. Let me participate instead of just following your orders all the time."

"What is it you want us to do?"

From her notes Jenny carefully read a ten-item list of specific requests. Dr. Hanes listened patiently without interrupting or arguing.

"I can't make any commitments now," he said when she had finished. "But I will consider your requests. And I'd like you to consider coming in so we can discuss them further. I can see you tomorrow, but the day after I'm leaving on vacation, as you know."

"I'll think about it," she said. "But first I want to talk to Dr. Reynolds."

"Please do. And remember, Jenny, we're all very concerned that you keep yourself safe."

"I will, Dr. Hanes." *I do like him,* Jenny thought, *at least when he's not so controlling. Even then, he's firm without being mean.*

Dialing her other doctor, Jenny counted the rings, waiting impatiently for Dr. Reynolds to pick up. After nine rings, Dr. Reynolds answered. The doctor's "Hello" was curtly spoken.

"It's Jennifer, Dr. Reynolds."

"Oh, yes. The hospital informed me you'd left."

"Have you talked to Dr. Hanes?" Jenny asked.

Dr. Reynolds responded icily. "Not yet, Jennifer. But I've decided he should handle all contact with you and your parents while you are gone."

"Why?" Jenny asked in a faltering voice, feeling her resentments resurfacing.

"It's too confusing for you to deal with both of us."

Bullshit, Jenny thought, *you've only kept me in that state of confusion for nine months.* "So, that means you won't talk to me now?"

"That's correct, Jennifer. And now I really must go. Sorry."

Jenny sat in consternation, listening to a buzzing dial tone.

After a fitful night's sleep and a breakfast of fresh grapefruit, bran flakes and yogurt, rye toast with butter but no jelly, all eaten without fear or guilt, Jenny called her father.

"I'm so relieved you're okay," he said.

He sounds tired but not upset, Jenny thought. *And like Dr. Hanes he didn't ask me where I am.* She told him where to find her car and car keys.

"I drove by the same Holiday Inn last night—twice," he said.

"You were out looking for me?"

"Yes. I had to do something. I couldn't just sit at home."

"Didn't the hospital tell you I called in safe?"

"No, honey. They notified us when you failed to show up for dinner, but they didn't let us know about your call. Dr. Hanes informed us late last night."

Jenny felt a twinge of guilt. "I'm sorry, Dad, that you went all that time without knowing."

"It was harder on your mom. She stayed home calling places where you might have gone."

"Is Mom mad at me?"

"More like concerned. She was worried you would have a car accident . . . hurt someone."

"I'm sorry for Mom, too."

"It's okay, Jenny. You had every right to expect the hospital would keep us informed. Although they won't apologize or admit it, they screwed up. I've unloaded on them already."

Jenny smiled. "So you got mad at them?"

"Yes. Thoughtfulness is rarely an institutional strength."

"Are you mad at me, too?"

"No, honey, just sad . . . and worried."

"It isn't working at Mountain View, Dad. There's too much control there."

"I know. Are you still talking to the doctors?"

"I'll call Dr. Hanes now. I had a good talk with him last night, but Dr. Reynolds . . . she wouldn't talk to me . . . " Jenny's voice faltered. "She . . . she hung up on me. I don't know why."

"I think I know why. Dr. Reynolds is running scared, afraid she might be implicated in some kind of negligent care assertion."

"She's trying to protect herself?"

"Yes. Dr. Hanes told me this morning she's persuaded him not to make any decisions about you until they have consulted with an attorney. I don't think Dr. Hanes realizes that Dr. Reynolds has set him up to take full responsibility for your case."

"So my psychiatrist is manipulating my psychologist?"

"That's what it looks like to me. Now we can't rely on either one to act in your best interest because they're both too conflicted by self-interest."

"And you're angry at them, too?"

"Yes. I've told Dr. Hanes what I think, that his inaction and Dr. Reynolds's insistence on involving an attorney are unconscionable. A lawyer can't help them make a professional judgment about what's best for you. He can only advise them how best to protect themselves. Meanwhile their indecision only keeps you at bay, increases your jeopardy."

"Do you think I'm in jeopardy?"

"Not right now. Now you sound strong. But I'm worried about what happens when the excitement of flight wears off."

"I'm really sorry, Dad. It's like I've left you in the middle. Maybe I should come home."

"Please come home, Jenny."

"I'm scared my doctors will force me back into Mountain View."

"No one wants to punish you."

"They may feel they have no choice."

"You know I can't promise anything. I just want you to stay safe and have help when you need it."

Indecision plagued Jenny after she got off the phone with her father. Reality also set in. *It doesn't make sense to stay here. I'll soon run out of money, and I can't enroll in Rice for several weeks. I don't have my things and can't get them without revealing where I am. What happens if I start starving myself or bingeing and purging again? But what happens if I go back and my doctors have the police search for me?* Confinement fears conceded to reality as Jenny called Continental Airlines and booked a return flight to Denver.

An "against her will" hospitalization became academic when Dr. Hanes left on vacation the day after Jenny returned to Denver. Dr. Reynolds had severed her involvement in Jenny's case, and there was no one physically present or professionally connected to make any kind of treatment decision other than Jenny herself. She decided not to go back to Mountain View.

When Dr. Hanes returned, he refused to treat her unless she rehospitalized. Jenny remained adamantly opposed. She faced an abrupt transition from a rigorously controlled environment to independent living with no professional help. An unassisted dive into the deep end of the pool, sink or swim. She leased a small apartment, which her meager possessions only partially filled. She committed to a full work schedule at Pennington Drugs, continued her Thursday night support group meetings, joined an athletic club, and plunged into a wildly excessive exercise program.

As Christmas approached, Jenny realized she wasn't coping with independent living. Her eating habits were locked in a vise of ritualistic avoidance interrupted by binge/purge bouts. Her fanatic exercise routines—biking 30 miles a day, running 6 miles a day, or swimming 2 miles a day—no longer eased her mind pain. She knew she could not maintain her pace without improving her nutrition. Her sick mind denied all thoughts of balancing need and satisfaction. To do less or eat more were equally rejected. She called in sick to work more frequently. Nightmarish abuse flashbacks tormented her daylight hours. Sleeplessness haunted her nights. A case of flu further debilitated her. The thought of continuing to face the future on her own terrified her.

CHAPTER TWENTY-THREE

Perretons 3 — Languishing

Two days before Christmas Jenny called Perretons and was accepted for readmission after the holidays. She felt elated. *I did it on my own,* she thought, *without anyone pushing me. They sound like they really want to help me this time. And I'm going to make it work . . . no matter how long it takes.* She enjoyed an anxiety-free dinner out with her family that evening, worked a full shift at Pennington Drugs on Christmas Eve day, went to midnight mass with her mother and siblings, and enjoyed a relaxed family Christmas dinner at her aunt's with all her cousins.

Jenny flew to Missouri with her mother on January 4 and checked into Perretons's eating disorder unit the next day. "Thanks, Mom." Jenny hugged her mother fiercely at their parting. "Thanks for helping me face returning here. I'll do my best. I'll work really hard."

"I know you will, Jenny." Her mother held her earnestly, tenderly, reluctant to say good-bye, as tears streamed down both faces. "We're so proud of you for trying again."

At check-in Jenny weighed 69 pounds. Once again her treatment program had but one initial focus: weight gain. Her mind is too nutrition deprived to work on anything else. First restore her physiological balance until she's out of harm's way. Then back to behavior modification. No privileges. No external activities. No patient discretion for anything.

Nor would Jenny be informed of her progress. Her nurses would weigh her backward, as she listened apprehensively to the clinking of metal balances behind her and tried to guess their direction from the day before. Each day Jenny would have to eat a calorie quota from a tray under a nurse's supervision. She would have no input into meal planning. After each meal she would have to sit quietly and remain under observation in a common area until her meal digested—to prevent purging. She could not go to the bathroom unaccompanied. There would be no recreation, no walks outside, no individual therapy of any kind.

January 7. I've been here two days now and am doing well but scared they won't let me stop gaining weight at 75. I feel good about my decision and am glad I came. I just talked to Dad. He was very complimentary about how I've handled things. He told me that before I called Perretons he talked to Johns Hopkins but got nowhere. He said he got angry and burned a bridge. I guess Johns Hopkins told him patients should decide to give up anorexia before going to Baltimore. Dad accused Johns Hopkins of being hypocritical by claiming anorexics choose their illness and then refusing to develop a program to influence choice. "Johns Hopkins won't help their patients with the hard part," Dad said. Maybe Perretons can help me make a choice, help me with the hard part. I know I need to persist with a good attitude and stay positive, trusting, and open this time.

Monday I have a fasting blood test at 8:30. How ironic. I'm here for refeeding but have to fast already. Why didn't they test me when I came in? I was supposed to get bran for breakfast, but the order didn't get communicated—so, of course, no bran. Perretons is off to a poor start.

January 8. Perretons says I lost 10 pounds in two days so they rushed a blood draw. My electrolytes are really bad so I'm taking potassium and salting my food for sodium. I got kinda high off that weight loss and didn't wanna gain it back. I'm afraid I did, though. The nurses didn't look as panicked when they weighed me this morning.

January 9. It's 4:45 A.M. and we don't have to get up till 6:30. I can't sleep I feel so fat. All my fingers are swollen. I know because I tried on my ring and could barely get it on. There's no telling what a fat pig I've become. I feel like I weigh 110—my stomach is so bloated.

January 10. It's 5 A.M. and I can't sleep again. Yesterday the lab was an hour late, so I didn't finish breakfast until 10:00. Then I got a stomachache at lunch, having to eat again so soon. They wouldn't let me off the unit yesterday, and it reminded me of being stuck at Mountain View.

My electrolytes were normal today, so I was allowed to walk to the canteen. My ankles and fingers are swollen, and I wanna start walking daily as soon as possible. All I do is sit and fight off self-destructive impulses.

I do not trust Tim, my associate nurse. In fact, I strongly dislike him and will never go to him with anything, I promise. He is an asshole. Everyone thinks so. He has no understanding of eating disorders and tells me to blow off how I feel and just do what he says.

January 11. Today we had a "team meeting" where you make your requests in front of all the patients, nurses, social workers, and doctors. I went first and asked for no bathroom supervision, at least in the evenings. I doubt I'll get it. Then I asked for walks. I am so desperate for exercise I paced in my room before breakfast and again before lunch. I feel like one big piece of lard.

Notes from Genogram Group Therapy Session. How do I see eating in my home? Mom eats all day long nonstop unless she gets involved in something that separates her from food. If she is going to church she skips breakfast and continues her "fast" by only eating an apple and maybe some cheese for lunch. Then she pigs out in the afternoon and is too full for dinner. She'll fix a tiny dinner for us kids and Dad because she's not hungry and assumes we aren't either. So the rest of us starve. I think this perpetuated my early stages of anorexia because I didn't eat between meals, and there was no way I got enough nutrition from the lousy dinners she prepared.

My big sister starves herself all day long and binges at dinner. Not an uncontrollable, crazy binge, just more than you should eat in one meal. Both Janis and Brian skip breakfast. Janis eats very little but drinks like a horse, and I worry she could become alcoholic. Brian parties a lot, too, but eats more normally than the rest of the family. Both he and Janis are good about eating only till they are full.

Dad is perhaps the most neurotic. He has to have his three squares and vitamins every day. He goes through phases where he gets hooked on and swears by a certain cereal. Now it is Health Valley Bran Flakes or something. He won't eat anything else at breakfast except maybe hot oatmeal. He walks around feeling his stomach and catches psychosomatic diarrhea anytime he hears of anyone else having that problem.

Birthdays and Christmas and Easter used to be big traditional dinners for us. Now that everyone is gone and my mother has thrown motherly pursuits to the wind, we barely have any celebration at all—unless my aunt takes up the burden.

Meme made functional dinners as far as I can tell. Perhaps Mom rebels because Meme is very much three organized squares a day, and Mom does everything the opposite of Meme. Mom's become a slob now and dresses like a bag lady at home, while Meme is very neat and always dresses well. Mom throws together shit for dinner, while Meme always prepares a good, complete meal.

January 12. It's early morning again—5:45. I talked in group last night about my fear of getting fat since I'm not exercising. They assured me I am too sick to exercise. Then Nurse Bev, who I like a lot, made a mistake and told me how much better I look this year. She made me feel I don't deserve to be called anorexic this time.

I'm worried and the nurses are concerned because now I'm peeing more than I'm drinking, and we don't know why. It happened once at Mountain View where they ran all these tests on me and couldn't find anything wrong. My theory is that when I starve myself, a lot of my cells fill with water where the nutrients are supposed to be. So when my body starts to receive nutrients it washes out the old water, causing me to pee more than I drink.

January 13. Today I'm really tired. I haven't been sleeping well. I get hyper around 10:00, and then Desyril knocks me out from 11:00 till 1:30 when I usually have to get up and pee. After that, sleep is erratic. Woke up at 3:00 this morning and didn't get back to sleep.

Today I see a medical doctor, and he can write an okay for me to exercise if I am healthy. Part of me wants him to find something wrong so I can feel anorexic and sick. Part of me wants him to say I'm healthy and can start exercising.

January 14. Nurse Marian yelled at me this morning about being nude in my own room. She said I must cover up even when I'm putting on lotion. She was really nasty. I wasn't doing anything wrong, but she treated me like I was breaking structure and should know better. I wonder why she got so mad. My theory is she was embarrassed she walked in on me.

Kathy moved downstairs today and that leaves me alone with Sharon, Felanna, and outer space Anita. Sharon is totally withdrawn. Felanna talks a little only when she feels like it, and Anita is so self-centered she'll babble on for hours about nothing.

We are supposed to get two new patients next week, which means I'll probably have a roommate. This brings up three fears. (1) I'll have to stop pacing. (2) I'll have trouble negotiating shower and bathroom in the morning. (3) The threat of a new anorexic sicker than me. Anorexia is my whole identity, and I am used to being the sickest.

January 15. Today staff scolded me about not sleeping. Then Kathy told me they make her stay in bed until 6:00 A.M. I hope they don't do that to me. I like time in early morning to pull myself together, read my daily affirmations and Bible, write in here, and get ready for my day.

I saw Lacy McCoy who was here last year. She's transferred to the alcohol and drug unit and looks more anorexic than me. I feel like one big piece of blubber compared to her. All my jeans are tight around the waist. Yuk, I am so fat.

I'm afraid they are going to increase my calories, and I wrote Dr. Stormeier asking him to give him input into meal planning first so I can consolidate my food exchanges.

January 16. Well, I've done it. May scolded me about overexercising in the morning by going down to the laundry room. She said my weight hasn't stabilized yet. So I need to prepare myself for an increase in calories. That means lots of extra food, tater tots, double fruits, potato chips—all these things I've seen Anita get. I'm so scared, but I'm determined to handle it as an adult, stop pacing, and do what I am supposed to do. Please, dear God, don't let me get too full, panicky, or self-destructive. PLEASE help me.

Tim is on duty, which makes me feel insecure. I still don't trust him. He has no idea what it's like to be anorexic. Nothing gets through his thick skull. He thinks life is all fun and games.

I wonder if I should stop hanging around Kathy. Her ritualistic behavior appeals to me. I used to be that way: totally organized, totally controlled twenty-four hours a day, seven days a week. She's so compulsive she has separate boxes for her earrings—I never did that. She even irons her pillowcase, jeans, shirts, everything. I think I'm jealous that these rituals still work for her.

I just had breakfast. It included yogurt and bran. Yea. Please, dear God, don't let my calories go up. I promise to stop pacing if they don't.

God heard me because they didn't increase my calories, at least not this morning.

Felanna and Anita both got meal planning today so that means Sharon and I are the only ones still eating from trays. I know I'm gonna be stuck eating a whole lot of shit. Today I had corned beef—what a horrible scary meat that is. I'm also sick of being watched while I pee, having to do my hair in the day room, not being able to exercise, and eating all day long like a fat pig—just disgusting. Oh how I hate HATE HATE my life. I can't live with anorexia and I can't live without it. I feel so gross I wanna go back in my room and exercise and beat myself.

I wish I knew what I weigh so I could know if I'm as fat as I feel. I'm so obsessed today I'm gonna make dinner unbearable for myself if I don't calm down. I gotta relax and be glad I don't weigh 100 pounds yet, be glad my calories haven't been increased yet.

January 17. Hooray! I didn't pace this morning. Here is why I must not relapse: (1) My deal with God. (2) The bind I would be in if I were to get my calories raised while still pacing. You see, then I would feel twice as desperate about keeping it up. (3) The fact that I'm going to get a roommate. What a drag. Reality is that I won't be able to pace when I have a roommate.

January 18. Yesterday when Nurse Trina passed out meal planning request forms, I didn't fill one out because I wanted to wait until later. After wrap-up she took me to the bathroom and asked why I didn't fill out a request. When I told her, she got mad and said it doesn't matter anyway, you aren't ready for meal planning. Later she came to my door and asked if we could talk some more. I said sure. Then, she continued to tear into me. Why do you think you should have meal planning now? Because I want to start planning before my calories are increased, before I start having to be so full. Who cares if you are full—we are going to do things differently this time. We are going very slowly. You're gonna be here five years.

We may even keep you on trays for five years. You are making yourself precious to the other patients. You thank them for supporting you, but you don't give them any reason to support you. I said I disagreed, that she hadn't been here all day, and she didn't know what kind of support other patients had given me. It was the most painful and needless confrontation I've had since those early days with Weintraub.

I'm so confused. You see, since I am the crazy one I tend to believe everything a nurse tells me. Trina was so vicious, though, that I got really upset and disbelieved her.

January 19. I'm constipated today. I must weigh 10 pounds more than yesterday, and I'm so fat fat fat I wanna die. My fingers are swollen, and my stomach is bloated. I'm pissed at God that he let this happen and pissed at Dr. Stormeier that he denies me bran and keeps me sedentary all day.

Also today I woke up at 5:00 and read my Bible in bed. Nurse May came in and said, "You're up awful early." I explained to her I was just sitting in bed reading my Bible. "Well, we'll have to watch you." She is so dumb, she thinks everything I do is meant to burn calories. She makes me mad when she's this way, so I told her I thought she was ridiculous thinking I did anything bad early in the morning. I pointed out the door was open, and if I were exercising I'd close the door first.

I'm disgusted with constipation. I feel like ripping my body apart, taking laxatives, taking a razor and slicing and dicing all up and down my stomach. When I talked to Dr. Stormeier, he told me constipation is all in my head, and he won't do anything about it. Nothing.

We just had videotaping, and I need to write down the nice things others said about me. Marie said I was very thoughtful and careful when I talked to people and "never say anything flippantly." Anita said I was trying really hard to get well. Sharon said I used my "keen intelligence" in helping people, and she admired my perseverance in battling this disease.

Today's new patient, Susan, is thirty-six, a compulsive overeater, and somewhat psychotic. She is definitely sicker than just an eating disorder.

I had a long talk with Nurse Marie today. She thinks it's important I take off my blinders and see what others say I am and do well. She said to focus on what I am today. She also said I should write down how I am different from others. So here goes. Differences from Kathy—older, more experience, more insight/honesty, draw, willing to see myself as less than perfect, not as compulsive, not in as much denial, not as obsessed with food. General differences, basically artistic, my own taste in earrings, have two supportive, loving parents, am honest and don't play games, try to see others' points of view, have some supportive friends in Denver, try to vent my feelings in an assertive and acceptable manner.

January 20. Thank God, today I had a bowel movement.

Please God let me have an apple or pear with breakfast—no bananas, oranges, or juice—or let me have yogurt so I can have bran. The morning kitchen staff is so dumb, they always give me eggs and don't realize you can have yogurt with cereal instead of milk. The only time I've gotten yogurt was when Carmen switched my tray around. My dream breakfast would be All Bran, one-half plain yog, one apple, one bacon, but I never get it. Enough obsessing over breakfast.

My new roommate is here. Her name is Pam. She is twenty-five and rambunctiously high. She didn't eat anything at lunch. I can't figure out if she's fatter or thinner than me because she's wearing a jacket and won't take it off. She says she weighs 95 and she's about 5'3", so obviously she is not thinner. Pam and I are both anorexics, but she has personality and I don't. I am scared the other patients are gonna like her and reject me. Already I wanna isolate myself.

January 21. Marian gave me a bad time about getting up before 6:00. She upset me because all I do is write in this or read my Bible or my book.

Today I'm such a fat cow it's grotesque. I want to pace but can't figure out when or how. Dr. Stormeier told me that he might increase my calories just to maintain me. He said I am still losing weight. This doesn't seem possible. My inner voice is saying BURN BURN BURN, and Dr. Stormeier is saying I am burning too much. I don't know what to believe.

Had a good talk with Laurie last night. Told her how much I admire her and want a relationship with her. Now how about this! Already Pam is submitting a three-day notice. I'll bet she doesn't leave. I kind of wish she would, then I could have my privacy back.

Sarah is driving us all crazy. She paces twenty-four hours a day, and Perretons can't control her because she's not legally here. Something about she signed in as a voluntary patient without consent from her guardian. Don't ask me how this works—all I know is they can't force her to follow structure. So Sarah paces all day, leaves the table in midmeal, refuses to eat anything scary, interrupts groups, water loads—you name it, she does it. It's all very irritating. I can't stand her pacing—whoosh, whoosh, up and down all day.

Bev wants me to think about what identity means. I think it mainly has to do with how you define yourself. I also think it has to do with the way others saw you and communicated this—verbally or nonverbally—to you throughout your formative years. Like Mom and others may have done to me. I think once you've formed this sense of yourself from others, it is very hard to believe contrasting points of view. I think identity centers around those features you exhibit which attract the most attention over the years. Identity can be transitory: while in school, I am a student; when at work, I am an employee; when playing sports, I am a runner.

January 22. Last night in group they asked me how it felt to have Pam here and my worst nightmare come true. I took this to mean they think Pam is skinnier than me. But I live with Pam, and I've hugged her. She is nowhere near as bony as I am.

I need to work hard on figuring out who I am, where I fit in, what my talents are. Some more thoughts on identity: I am hopeful identity can be changed by conscious attempts to see yourself differently than in the past, and—ideally—identity should be based upon your own sense of worth and not what others told you when you were a child.

Sarah leaves tomorrow, and I think the unit will finally relax. She's really made it crazy here, and the tension is palpable.

It's hard to be social with other patients sometimes. I don't know what they are talking about. It's like my brain won't zone in, like I'm totally disinterested. A lot of the time I just plain do not know what to say.

January 23. Last night the group confronted me about a lot of things, and I felt attacked. It was one of the hardest sessions of my life. I began by talking about how difficult it is for me to feel part of the group, and

Laurie said she thinks some of it's my not knowing current events, but most of it's my depression and preoccupation with other things. I agreed with her and then Trina chimed in, "What is Jennifer preoccupied with?" I had a negative reaction to this, because I assumed Trina wanted them to say, "With food and calories." I said that it's not food and calories that have me preoccupied. (Now, when I look back through here, I have to admit Trina may be right.) Then Sharon said I'm always asking the time when we start to eat, and Laurie picked up on this and said I irritate everyone by using the whole time allotted, whether for one Wheat Chex or ten apples. I agreed with them. I have a fear of finishing early because then I feel I am a pig—and I get scared watching other people eat. At those times I'm acutely aware of my hunger and how easily I could eat everything in the room. They went on to confront me about what a stickler I am for rules and how I always compete to get less food. Why? they asked. I answered that it's hard for me to eat more and follow a more restricted structure than Perretons requires of others.

I couldn't stop crying after group concluded, and Trina really was decent to me; she gave me a hug, said she appreciated my honesty, and said somehow we were going to teach me to be a fun person—not just a likable, nice, sweet person, but a fun person. This hit home because that's what is missing when I'm in groups or with my family—I'm no fun. I am boringly serious and a real drag to be around. I remember back in the days when Diane and I used to go crazy together, and I wonder where that Jenny has gone. Will I ever find that spontaneity and gaiety again?

January 24. *Am constipated and bloated today, also menstruating a little. They are increasing my calories to 1,400, which will mean an extra starch and fruit at breakfast. I have this tremendous need to burn calories any way I can.*

Bev gave me perfection as a topic to work on. The dictionary says: The doctrine that perfection (freedom from fault or defect) of moral character constitutes man's highest good. To me perfectionism is the constant struggle to be good enough, better, best. I think this drive centers around two things: the desire to control exterior elements in order to define oneself, and the desire to be good enough to be loved; in my case; first of all by my mom, but now extended to just about everyone. But defining good is hard—are you ever good enough? What is good enough? My drawings, for example, would be perfect if they looked exactly like what I was trying to draw—but who says what I am trying to draw is perfect? I always think things other people do are perfect, and my best is never as good as theirs.

I paced a lot today, about two hours' worth.

January 25. I'm jealous of Pam. After two days here she was allowed to shower unsupervised, given a 3:00 activity, and exercise, privileges I still don't have. Today, after less than a week, she is asking for meal planning. I'll bet she gets it. She's on a twenty-eight-day program, but I'll bet they keep her longer and give her full privileges and me none. I like her, but I know it's going to be hard seeing her progress so much quicker than me.

I'm menstruating today. It's so gross.

Last night I had nightmares about molestation. This old man was squeezing my breast, and I couldn't defend myself. It was like my arms were tied. This morning I went into a catatonic-type shock, and no one could understand what was wrong. Staff pressured me to keep performing and be the perfect patient, so I suppressed the shock and pretended everything was okay.

January 26. Yesterday I was confronted about exercising in the bathroom. They told me I'm an unstable person who should be locked up under full supervision for a very long time.

I saw Dr. Stormeier yesterday, and he explained some of his distrust to me. He was pretty gentle, and I was pretty hysterical. He said he just wants to get my weight going in an upward direction, and then I can exercise. He doesn't want to take any big steps with my privileges until I have formed some relationship with a therapist.

January 27. Woke up in a crazy, angry, destructive frame of mind. My body is so gross. I got eggs again this morning for the sixth day in a row. I'm supposed to pick out one good thing to focus on today. It was nice seeing Auntie Lynn last night. I love her so much. It was nice of her to visit me, and she is going to send me a picture of her and Uncle Tom.

Nurse Bev told me to think about contentment. To me contentment is acceptance and peace with yourself. You don't feel angry at yourself. You accept your body, your ideas, and your thoughts. You don't think you are less than others. You are not resentful or jealous of others. I want people around me who care about me and who I care about. I want to care about myself enough not to be vicious to myself.

January 28. Today I'm still constipated even though I took milk of magnesia last night. Please God, let my breakfast be different than eggs. Help me to get through the sedentary times.

Good things to think about today. I have some goals (see above). I am loved by some people, particularly Diane. I miss her so much. Here is a nice letter I got from her today. It made me cry. "You are going to do amazing things for yourself there, Jen. Don't ever doubt it. Last year when you decided to take the reins of your life and leave Mountain View, I cheered with joy. Do you know how inspiring it was to witness such an act of courage? It made me feel proud to be your friend.

"None of us survives alone. We all need support many times in our lives. You need it now and are getting it. I have no doubt you will leave Perretons one day and not look back. Just surviving as long as you have shows immense strength, courage, and will. Begin refocusing your anger, Jen. Stop turning it against yourself, and get angry at those who hurt you so long ago. They deserve it, not you. Don't keep giving them the tools to hurt you. Realize how special and unique you are. Don't keep hurting yourself. You deserve better!"

After I read Diane's letter, I got that depressed, foggy feeling, worse than any time yet. I felt catatonic.

January 29. PRAISE BE TO GOD! Today I have to go to the bathroom! This is what I did with my water yesterday: three cups before breakfast, one cup plus one tea at breakfast, one cup between breakfast and lunch, two tea at lunch, three cups between 2:00 and 4:00, two tea dinner, one cup plus one tea snack, one cup before bed. Follow that.

Good thought for today: I'm loved by Melinda and Jim. Here are the cards I received from them. Melinda—"We're with you 100 percent and look forward to having you well and home. We miss your special visits and love you lots." Jim—"I miss your smiling face, and I'd just as soon you were here . . . but you can't be here until you're done there."

I'm supposed to write down things that make me contented. Last night it was sitting quietly with everyone while we watched Broadcast News. Then it was crocheting and working on my "I want" collage. I also found peace in talking to Bev and Carmen.

January 30. Good thought for today: I am a gentle person. Contentments of yesterday: crocheting, talking with Carmen, working on my collage with Anita, playing backgammon with Felanna.

Today Bev wants me to focus on "positive attitude." I think a positive attitude is like the proverbial person who sees a cup as half full instead of half empty. Positive means hopeful despite the odds, attitude means the way you approach your life—what color sunglasses you wear when you look at the world—do you try or do you not try.

January 31. Pam got meal planning, and that makes me really jealous because I know they will keep me on trays forever. Please NO EGGS FOR BREAKFAST. PLEASE NO PANCAKES.

Yesterday my contentments were working on Bible verses with Kathy, working on bracelets in the evening with Tim, listening to Dr. Stormeier talk. Today my positive focus is: people like the way I braid their hair.

February 1. Contentments of yesterday: going outside between art and gym, working on my cross-stitch, talking to Marie, watching the Georgia O'Keefe movie.

Last night Felanna said I shouldn't get meal planning because of my food rituals. Laurie said I needed more time on trays. This made me mad—why won't they give me a chance like everyone else? Positive focus for today: I am a child of God, and He loves me.

February 2. Team meeting was not so awful as I expected. None of the staff responded to my requests, though, so I wonder what they were thinking.

Contentments of yesterday: cross-stitching, crocheting before bed, talking to Vera, reading the paper. Positive focus today: Listen to feedback from others, and if I get defensive, try to explain why and work with it.

They give me too many combination foods. That makes me remain too hungry. I am so jealous of Pam. She gets to order All Bran for breakfast and whatever she wants.

Today I went to art feeling so pessimistic that all my drawings turned out really dumb, and that made me feel even worse. Perretons won't give me a chance so why bother with requesting changes; it's humiliating and a waste of hope and energy. Today I felt that burning anger I used to feel at Mountain View, knowing they don't care what I think I'm ready for.

February 3. Well, neither of my requests were granted, and today I am fat, bloated, constipated, and depressed. I feel like cutting on myself. I'm so angry they will not give me meal planning. They said I'm losing weight, and I'm paranoid they are going to increase my calories again.

I'm going to try and think of some good things—that'll be hard today. Contentments of yesterday: writing Meme, creating a new character for my drawings, having Laurie come in and say good night. Positive focus for today: Dad loves me. Here is a note he sent me today. "Courage, patience, and perseverance to you—perhaps the third time is a charm. Mom and I have been talking about how hard you tried to be a normal person during the holidays—and, more important, that you succeeded! May the memory of that success, and the knowledge you can be enjoyed and accepted in a normal environment help sustain you as you again work through a structured program. Your courage to keep trying is an example to us all."

I think this is why Perretons is keeping me so confined. (A) I am worth taking care of, and because my body is still sick and I am still frail psychologically, others need to care for me. (B) The issues I need to work on are not related to food. Staff will do anything, including denying me meal planning, to make me separate food from the real issues. (C) Meal planning, exercise, and other privileges will come eventually, but they are not a goal for right now. Now's goals are to stabilize my body into a slow upward gain, express my fear and rage in an acceptable manner, accept my worth as a person. (D) I am like a baby who fails to thrive. I need to be cared for and watched closely until I begin to thrive again.

CHAPTER TWENTY-FOUR
Victimized

Although Jenny resided in a mental institution, the mental side of her anorexia remained untreated. Perretons again denied her early access to a psychotherapist. Like an automated factory staffed with robots, Perretons continued with its single-minded purpose—hold everything until Jenny is fattened up—and witlessly aggravated the very condition it sought to improve. Most of the time Jenny was the only patient denied meal planning, which reinforced her notion that she was unworthy—the least worthy—of trust. Rather than rebuild self-image, Perretons promoted its diminishment. In such inflexible captivity, Jenny's moods darkened and her depressions intensified.

On the morning of February 4, she began her day writing in her journal and resolved: *I never give up. No matter how hard things get I always keep going.* But she couldn't keep despair from dominating her journal entries. On February 5 she wrote: *I hate my body so much today. I feel like ripping it apart limb from limb, slicing and dicing.* Breaking her commitment to Perretons staff, she acted on her desperation the next day—and recorded her act. *I cut my breast this morning even though I'd contracted to be safe.*

On February 10, Jenny's nurses informed her that she was not gaining weight, even with a supervised intake of 1,600 calories per day. Over five weeks of controlled refeeding had passed with no weight gain. Despite failure of its refeeding program, Perretons made no treatment modifications. Dr. Stormeier remained as obsessively intransigent in his approach as Jenny was in her addiction. Irrationally immovable minds, physician and patient alike, collided and became hopelessly deadlocked. Jenny's treatment plan continued to focus blindly on food and sought to combat

243

her depression with stronger drugs. She accepted the drowsy, surreal world of Thorazine, and despite its numbing of her senses, she continued to decline in motivation and spirit. She railed at herself in her journal.

> *Every FUCKING time I menstruate I get all bloated and constipated. I hate it. I wanna leave the hospital and go to a nursing home. I hate my body. I hate my life. I wanna be dead. I'm so depressed today that, were I able, I would commit suicide. I don't care. I wanna be dead. I hate living. I hate my body. I hate everything. I JUST WANT TO BE DEAD. Dear God, please let something kill me today. Please. I do not want to live anymore. My stomach is bloated beyond recognition. I feel like I'm going insane, banging my head against a wall, totally losing control. Thorazine doesn't help. It just makes me sleep. Why is this happening to me, God? I HATE MY BODY.*

Petty conflicts with other patients erupted.

> *Yesterday they jumped all over me in wrap-up. Laurie accused me of asking Kathy about her weight and upsetting her. She said I was jealous Kathy doesn't have to eat and I do. I don't remember asking Kathy about her weight, and I'm not jealous that she is fed by a tube down her throat. I would much rather eat than be tube fed. Then Laurie said I am a pity pot and nothing has happened to me that hasn't happened to the rest of them. All nodded their heads in agreement. Marlene chimed in that I eat slowly so I can be the last person done every meal. She said my behavior makes her sicker because it reminds her of her own competitiveness. Laurie said I was being passive aggressive and controlling the group by finishing last. After saying I had complained Sarah was competing with me, Felanna accused me of competing with everyone else. They said I never let go of depression. Then they confronted me about how hard it is to confront me because I'm small and I cry or get defensive. They laid into me for thirty minutes. It was my worst confrontation ever.*

And more confrontation—this time by the nursing staff.

> *This morning Marian accused me of throwing something in the toilet. I don't know what she thought I'd done, but she made me turn on the light so she could look. I just wrung my hands and said I didn't know. I ended up feeling guilty when I'd done nothing wrong. Having been under scrutiny for so long, my only reality is how others see me. If they say I am bad, I must be. I don't have much sense of self left.*

Jenny's relationship with her roommate grew strained.

> *Pam wants to move into a single room. First she says she needs privacy, that she's never had any private time. Then she says she's always alone at home. I think she's just selfish and doesn't like having to compromise, so she wants out of a double room. She says we are stressors for each other, and neither of us needs that. I guess there are things I do, that she doesn't tell me about, that bug her and she feels she can't live with. I've always liked her a lot and liked being her roommate. If she does get a private room, I'll have to adjust to a new roommate and that scares me.*

On Friday evening, February 17, Jenny sat at her tiny, uncluttered desk and wrote a long letter to her grandmother, who was scheduled for abdominal surgery in Florida. "I know you are going to be okay, Meme, just as I know I will be okay someday," she closed the letter. Pleased that she was able to leave her illness for a time, think positively, and attempt to cheer another, her mood brightened. "I'm going to the lounge," she said to Pam. "Can I bring you anything?"

"Thanks, Jen. But no," Pam responded. Jenny didn't notice Pam's shadowed frown.

For the first time in a week Jenny was able to concentrate enough to read and digest an entire newspaper. She also thumbed through a recent issue of *Mademoiselle*, envying the thin, shapely forms she saw presented there. When she returned to her room, Pam was sleeping. She donned a flannel nightgown hanging from a hook inside the bathroom door, returned to her desk, and logged the day's meager events on her calendar. She grimaced when she noticed a "Menstruating" entry from the day before and silently mouthed "yuk" as she repeated the same entry for the current date. *At least the hormone pills work,* she thought. *Too bad most of the others don't.* She reread a Norwegian proverb occupying the current calendar page: "That which is loved is always beautiful." *Mom and Dad still love me.* She admired the scripted proverb with its white lettering contrasted against a dark purple background, and she smiled when she saw decorative hearts sketched into the page design in a soft lavender shade identical to her pen—her favorite color. *A sign of better things to come?* Jenny went to bed relaxed and pleased with the end of her day. She was asleep by 9:30, her slumber peaceful, unmarred by dreams or nightmares.

At 11:30 a hand shaking her shoulder awakened her. Rising up on her elbows, she blinked rapidly to diffuse a bright light shining directly into her eyes. Her heart pounded in fright as she strained to see into the darkness behind the flashlight. Two shadowy figures hovered there. A familiar voice spoke from one of the shadows. "Are you awake, Jennifer?"

"Vera? Is that you, Vera?" she asked. "Is something wrong?"

"No. We just need to check you, Jennifer," the other shadow spoke.

"Marian?"

"Yes. We need to check you."

For a moment Jenny panicked. She remembered Marian's confrontation about something down the toilet from two days before. The same irrational guilt she had felt then returned. *They know about the cut,* she thought. *They know I cut my breast.*

"N-n-now?" Jenny managed to stammer.

"Yes. It'll just take a minute."

"But what for?"

"Bleeding," Vera said. "It was reported you had blood on your legs today."

Jenny was relieved. "It's from shaving my legs," she said. "I cut my left leg this morning. It's just a small scrape. I'm okay."

The nurses ignored her explanation, and she didn't think to insist they check her leg. "No, Jennifer, we need to check you for vaginal bleeding." Marian was gruff and confrontive, as she had been on Wednesday morning when she had intimidated Jenny. "Can you get up for a minute?"

"Wh-what?" was all Jenny could manage.

"We need a vaginal smear."

"Wh-what? Now? I'm having my period. Why are you doing this? Wh-why now?"

"We want to be sure you're safe," Marian said.

"What do you mean?" Jenny asked.

"To be sure it's just menstrual blood," Marian said. "I'll come with you into the bathroom."

Still groggy from the rude awakening and numb from fear, Jenny struggled to the bathroom. "Why are you doing this—why now? I haven't done anything wrong. Why should I prove I'm having a period?"

With Marian eyeing her suspiciously, Jenny took a cotton swab, produced a blood-spotted sample from between her legs, and gave it to Marian.

Marian's scrutiny of the sample was perfunctory. "Okay, Jennifer, now we'll have to examine you," she said.

"Wh-what? Here?"

"No. On your bed."

As Marian led Jenny back into her room, Jenny glanced at her still-sleeping roommate. *Did you do this to me, Pam? Did you tell them I had blood on my legs? Why did you tell them? Why didn't you ask me? I didn't do anything wrong. Why are they humiliating me?*

"Pull up your gown, lie on your side and lift your leg," Marian instructed.

Embarrassed and ashamed, Jenny complied. She felt Vera's fingers probing briefly inside her and watched Marian peering intently with the flashlight focused between her legs.

Apparently satisfied with their examination, the shadowy figures disappeared as silently as they had come. Jenny's heart continued to pound. Part of her was relieved the nurses didn't find the cut on her breast. Part of her was angry and bewildered at such a senseless invasion of her privacy. She sat up on her bed, pulled her legs to her chest, and pushed her nightgown down until its edge covered her ankles. Then she clasped her arms around her shins, rested her head on her fleshless knees, and rocked slowly back and forth on bony haunches until her tears finally came. Her muffled sobs haunted the darkness far into the night.

Still feeling angry and humiliated on Saturday morning, Jenny developed a course of action. She hoped she could act in a mature and rational fashion. She avoided discussions with other patients, even Pam, or any staff. She knew the administrative officials she wanted to talk to would not be available until Monday and that her social worker, Paula Jacobs, and Dr. Stormeier would be off duty all weekend. When she called home, there was no answer. *Mom's at church,* Jenny thought, *and Dad's probably at his office.* She reached her father on his office line, calmly reported what had happened the night before, and explained her plan to talk to a patient's advocate, realizing if she sounded too upset her father might overreact. Her father encouraged her plan and indicated he would speak to Dr. Jacobs.

Although Jenny resolved not to initiate discussions with anyone on the unit, an institutional grapevine circulated news of a midnight strip search more effectively than anything she could have started. By Sunday night most patients had contacted Jenny and expressed fearful concern, sympathy, and support. Pam, however, avoided Jenny. *She's afraid I'll confront her about her big mouth,* Jenny thought.

On Monday, Jenny first called Dr. Jacobs. "She's in a staff meeting, Jennifer," a secretary said. Then she tried to reach Perretons's hospital director, whose secretary promised a return call.

Monday passed without any of Jenny's calls being returned. She avoided Dr. Stormeier and staff and spent most of the day in her room. Nurse Bev stopped in to see Jenny and assured her, "Nothing like this will ever happen again." It was the first contrition shown by any nurse.

Vera and Marian were absent from the unit's group meeting on Monday night. Jenny maintained her resolve not to discuss what had happened. In an effort to quell unease spreading like a plague among other patients, Elena, speaking for all the nurses, acknowledged grimly, "Although Perretons had valid concern that Jennifer might hurt herself, our concern was improperly handled. Midnight strip searches will not occur again." *Not exactly an apology,* Jenny thought, *but better than nothing.*

After group meeting, Elena took Jenny aside and explained gently, "They were concerned you might cut your genitals. That's why they examined you."

"But I've never done anything like that. Why were they concerned?"

"They said self-mutilation was discussed with you several weeks ago, and you knew they were concerned about it."

"They're lying. It wasn't discussed with me."

Elena's discomfort with the conversation was evident in her response. "All I know is that Dr. Stormeier has written an instruction to be alert to genital mutilation."

"But why?"

"I don't know."

"And did he order the search?"

"I just don't know."

Later Monday night, Jenny talked to her father, finding him still at his office as she expected. She felt calm and in control, angry but not overly upset. She related her conversation with Elena. "I don't know what's going on, Dad."

"I'm confused too, honey. I talked to Paula Jacobs today, but she was defensive, distracted, and very uncomfortable talking to me about what happened. She told me Dr. Stormeier instructed your nurses to be alert to bleeding of unknown origin."

"But I told the nurses I'd cut my leg shaving."

"I guess they didn't believe you. Paula also mentioned their concern about self-mutilation. She said you had previously cut yourself to simulate a period."

"That's crazy. Why would I want to simulate something I've tried for years to avoid?"

"That's what I told Paula. Have you ever done anything—cut yourself in some way—that might cause staff to be concerned about genital self-mutilation?"

"No. Last time at Perretons I cut on my stomach once when I was really upset but never on my genitals."

"Has the staff ever talked to you about simulating a period?"

"No, Dad." Jenny was exasperated. "There's no reason for staff to doubt I'm having a real period. They know I had one in January, after they started me on the pills."

"It doesn't make any sense to me either. Have you talked to Paula Jacobs yet?"

"No, I think she's avoiding me."

"That's not like Paula. She's generally very responsive. I think you should keep trying to talk to her. I've always been impressed with her sensitivity."

"I think she's worried because there's a rumor circulating that Vera is gay."

"My God, Jenny, you were strip-searched and pelvicly examined by a lesbian? No wonder they're defensive. It's outrageous. Paula says the nurses denied touching you. It sounds like they're lying to protect themselves."

"Calm down, Dad. I wasn't hurt, just humiliated. And it's only a rumor about Vera."

"Goddamit, they victimized you. Right there and officially sanctioned. They should at least apologize."

"I know, Dad. But please don't escalate the situation. I think I can handle it."

"Okay, honey. Have you talked to Mom?"

"Yes. This afternoon. She thinks the hospital was wrong and should apologize."

"That's good. Jenny, you're handling this very well. Better than I am. I'm proud of you."

"Thanks, Dad."

On Tuesday morning Jenny reached Perretons's hospital director. His impatient "Yes, Jennifer" revealed his distaste for personal interaction with hospital patients. He didn't apologize for failing to return her call.

"I was calling for an appointment. I'd like to talk to you."

"I'm sorry, I can't see you today." He didn't sound sorry. "But I have arranged for you to meet with our director of nursing, Ruby Jefferson, this afternoon."

So he knows why I'm calling, Jenny thought, *and doesn't want to talk to me. Just as well. I'd rather talk to a woman.* "Thank you, doctor," she said.

Jenny also finally reached her social worker. Paula Jacobs sounded genuinely contrite. "I'm sorry I didn't get back to you yesterday, Jennifer, and I've scheduled time for you to come in after you talk to Ruby Jefferson."

Jenny ate a relaxed lunch of grilled cheese sandwiches, vegetable soup, and a peach cobbler, all food she enjoyed. Staff had no objection to her walking unaccompanied to Perretons's administration building after sitting for an hour to digest her meal. As she left the unit she felt elated. *For the first time in weeks I'm free. Really free. It's the only time I've been permitted to walk outside alone, and the first time I've walked this far on hospital grounds. For once, although I know it won't last long, I feel like I'm in control rather than dancing at the end of someone else's strings.*

She walked slowly with her head bowed in thought, going over in her mind what she wanted to say. As she crossed the quadrangle, Jenny admired grass greening in unshaded areas and fresh buds forming on long, spare hedgerows that separated the compounds. *There's renewed life here—at least outside.* An old brick building loomed ahead, in its original red, the only contrarian color in a sea of green. The first building constructed by Perretons's founder, it represented realization of his dream to provide a nonurban, residential facility in a quiet, campuslike setting. It seemed less intimidating than Jenny remembered.

A gray-haired woman whose eyes sparkled with intelligence and compassion, Ruby Jefferson was kind and attentive. The woman's warm, receptive manner helped Jenny feel comfortable, calm, and resolved. Jenny described Friday night's events and her feelings of humiliation. She summarized why she felt she had been unjustly treated and concluded with, "They searched me at 11:30 at night, and everyone knows I have sleeping problems and nightmares relating to sexual abuse."

Ruby Jefferson listened patiently. When Jenny finished, the older woman remained quiet, looking intently into Jenny's earnest eyes. For a moment sadness greeted sadness, and Jenny felt a silent but powerful expression of sympathy.

The nurse finally spoke. "You were right to come to me, Jennifer. It took courage to do that. What was done to you was wrong—inexcusable really. I've ordered an investigation into the nurses' role in the incident. And I've recommended a similar investigation be undertaken of Dr. Stormeier's actions. Although I must ask you not to discuss it with others, a number of nurses from the unit have called me to express concerns similar to yours. I want you to know you have staff support from the unit as well as from me. What happened to you will never happen again."

Jenny left feeling vindicated. She walked briskly back to the unit with her head unbowed.

Her meeting with Dr. Jacobs was less satisfactory. The social worker was nervous and edgy. Jenny sensed more distance than usual in their conversation. Dr. Jacobs spoke mechanically, without conviction, as if she struggled to keep her thoughts focused on her patient's circumstance. "You've handled this very well, Jennifer," she concluded, "very maturely, particularly in asserting yourself without becoming hysterical." Dr. Jacobs remained noncommittal about the search itself, neither apologizing for it nor attempting to justify it. Jenny left the meeting confused. *Paula is out of it today*, she decided.

When she returned to the unit, Laurie, frequently a harsh and outspoken critic, approached Jenny with a remorseful hug. "I'm sorry I've been so bitchy sometimes," she said. "I'm really sorry about what happened to you. I had a long talk with my father today. He's a lawyer and deals with medical malpractice all the time. He says you have grounds for a case, and he gave me the name of a local attorney if you want to go after Perretons."

"Thanks, Laurie. I've thought about it, but I think a suit would detract too much from my real purpose . . . to get better. But if anything like this happens again, I'm going to sue the bottom out of this place."

"My father is going to call the hospital director."

"Good luck." Jenny smiled. "Herr Direktor doesn't like to talk to people."

"Dad says if he doesn't get the assurances he's looking for, he wants me to leave Perretons. He thinks the shrinks here are all a bunch of quacks, anyway."

Paradoxically, her ordeal seemed to strengthen Jenny. It continued to be a subject for group meetings, where Dr. Stormeier and the involved nurses insisted their actions were appropriate. In an attempt to terminate discussion of the incident, Dr. Stormeier spoke to all patients in a joint meeting with staff the following week. His professional, expressionless mask was in place, and his visage revealed no feeling or emotion as he spoke.

"I ordered the procedure," he said, "to determine the cause of inexplicable bleeding. We have an obligation to take care of all of you no matter how painful or uncomfortable some of our procedures may be. What was done was necessary for us to fulfill our care responsibility.

"I know this has been difficult for all of you, as well as for Jennifer." Turning to face Jenny and posturing accusation, Dr. Stormeier spoke directly to her. "I realize she has initiated discussions about this incident in each group meeting since it occurred. However, all of you need to put the matter behind you, in the past where it belongs, and return your focus to working with us to improve your conditions."

"Dr. Stormeier," Jenny interjected.

"Yes, Jennifer."

"I need to correct something."

"Yes." The doctor's tone was haughty but polite.

Jenny said calmly but firmly, "I have not brought this up in every meeting. In fact I've never brought it up. All of the discussions last week were initiated by the nursing staff or other patients, and tonight you started the discussion." Jenny was seething inside. *Why is he purposely trying to humiliate me?* She remained calm and continued, "And I resent the implication I am continuing to use what happened as an issue to avoid working on my anorexia."

"I'm sorry, Jennifer. I did not mean to single you out." The doctor seemed gracious.

"I don't think so," Jenny said. "You knew exactly what you were doing and so does everyone else. You were trying to make me responsible, victimizing me again, to divert staff and other patients from criticizing you or the nurses."

The open confrontation between Dr. Stormeier and his toughest case smothered whatever remaining discussion might have taken place. Several nurses stopped to hug Jenny and express support for her public defiance of the unit director. "You were right to protest, Jennifer," Elena consoled her. "He can be such a bastard sometimes."

March 6. Contentment of yesterday—class and exercise. Positive thought for today: God loves me. Mirror says: I have nice earrings.

My roommate is being a real bitch talking behind my back to everyone.

Staff wants me to think about psychotherapy—after they've deferred therapy for over two months! Four things I'm supposed to ask myself. (1) Am I scared?—Yes. I'm afraid we will find out I wasn't abused and there is no reason for my anorexia other than neurotic brain damage. You know, I really think I made it all up. I know Mom never abused me too bad—maybe Tony, my trainers, the men in the mountains, the baby-sitter in the basement, Maria, never happened. Or didn't happen like I think it happened. But if it didn't happen, why did I show all the symptoms as a small child before anorexia began? Was Weintraub wrong about that, too? (2) What do I want out of therapy?—Simple, I want a miracle. I want to live. (3) What will I put

into it?—Honesty, mostly, no matter what it costs me to tell the truth.
(4) What kind of commitment will I make?—None, really. If the going gets
too rough, I may pull out and go to a nursing home.

Contrary to their assurances, Perretons continued to delay providing a
therapist for Jenny. Discouraged with lack of progress, she again convinced
herself that Perretons wasn't right for her. *All I'm doing here is eating and
menstruating,* she wrote in her journal. *Now the hormone pills have me on a
two-week cycle . . . I hate it!* After another unpleasant confrontation in a wrap-
up session, she called home to talk to her father about leaving Perretons.

"It's not working, Dad." She wasn't apprehensive about her father's
reaction, knowing he too had soured on Perretons.

"I'm sorry, honey. They don't know how to treat you, do they?"

"No, but they won't admit it."

"What do you want to do?"

"Remember Dr. Hanes telling us about a patient who got better in a
nursing home?"

"Yes. The story intrigued me."

"I'd like to try a nursing home." She wondered if he might object.

He didn't. "Yes, it's time," he responded cryptically. "Shall I do some
checking?"

"What about Resthaven? I was a candy striper there once. Could you
talk to them?"

"I'll talk to them tomorrow," he said. "And Jenny . . . are you sure?"

"Yes."

"It's a give-up, you know. You're giving up on mental health care."

"I know. I'm ready." Her father paused, and she could hear him clear
his throat. *He always does that when he's upset,* she thought. "I'm . . . I'm
ready too," he finally stammered. "But, you know Resthaven may not
be able to help either. You . . . uh . . . you may die there."

"I know. But I'm so tired, Dad. Nothing seems to help. I'll give
Perretons till the end of March. Then I'm out of here, even if I have to
leave against medical advice again."

"Resthaven may refuse you. It will look bizarre, even to them. They may not understand."

"Please, Dad, try to make them understand. I just can't handle another mental institution."

"I'll try. At least a nursing home provides you with structured assistance. A live or die option is still available to you there. But the director may insist you have some kind of doctor."

"I've already contacted Dr. Steiner."

"Who?"

"Dr. Steiner. You remember. He's the Metro General staff physician who was so nice to me when I was at Mountain View."

"Oh, yes. The doctor who does house calls."

"I really like him. He's a caring person. He's agreed to take care of me medically."

"And—and what if you quit eating?"

"We talked about that. He agreed not to intervene, just to keep me comfortable and free from pain. He said he'd call you and talk to you about making the same commitment."

"He sounds like a remarkable man. I wonder why he's willing to risk sanctions by only standing by while you starve to death."

"I think he understands, Dad . . . maybe the first who truly understands. I asked him why he was willing to help me, with all my negative history . . . and do you know what he said?"

"What, honey?"

"He said, 'Because you asked me to.'" Jenny could hear her father clear his throat again and struggle to speak. *He's going to cry, and he generally controls his pain so well.*

"I . . . I'm sorry, Jenny," he finally stammered huskily, in a breaking voice. "It's just that I'm very moved . . . overwhelmed actually . . . and very humbled by this man's compassion, his courage, and—and his generous heart. How will I ever thank him when he calls?"

"The same way I did, Dad. Just say thank you."

For several years, insurance reviewers had required periodic recertification of medical necessity for Jenny's long hospitalizations. Psychiatrists from an independent service evaluated her case on a biweekly basis. Their review added yet another layer of bureaucracy to her illness. When her care costs breached the million-dollar level, the evaluation service grew reluctant to continue its certification. Dr. Stormeier spent long hours counseling with reviewing psychiatrists and providing them information. Answering their questions was like pouring water down a drain. Never fully satisfied, they regularly challenged Perretons's long-term program.

In mid-March the insurance company wrote Dr. Stormeier, "Certification of medical necessity has been withdrawn, and insurance benefits for Jennifer's care at Perretons will no longer be available after March 10." The retroactive denial of coverage intensified the doctor's dilemma. He knew insurance withdrawal generally terminated institutional care. Few patients could afford a $15,000 monthly price tag for long-term care. He was torn between accepting the denial and fighting the decision, which he knew was based not on professional judgment but on pressure to find a way out of a major case.

He also knew insurance denial could be a death sentence for Jenny. She would be unable to function outside an institution. How could the reviewers not see that? How could they turn their backs on her? But she had shown so little sign of improvement at Perretons. Insurance denial could be a convenient excuse to discontinue responsibility for a risky patient.

Dr. Stormeier wrote one appeal letter, hoping the insurance company would reconsider.

It didn't.

On St. Patrick's Day, Jenny awoke to severe stomach pains. She was rushed to an emergency room where she was treated for pancreatitis. Upon discharge, Jenny acted on her resolve to leave Perretons, now endorsed by the insurance company's denial of coverage. After arranging a return to her former job at Pennington Drugs, she gave notice to

Perretons, refused Thorazine for a week, and paid the price with an Easter Sunday filled with terrifying flashbacks.

After a day of packing and tearless good-byes, Jenny left Perretons on March 28. She checked her suitcases at the airport, found a weight scale, deposited a penny, and fought a conditioned reflex to stand backward. She watched the needle settle at 72 pounds. *About the same as when I came,* she thought. *They never told me. Two times I left against medical advice when I was in pretty good condition. Now I feel rotten, worse than when I admitted, yet they calmly say good-bye and let me walk out the front door.*

With an hour before flight departure, Jenny headed to the cafeteria. She selected a fresh green salad with cottage cheese, took a table next to the window, and slowly ate her lunch. When finished, she returned to the food counters, picked a bag of potato chips off its clip, hesitated, and then picked another, stopped at the dessert case for a piece of apple pie, then added a second, and finally filled a large cup with Diet Coke. Reversing direction, she went back to the pastry shelf and selected six chocolate donuts. Avoiding the cashier's curious gaze, she paid for her second meal. After wolfing down her food, she walked to the ladies room, where she selected an end stall, induced a gag reflex with her fingers, and relieved herself of both meals. She returned to the cafeteria, bought another Diet Coke, and departed for the concourse to board her flight to Denver.

Searching for Release

CHAPTER TWENTY-FIVE
After the King's Men

A dirt path wound through a cottonwood grove behind Resthaven. The path was wet from a hard rain the previous evening. As if spirits breathed from the earth, steam rose among the trees and dissipated into sunlight above. On leaves and branches, condensation formed into beads and dripped back down on the path and its wooden benches. The benches were spaced to accommodate the resting needs of those who trod the path with hesitant steps, the elderly and infirm. Nearby, a tiny intermittent stream announced itself with the soft babble of rushing water. From a field beyond, two meadowlarks sang to each other in a lyrical union of happiness. Voices of spring danced in and out of the early morning sun and shadows.

Two figures walked along the path. Jenny was pleased her father had stopped to see her on his way to work, a departure from his routine of evening visits. When she looked up at him, he glanced at her, smiled, and looked back toward Resthaven. "Forget something?" she asked.

He laughed. "Just checking to see if Dr. Weintraub is spying on us."

Jenny laughed. "My Oedipus complex. A ghost from the past."

"I'd forgotten. Really. Until just now. I was only teasing."

She poked him in the ribs, and he took her hand. "You're getting your good shoes muddy, Dad," she scolded, "and your suit is all wet."

"Not a problem. One more spring and my work clothes are history."

"And me, Dad? Will I last for one more spring?" She could see him struggle with an answer. *Sometimes he's too honest*, she thought, and continued, "You've quit telling me there's still time left for me. It's okay. I know you won't tell me something you don't believe."

He cleared his throat and then spoke softly. "I'm sorry, Jenny. It took a long time for me to accept reality. Until you were victimized at Perretons, I was always confident that somewhere we would find a program that would work for you. We only had to keep trying."

"And now?"

He stopped then, turned and then faced her. "I don't know how to help you fight your illness anymore, without fighting the crazy health care system itself, forcing it to change."

"They all tried to fix me, Dad. I'm just too broken."

"Like Humpty Dumpty?"

"Yes, and after all the king's horses and all the king's men have given up, what happens to me?"

He gestured toward Resthaven.

"Nursing homes take over."

"Most days I feel okay here, some days almost normal."

"I'm grateful for that."

Jenny detoured around more troubling questions, to protect her darker feelings—or his, she wasn't sure. "I like it here, Dad. Here in the woods, I mean. So small, yet so secluded."

"A private haven?"

"Yes, that's just what it is. A patient could get lost in here and never be found. I wonder . . . most of Resthaven's patients are such hopeless cases. Do they ever come here, just to lie down on the ground and die?"

"Like a wild creature choosing to die in solitude?"

"Not in solitude, Dad," Jenny sighed. "There is the earth, the sky, the company of trees and small creatures. When I walk here by myself, I don't feel alone. Not really." Jenny motioned above her. "A cool breeze talks to me through the cottonwoods. And squirrels gossip up there, sounding just like some of our old neighbors. Meadowlarks sing to me from the fields, and the stream teases me . . . gently, like you do."

"Your best company?"

"Yes, except when Diane comes."

"She still sees you?"

"Yes. She still believes in me. I don't know why. Most everyone else has given up."

"I'm sorry, Jenny."

"It's okay. It's not as bad as I make it sound."

"Because nobody orders you around this time?"

"Yes, I'm more comfortable this way."

They turned and retraced their steps in silence.

"Remember about tomorrow," Jenny said as they parted.

There was mischief in his smile. "What's tomorrow?"

"My birthday, silly."

"Oh, yes. Your mom and I are bringing balloons, twenty-five of them. We'll come early and decorate Resthaven's dining room."

She stood on the nursing home steps and waved good-bye. He waved back. Their gestures lingered in the morning mists.

"Resthaven. Foothills Parkway and Harvard Lane. Okay, I have it." Father Paul cradled the phone receiver between his shoulder and ear, used one hand to scribble the address on his desk pad and the other to open the wrapping on a ham and cheese sandwich left over from a missed lunch. "You want me to give her last rites, too?" he asked. He stooped over his desk in his tiny office. His spare figure cast a long, narrow, slightly humpbacked silhouette onto a bare wall opposite the desk lamp that provided his room's only light.

"No, not last rites," Jenny's mother responded. "Father Potter is doing that now."

"Are you sure you need me?" Father Paul felt perplexed and a little rushed. He'd left a dying cancer patient's bedside to take the call. "I'm not sure what I can do. I'm only conversationally familiar with anorexia. Other than the very elderly who think they're too sick to eat, we don't see eating disorders here at the Hospice."

"Please come talk to her, Father. We'd be very grateful. I think she fears condemnation. It's hard for her to accept she's really going to die this time. Father Potter encouraged me to call. We know you're the best for counseling terminal patients, helping them accept reality."

"Are you sure she's terminal?"

"Yes, her doctor told us she's beyond hope . . . beyond rescue through medical intervention. She only weighs 52 pounds, hasn't eaten for twenty-two days since her birthday, and only sucks on ice occasionally. She's nearly blind, and—and she can't walk without assistance. Her . . . her electrolytes dropped to th-the fatal level yesterday." Father Paul recognized the halting strain in a voice stressed close to breaking. "Her kidneys are failing and she sleeps most of the day. She has di-difficulty breathing . . . and . . . and . . ." Father Paul waited for the voice to regain composure. ". . . her heartbeat is erratic, Father, and she only speaks in whispers. She's nearly comatose. We . . . we don't think she can last much longer."

"How does she feel about seeing me?" Father Paul asked gently. "Some fear me. They think I'm a harbinger of death, like the grim reaper!"

"She's willing. For all her fears she's really quite brave."

"What about the rest of her family?"

"They're all supportive. They know she can't come back this time. They're all here, waiting with Dr. Corbin and Dr. Steiner . . . waiting for her to . . . to die."

"Why so much trust in someone you don't know . . . blind faith, perhaps?" Father Paul asked, smiling.

"I guess so. No, it's more. You're so highly regarded, and there's no one else."

Father Paul smiled again, tiredly. "What does Jennifer's psychiatrist think?"

"She doesn't have a psychiatrist. Jim Corbin came down as a family friend, not as a doctor, to do what he could to help all of us, be here with us . . . all day if necessary. No psychiatrist will treat her. They've all abandoned her as an impossible case. Please come. Tonight if you can. There's so little time."

"All right, Mrs. Hendricks, I'll get there as soon as I can. But please understand, my mission is with Jennifer. I won't have time to talk to her family."

"We understand." Jenny's mother could hear gentleness and compassion in Father Paul's earnest voice. She felt reassured, confident she had marshaled all the strength available to her from her Anglican faith—to comfort her daughter in the last hours.

Jenny's mother greeted Father Paul in Resthaven's vestibule. "Thank you for coming, Father. Jenny's in the west wing, last room on the right. She's awake and expecting you. Don't be alarmed at what you hear in the corridor. Resthaven has a noisy patient in the first room who won't close her door."

Relieved that Jennifer's mother made no attempt to accompany him, Father Paul walked through an elegant but empty lounge. He admired the moss rock fireplace and resisted a temptation to reach out and touch its flanking walnut bookshelves. He glanced with fleeting envy at a deep leather couch that faced the fireplace.

Quickening his pace, Father Paul opened the west wing door and was promptly greeted with a disembodied shriek from the dark emptiness beyond, "Help me, please help me." Father Paul shuddered as he hurried down the hallway. A second screech, "Help me, please help me," echoed behind him as he knocked softly on Jenny's door and then entered.

After her encounters with the two priests, Jenny was beset with unsettling thoughts, but she was determined to finish her will, despite her exhaustion and confusion. She had executed a statement denying extreme measures weeks before. Now she wanted to arrange disposition of her few possessions, while she could still think, still force a few words. Counselors of God had prepared her for a spiritual afterlife. Her father would deal with remnants of a materialistic life she was about to leave. But there was something she wanted to give him, something she wanted to ask him to do. Her last gift would be her last request.

After signing her disposition statement, Jenny closed her eyes and rested. Her father sat quietly at her bedside, and she clutched his hand fiercely, as if trying to transmit something further by touch alone. After a moment she opened her eyes and released his hand. Her vision was blurred, and when she tried to talk her lips formed soundless words. Realizing she struggled to speak, he rose to his feet and bent over her, leaning on his hands, which he placed on either side of her shoulders. She extended her arms up toward him and cupped his face in her hands. Her vision clouds parted and her eyes cleared. She looked at him intently, burning his grief-stricken image into her mind to take with her into eternity. A bond stronger than words held them. "Keep my journals, Dad," she whispered huskily, their faces only a few inches apart. "Read them . . . and tell my story. Please tell my story . . . so I can still make a difference."

He dropped his head, but she could still see his tears. "I'll try, honey . . . I'll try," was his halting response.

That night, Jenny slipped in and out of a dreamless sleep. Conflicting thoughts tormented her. Her death resolve weakened. A more fundamental force strengthened.

"She's run away?" Dr. Steiner was aghast.

"Yes. Metro General just called. An ambulance took her there from a donut shop up the street."

"My God, what has she done? Does her family know?"

"I reached Mr. Hendricks at his office and Jenny's brother, David, at home. I left a message for Mrs. Hendricks at her church."

Dr. Steiner hung up and sat at his desk shaking his head in disbelief. Jenny had broken the nonintervention pact. He wondered what had happened to cause her to start another rescue cycle. Then he realized . . . *her father won't accept this.* Dr. Steiner sprang to his feet, alarmed. "I've got to intercept him," he shouted at a nurse as he sprinted from his office.

Stopping for a brief verbal report from Jenny's attending physician, Dr. Steiner reached the emergency room entrance as a visibly distraught

Mr. Hendricks burst through the doors brandishing a sheaf of papers in front of him. "They can't do this," he shrilled at Dr. Steiner. "They must not treat her. They don't know what they're doing to her."

A much bigger man, Dr. Steiner grabbed Jenny's father by his arms and shoulders, restraining him in a bear hug. "Don't," he said firmly. "They have no choice. She's asked for help."

"But . . . but, she doesn't know what she's doing."

"You and I know that, but we can't prevent the emergency room staff from responding to her appeal."

"Not even with this?" And he waved some papers in front of Dr. Steiner's face.

"Her living will?"

"Yes. It denies extreme measures."

Dr. Steiner wrested the documents away. "Not even with this. You've borne the burdens of decision too long. Let me keep Jenny's living will. I may be able to use it later. I can't now."

"But you're chairman of the Ethics Committee here. Can't you make them stop?"

"There's no way. My committee would never deny her plea for care."

Beaten in spirit, Jenny's father permitted Dr. Steiner to lead him to a waiting room chair where he collapsed. "Thank you, doctor, for stopping me," he finally said. "I know you could be sanctioned for what you've done these past few weeks . . . attending her death from starvation without trying to prevent it."

"I've only done what was right."

"Right for your patient, but unacceptable to your profession." He struggled with difficult emotions and looked at Dr. Steiner with eyes blurred with fresh tears. "I . . . I'm overwhelmed by your courage and your compassion. And . . . and, doctor?"

"Yes?"

"I'm forever grateful."

"You understand why I'm powerless to act now?"

"Yes."

"I'm sorry, Gordon . . . that we've come so far, you and I, only to start all over again."

"We've both been beaten by the system?"

"I'm afraid so. What they don't understand is that she will soon deny nutrition, and forced refeeding will once again send her into a terrible anger and suicidal depression . . . which no one knows how to treat."

"Will they honor her denial as they have honored her plea?"

"No."

"So . . . they will torture her to death?"

"Yes. They don't understand Jenny's torture can be ended humanely only by breaking her cycles . . . save-me/leave-me-alone/save-me . . . and her cycles can be broken only by not beginning another save-me cycle."

"But you understand. Why can't other doctors?"

"I've been touched by your daughter's illness in ways they will never know. Avoidance of personal involvement is both a curse and salvation to most physicians. They can't be expected to follow a course of action that is contrary to their training and commitment or to their perceptions of humanity."

"They save her life so her slow death can continue?"

"Yes. She's actually responding to IVs. I wouldn't have thought it possible. Do you want to see her? She's asked for you."

"I can't just yet. I won't be able to meet that tragic pleading in her eyes, when I know she will see only an absence of hope in mine."

CHAPTER TWENTY-SIX
I Cannot See the Sun

*L*egs drawn to her chest, Jenny lay on her bed curled on her side, conserving her meager body heat. She'd left her door open, and sounds of morning activity on Glenbrook's adult unit drifted into her room and touched her consciousness. Although she couldn't make out the words, she heard nurses talking quietly with another patient in the hallway. She frowned and thought, *They have time for others, but not for me.* Blocking the conversation, Jenny stared at the empty white wall in front of her. A sterile, accusing, and unrelenting sameness stared back. She extended her hands in a supplicating gesture, but touched nothing. The wall was inches beyond her reach.

On the adjoining wall, her room in the East Building had windows overlooking a parking lot on the edge of the campus. Jenny hated that view of the outside, of freedom.

Jenny wished she had a south window, which would permit her to bask in rays from the afternoon sun, or a west window, which would let her gaze into Glenbrook's courtyards with their manicured lawns and shrubs, their mature trees—elm, maple, pine, and a few spruce. There she had a glimpse of order, of reason. There she could see an oasis of green in a disordered desert world of disturbed lives with dismal pasts, a world where silent, solitary figures with vacant faces sat on harsh stone benches. Concrete walkways crisscrossed the quadrangles where doctors and staff walked with brisk, purposeful steps and patients shuffled along, aimless and detached. Trying desperately in small ways to separate herself from the haunting and self-deprecating cadences of the mentally ill, Jenny avoided sitting alone outside or walking slowly like the other patients.

Although resolved, Jenny felt sad, angry, exhausted, afraid, and alone. She sat up slowly and confirmed that the sweatsuit she wore—the pink one, her favorite—was still clean and wrinkle free. She reached down and covered herself with her appliqued quilt, frowning back at the smiling hedgehog. She lay on her back and stared at the ceiling. She smiled when she saw a vagrant spider web clinging to a corner. *How'd they miss that? They keep everything about this place perfect—except me. Already seven weeks here with no progress. I'm still bingeing and purging, but the staff isn't smart enough to figure it out. They're tired of me. And I'm tired of trying, tired of eating, tired of puking, tired of fighting the flashbacks . . . tired of everything. I feel so . . . so dirty inside.*

She closed her eyes and her mind skipped back a season, to spring, and then replayed her past few months of despair. Images flared behind her eyelids. For nearly an hour she remained motionless, remembering, fueling her resolve.

Returning to the present, Jenny rose slowly from her bed, wrapped her quilt about her, and walked to her desk. She began writing in her tiny, laborious script. She wrote steadily, without emotion, as if she had already detached from the world about her.

> If I somehow live through this, I want to come back to Glenbrook. Start over and try again. Right now I am concerned with thoughts of death. The sadness and rage and self-destruction I feel are too powerful. I cannot see the sun anymore and fear I'll never find it. Never get past the fright of eating too much, too little. No one can understand the exhaustion I feel having this disease every day. I am so afraid of people, yet desperately ready for them at the same time. I've called and called out for help the past two days as the very physical sensation of my sexual abuse has been inescapable; the dirty penetrated bloated full feeling inside is uncontrollable right now, and all I want to do is cut and escape it. CUT HARD. I've tried to make contacts today, but no one has time. They assume I always can control it from within. There is nothing within anymore. Just hunger and the fear of satiating it.

I love you, Dad—more than anyone I've ever loved. You've tried so hard, and I've demanded so much. I'm so sorry, but I cannot live with the pain anymore—heaven and hell don't even matter. I do this, once again, hopefully for the last time, and maybe it will be freeing for us all—maybe you and Mom will be set free from your worries.

You see the pain I feel and have felt is not counterbalanced by the people who care (I wish it was so badly), but the fact is I am empty and have nothing to give you all. All this adds to my guilt. Besides Dad and an overwhelming "need" for Mom and spurts of what I think of love for others, I am void and afraid and only know safety in my rituals which will eventually cause my death anyway. Hopefully this is the end of that.

The waiting area wasn't a room, just a drab, vestibule-like space, partially separated from traffic by shoulder-height yellow partitions and containing a few gray ill-formed plastic chairs. The partitions faced an elevator bank that served as a barrier to the operating rooms. *This part I really hate,* Dr. Price thought, as she entered the partition opening and saw a middle-aged couple waiting quietly and uncomfortably before her. *It's those anxious faces, the same tired, anxious faces . . . and all those questions, so many I can't answer or can't take the time to answer. I always have to remember to smile so they don't mistakenly conclude the worst from the way I look.* "Hi," she said, briskly shaking hands and continuing rapidly, "I'm Dr. Price. She's fine," anticipating the first question. "She's just fine."

Ten years of anguish screamed from her eyes, but Jenny's mother spoke softly. "It took so long."

"We had to use a local, and the interior repair was intricate work."

"Was it bad?"

"Her wounds weren't as serious as they looked. She missed the jugular and carotid." The doctor noticed both parents shuddered, as if her words created unbearable images.

"How could the hospital let her hurt herself so?"

For a moment, surprise pierced the doctor's mask. "She was hospitalized? Here?"

"Not here. She's been at Glenbrook Psychiatric. How could it happen?"

"I'm sorry. I don't know. I just don't know."

"Can we see her?"

"As soon as I release her from recovery. That should be in about an hour, and she'll be transferred to the surgery ward . . . you can see her there. She'll probably want to sleep. They'll watch her carefully for infection the next few days, but I'm sure there'll be no trouble." Dr. Price paused. "She's very strong, you know. Your daughter is incredibly strong."

"Too strong," was Jenny's father's mumbled response, as the doctor turned to leave.

Dr. Price knew what he meant.

The recovery room made Jenny restless. Her eyes darted about the other forms waiting under white sheets for a return to consciousness. Were they alive or corpses already? She couldn't be sure if any of the sheets moved up and down to indicate breathing. She listened carefully but heard no sounds, not even a wheeze. *So this is what they mean by dead silence,* she thought. *Like in a morgue. Maybe I'm dead and in the morgue.*

Her memory of the operating room was hazy. She remembered bright lights glaring from above, masked faces peering down, and human forms gowned in pale olive hovering over her and floating like spirit wraiths about the room. She remembered a peculiar feeling of weightlessness, as if her body was suspended and supported only by a cushion of air. *For once I was as thin as I wanted to be.* She sensed her mind was angry and somehow had detached itself from the rest of her, disassociated itself from the ministrations to her body and wandered off someplace where it had sulked and refused to function for a while. She thought her soul also had detached but without anger. Her long-suffering, ever-forgiving soul! At least her soul had rested—languished peacefully in limbo where it waited patiently for the doctors to confirm or recall its tentative release and, if confirmed, for God to resolve its destiny.

Jenny couldn't remember what the doctors had done to her—reattached her mind to her body, maybe? Restored her soul? No, that was God's domain. Or was it? Had she been returned to life by modern skill and technology? Or by God's will? Or by Satan's curse? She knew she had journeyed close to death this time, closer than the other times. She didn't feel frightened by the experience. Or awed. Mostly just disappointed.

Soreness in many places persuaded Jenny she was still a living thing. She surveyed the bandages she could see and ran her fingertips along the edges of a wide bandage on her throat. *I'll need a scarf.* She was relieved there weren't any tubes inside her, just an IV in her uninjured wrist. A nurse helped her walk to the bathroom. She felt weak and light-headed. *Nothing new about that, except for my neck. It feels like my head will fall off if I move it. And I don't feel a need to self-destruct anymore. I feel like the old Jenny's been expunged. I'm purged of depression and all the mind and body filth. Just like the other times. I wonder why. I wonder how long.*

She returned to her bed feeling remorseful. *Can't even do this right. Why are doctors so good at fixing me just enough to prolong my agony? Oh, God, what about Mom and Dad? I've made them suffer again. Why didn't the doctors just let me die?*

Dr. Price was surprised to find her young patient bright and alert when she checked Jenny a few minutes later. The doctor took Jenny's hand, careful to select the hand from the tubed but uninjured wrist. It was a tiny hand, a child's hand, except for thin spidery veins, which dodged freckles and mottled Jenny's pale skin like the inked lines on parchment appearance in hands of the elderly. As if seeking succor, Jenny's hand clutched back. Dr. Price shuddered when she saw Jenny's pallid skin stretched tightly over reddened knuckles and felt bones depleted of flesh padding. Dr. Price instinctively repelled, as if direct contact brought an unwelcome glimpse into a soul in torment. She tightened the handclasp, ashamed of her first reaction.

"Feeling better?" Dr. Price asked.

"Yes." Jenny could feel strength and gentleness in the doctor's touch. And compassion. She didn't sense the fleeting aversion.

"Stronger?"

"A little."

"Sore?"

"A lot."

"Still fuzzy from the anesthetic?"

"I don't think so. But I don't remember what you did to me."

"The wounds weren't as serious as they looked, and there's no sign of infection. They should heal fine." Dr. Price released Jenny's hand.

"That's good . . . I guess." There was resignation in Jenny's voice.

"You will have a very thin scar on your neck. After a few months it should be indistinguishable." *My God, is this all I can say to comfort her? Reassure her about an external scar, when her real wounds are still open and unstitched deep inside her. She's so vulnerable, like an abandoned, emotionally destitute child. She looks like she's only twelve or thirteen, except for her haunted eyes and those shrunken facial features where she's prematurely aged. I'm not going to ask her why.*

"I'll wear a scarf, a bright and cheery one," Jenny said.

Dr. Price smiled. "What's your name?" she asked, surprising herself since she generally avoided patient names.

"My name is Jennifer."

"Okay, Jennifer, I'm Dr. Price. Let's get you out of recovery and into your own room."

"Did you see my mom and dad?"

"Yes. I talked to them. They're waiting to see you."

"Thanks," Jenny responded without enthusiasm. "But I really don't want to talk to Mom and Dad yet. I don't know what to say to them." *I'm glad she didn't ask me why.*

Before leaving the hospital, Dr. Price stopped at the front desk, wrote out a note, and clipped it to a fifty-dollar bill. "Be sure a candy striper picks this up," she instructed. "At least there's one more superficial thing I can do." As Dr. Price disappeared through the door, the puzzled desk clerk read the hastily scribbled message. "Please get a scarf from the gift shop, the brightest, cheeriest one you can find, and take it to Jennifer on the surgical ward. No card. She'll know who sent it."

CHAPTER TWENTY-SEVEN

The Dilemma

*W*hen Jenny awoke, her first memory was that of a pretty smile, the face of Dr. Price. Gingerly she pressed her fingers to all her bandaged wounds, starting with her abdomen, then her left wrist, and finally her throat. *Not too sore. They did a good job.* Jenny looked at the IV tube still leading into her right wrist. *Maybe if I'd cut the right one, too, they couldn't IV me. I'm really hungry,* she suddenly realized, *and fear of eating isn't in my mind today. I wonder why. I hate it when fear drives everything else out of my mind.*

Jenny looked out her window to a familiar sight. Her room on the fourth floor overlooked Mountain View Sanatorium. From her treetop vantage point she could see the changing season. A rising sun captured autumn in a strip of bright light between the two buildings. Tree leaves advertised ebbing life. Color chronicled the decline. Many leaves were yellow or amber, some orange, a few already brittle brown, severed and falling to the ground in the September wind. She couldn't remember noticing changes in the trees and grounds at Glenbrook. *Maybe it's from being higher up. Or maybe I've slept for a month, instead of just a night.*

She tried to pick out one of her old rooms at the sanatorium. *Nearly a year I lived there. Maybe I should have stayed. Dr. Hanes was my best doctor—so patient. I think he could have helped me. I'm not sure what went wrong. I wonder if he'll be sad when I die.*

Jenny slept again after breakfast and awoke to find a nurse smiling down at her. "Has Dr. Wakely been in?" Jenny asked.

"Dr. Wakely? I don't think so. Who's he, Jennifer?"

"He's my doctor from Glenbrook. Has he called?"

"No. No one's called or been to see you."

"How about last night? I was sleepy and don't remember. Did anybody come? My parents? Dr. Wakely or any of the staff from Glenbrook?"

"I don't know, honey. There's no one here from last night's shift."

"Do I have a doctor here? Is Dr. Price my doctor?"

"Dr. Price is an ER surgeon, so she can't be your doctor. Our residents are checking you, and one should be by later today."

"Is there someone I could talk to now?" Jenny was feeling a little panicky—that old sense of abandonment.

"No. Not right now. I've checked your wounds and they look fine."

Then Jenny remembered. "How about Dr. Steiner? He's been my doctor, although I haven't seen him recently. He practices here."

"Yes, he's here. But he doesn't see surgical patients."

Jenny tried to decide if she should ask for Dr. Steiner. *I like him and I trust him. He's the only one who seemed to understand and didn't try to control or change me. But I'm ashamed for him to know I hurt myself again.* "Okay. I'll try to reach Dr. Wakely and then call Glenbrook. I'll need some of my things from there."

"Anything I can do for you?"

"I don't think so. Except if you could move the phone a little closer. It's my neck. Feels like my head will fall off if I move it very far." Jenny managed an appreciative smile.

"Oh. I almost forgot. There's a package here for you. A candy striper brought it by" Shall I open it?"

"No." Jenny felt a need to talk to someone else. Something nagged at her, something she needed to remember. "I'll get it later."

After the nurse left, Jenny paused before she dialed her doctor. *The letter! I almost forgot. I have to call Dad, tell him to get my letter. I'm afraid they'll destroy it.* When she dialed her father, Marty, her father's secretary, answered. "I'm sorry, Jenny, he has meetings out of the office this morning. How are you doing?"

Jenny felt relieved. Marty's cheerfulness indicated she didn't know. "I'm fine. Please ask Dad to come by this afternoon."

Then Jenny tried to reach Dr. Wakely. "I'm sorry," his receptionist replied. "The doctor isn't in. If it's an emergency I can dial his pager."

"No, that's okay. Please have him call Jennifer."

Next she called Glenbrook and spoke to a receptionist who promised to deliver the things she requested: clothing, a nightgown, her drawing materials, a new book titled *Courage to Heal*, her calendar, a new journal, and some toiletries. She didn't speak to any of her ward nurses and was relieved she could avoid a painful conversation.

When Jenny called home she got a busy signal. When she tried again, her mother picked up. "Hi, Jenny. We came to see you last night after surgery, but you were asleep."

"They gave me another sedative."

"Your father and I called the hospital this morning before he left for work. You were sleeping still, but we got a good report from the nursing station. How are you feeling?"

It doesn't seem like she's angry or trying to avoid me. Maybe the shunning is helping her. "I'm sore, but I feel pretty good. I slept well and ate a good breakfast. They've pulled the IV already." *I hope she doesn't want to talk about the suicide attempt.*

"I'm so glad you're okay, honey. I talked to Nancy and Janis. They send love."

Mom's just saying that. I wonder what they really said to her. "Did you talk to Brian, too?"

"We haven't reached him yet. I went to early mass this morning, and you're still on the prayer list at church."

No accusation in her voice. I always feel so guilty, and everyone seems so forgiving when I do this. It only makes my guilt worse.

Jenny stood at her window, waiting. The usual crowd gathered about the hospital entrance below. Patients looking antiseptic in bed gowns and robes shuffled about on sandaled feet, seeking fresh, unrecycled air. Visitors puffed on cigarettes. Tired hospital attendants captured an outdoor interlude as they slumped on long wooden benches and stared

at the sky, seeking temporary oblivion. A few glowing young faces—
the semester's new crop of interns, still enchanted by their ordination
into the mystique of medicine—talked excitedly among themselves.

Jenny saw her father then. *He's not hurrying like he generally does.* She
watched him pause and stare at a bronze sculpture in front of the hospital. Jenny had admired the sculpture, too. Something about it haunted her,
moved her to tears when she looked at it. Rising 10 feet from a cement
base, it comprised three forms intertwined in symmetrical grace. Delicate
hands of a small figure, the trusting child, reached up and clasped the arm
of a larger figure, the mother, the caregiver, whose arms, one about his
shoulder and one around his waist, embraced the father, the protector,
whose circumambient arms encircled both figures. Three featureless faces
turned skyward and sent their message of hope and faith into the heavens. It was a compelling work of compassion titled "The Family."

Jenny watched him detour and walk slowly around the sculpture,
then stop again, with a look of incredible sadness on his face. *It affects
him the same way.*

She glanced in the mirror. A figure even she had to acknowledge as
shrunken stared back. She appeared wan and haggard, gaunt and bandaged—but alive! She decided to greet him standing, so he would know
she was recovering. When he entered her room, she saw him try to smile
as he said, "Hi, Jenny."

She was relieved he didn't add, *how are you?* "Hi, Dad," she greeted
him warmly, without hesitation. Father and daughter embraced, and she
felt him wince, as if her wounds caused him physical pain. "I'm glad you
came." Unsteady on her feet, Jenny retreated to sit on her bed, holding
her neck stiffly erect.

He took her hand. "Are you sure it's okay to talk now?"

"Yes," she said, feeling calm and composed. She knew she needed to
talk to someone who wouldn't judge her. "I tried to talk to a nurse. Three
times. But she was too busy. She said I had to control it from within."

He cleared his throat before he spoke. "She was just trying to remind
you to be responsible for yourself."

"I know. But I couldn't, and they had forgotten to recontract me. I knew they wouldn't check me, even though they're supposed to. I was in bed cutting for a long time."

Fighting his own tormenting images, he sat silently for a moment without reaction, then spoke. "Did you talk to Dr. Wakely?"

"He spends so little time with me, only a few minutes each visit, and he's always in a hurry. I had already made up my mind when he came in. I didn't think talking to him would do any good. I tried to get three staff nurses to talk to me after lunch and they wouldn't. So I just gave up on the whole idea."

"Do you want to pursue a grievance against Glenbrook?"

"No, Dad. I want to go back. Try again."

He reacted with surprise. "After this?"

"Yes. Some there seem to understand. I'll talk to Dr. Wakely about going back."

Jenny feared he wouldn't agree. Instead he changed the subject, and they chatted briefly about her brothers and sisters. She found herself actually interested. As small talk waned, he asked her with a genuine smile that surprised them both, "How about a game, honey?"

Jenny smiled, remembering their visitation ritual in earlier years had included late-afternoon backgammon games. She had always looked forward to them as opportunities to divert her mind and conversation from her illness. "You always try to free me from myself in small ways. But now? We haven't played in a while."

"It's how I can tell if you're still mentally alert," he teased.

Giving in to a sudden drowsiness, Jenny lay back on her pillow. "I'm pretty tired, Dad, and I can't hold my head up unsupported for very long. Maybe tomorrow." Then she rose up again. She'd almost forgotten. "There's a letter for you at Glenbrook, and I want you to read it, Dad. Ask Dr. Wakely about it."

After resting most of the weekend, Jenny tried to contact the Glenbrook staff on Monday. She called and left word for Nurse Harrold to call.

Two hours later, when her call hadn't been returned, she tried again. the nurse was busy. "She won't call back, will she?" Jenny asked.

"No," the switchboard operator confirmed.

"Is there anyone on the unit I can talk to?"

"I don't think they'll let anyone talk to you, Jennifer. I'm sorry."

Feeling punished and abandoned, Jenny called Dr. Wakely. "It's urgent," she said to his receptionist to bypass a callback delay. "They're stonewalling me," she chastised her doctor. "No one at Glenbrook will talk to me. That's petty."

"It's hospital policy, Jennifer. They're not supposed to."

"Why not?"

"You're post–suicide attempt and in another hospital now."

"But I've talked with the staff psychiatrists here. They don't know what to do with me. I'd like to go back to Glenbrook and try again."

"I'm sorry, but I'm leaving for a meeting. Maybe we can talk more this afternoon."

Jenny felt better after lunch. She'd eaten well but not excessively. Her self-destructive impulses were closeted in the shadows of her mind. Her mind demons rested from their recent triumph. They remained hidden, satiated, and no longer a threat.

She was apprehensive about what would happen when Metro General discharged her. Where could she go next? What should she do? She was determined not to let apprehension feed her fears and lure her demons out of hiding. *I'll keep my demons undernourished, she thought, like the rest of me. I'll starve the little buggers, keep them in the closet. I won't feed them with my head. I'll try to read again, keep my mind active on other things so the demons can't grow, get strong, and take over again.*

Neatly folded on her bedside table, the scarf from Dr. Price caught her eye. Its bright floral pattern cheered her. She unfolded the scarf and admired its sweeping swirls of red and yellow, white and green. *Like the joyful creation of a bingeing artist. I wish I could create something as pretty from happy thoughts—and without bingeing.*

She wrapped the scarf around her still-bandaged neck and resumed reading *Courage to Heal*. The book suggested she analyze and write down her feelings about the effects of abuse. She began to write in her laborious tiny script, using her favorite lavender-colored pen.

First page in a new journal. Another new beginning. I wonder where it will end.

She wrote slowly and without emotion, not realizing *Courage to Heal* might sabotage her resolve and redirect her mind back to feelings she had decided not to nourish.

Any food in my intestine or feces in my bowel makes me crazy that it is a penis up my anus or wriggling around in my vagina. I do controlling, destructive things to avoid this feeling of penetration. I only eat things that pass straight through me I throw up I starve I exercise till I can't feel it anymore. I'm scared of all people who are not nurses, doctors, or mental health workers. I have terrifying flashbacks, but I'm not sure if they are real. I wanna cut my body and let the evil bleed out and death come in. I don't deserve to eat unless I have hurt myself first. I can't seem to gain weight beyond emaciation because that endangers me—I may become sexual and that is dirty and wrong. I seek the nurturance I missed in childhood and set up dependent relationships, though I'm not sure how. I also seek reassurance from my parents that they love me and won't leave me. I'm afraid of being independent, because that means lonely, abused, and unhappy.

Before a recent suicide attempt I was bingeing and purging twenty-four hours a day and sought no other activity in my life. Avoidance is my only goal. I have little self-worth and even less self-trust. I never know when that INCREDIBLE PERVASIVE urge to self-destruct will rear its compulsive head. Some days I wake up so dirty I know I must hurt myself.

On the other hand, I've developed strengths that will be invaluable should I ever recover. I'm able to perceive and interpret people's behavior. This gives me capacity for great compassion. I have unusual perseverance. I know anorexia and its symptoms better than most professionals. I know psychiatry. I can tolerate almost any living situation. I've had some rare and uncommon encounters with special people. I am STRONG.

Jenny finished her exercise more confident than she began. She waited impatiently for Dr. Wakely to call. She also chafed at not hearing from her father. She wondered if he'd found her letter and read the message to him she so desperately wanted him to see. She supposed she could tell him directly, and maybe it wasn't so important now. Now she had to focus on where to go next. Maybe returning to Glenbrook wasn't a good idea. In several phone calls to Glenbrook she'd managed one brief conversation with a ward nurse who told her to "work harder." *Always the same message. Work on what? Glenbrook obviously doesn't want me back. But where else can I go? I need to find something soon or Metro General will commit me to the state hospital.* Jenny shuddered at the thought.

The call from Dr. Wakely interrupted her thoughts. They discussed her options. "If you return to Glenbrook, we'll have to severely restrict you," Dr. Wakely said.

"Restraints?" Jenny asked.

"Only at night."

"You're going to tie me down? I can't believe it."

"Only until you've recovered from the emotional effects of your suicide attempt."

"You're afraid I'll hurt myself again, aren't you?"

"We want to be sure you're safe."

"But you don't understand. The pressure is relieved. It will be a while before it builds up again. That's always the way it is. I won't be a threat to myself—not for a long time."

"We can't take the chance."

"You still don't understand. The controls you use to prevent suicide attempts aggravate the feelings that produce my suicidal impulses in the first place. You should work on the problem—the impulse, not its consequence."

"I'm sorry, but the hospital has a policy we have to follow. Would you like me to explain the other restrictions to you?"

"No. You know I have a hard time dealing with controls dictated to me. I can support a program better if I can help develop it. I know myself and my illness better than anyone, and I know what works and what doesn't. Why won't you let me help develop a treatment plan?"

"It isn't appropriate. But you do have an alternative to Glenbrook."

"Not the state hospital. I won't go there."

"Not the state hospital. Community Care. I've talked to them again, since your visit ten days ago. They think they might be able to help. They only take the most difficult cases, chronic cases that don't respond to conventional hospital programs."

Jenny felt panicky. "I may not be strong enough for a change."

"They suggest you go over again tomorrow or Wednesday, meet more of the staff, talk to the doctors, maybe get a pass from the hospital and stay overnight. I think you'll find their program much less restrictive than at Glenbrook."

"Would you still be my doctor?"

"No. Community Care has its own psychiatric staff. You would be under the care of Dr. Walter, the program director, or Dr. Grunewald. Probably Dr. Grunewald because Dr. Walter leaves Wednesday for three weeks' vacation."

"Have you talked to my dad about insurance?"

"Once. I'll call him again."

After she disconnected from Dr. Wakely, Jenny felt frustrated. Others controlled her again. She returned to her journal.

No one will listen to me. The system is going to defeat me again. Dad says when I attempt suicide I abdicate my right to self-determination and others take over. He says the system reverts to a medieval medical monster. He's right.

The doctors here want to send me to the state hospital in Pueblo. I guess Weintraub was wrong about that, too; I'm outside Fort Logan's jurisdiction. I know I'll die in Pueblo, like Weintraub said. Dr. Wakely is afraid to treat me now, and the staff at Glenbrook won't even talk to me. I know Dad is tired, and he's out of ideas. He was impressed with Community Care's approach. Maybe I should try it there. I know I'll have to be more responsible for myself, and I don't know if I can do it. I don't know what to do. I need someone to talk to about it. Dr. Wakely is useless; he's always in such a hurry. Maybe Dr. Steiner can help me decide.

Dr. Wakely called Jenny's father. "Any word from the insurance company?" he asked.

"They use an evaluation service to certify all admissions. I've already sent in Community Care's information packet. You should hear from them directly. What does Jenny think?"

"She's undecided. I'd like for her to visit again."

"Is she strong enough?"

"Probably not."

"Will the hospital let her stay until she's strong enough to decide about Community Care?"

"I don't know how long. Probably just a few more days."

"That means another decision has to be made without enough time to make it properly."

"How do you feel about Jennifer returning to Glenbrook?" Wakely took a calculated risk but was confident Jenny's father would oppose a Glenbrook readmission.

"Very negative. I want my daughter to be comfortable. She's close to the end of her illness, and her comfort is more important than perceptions of her safety needs. Nobody, no institution, no restrictions can make her safe anywhere. It's an impossible task. With your controls, she might be less likely to hurt herself at Glenbrook, but because of your controls she will be less likely to want to hurt herself someplace else."

"I appreciate your candor. It helps."

After a good night's sleep, a rare experience for her, Jenny received permission to shower and wash her hair. She toweled steam from the mirror, smiled at the image, and admired her hair as the blow-dryer ruffled the auburn strands about her. *My hair really is pretty now,* she thought. *But, when I last saw Mom a month ago, hers had lost all its luster—gotten gray and lifeless.*

After lunch, Jenny called her father. "What do you think I should do, Dad?"

"Go where you feel most comfortable."

"What if the insurance company won't approve Community Care?"

"Not part of the decision, honey. If that's where you want to go, that's where you'll go, even if the insurance reviewer doesn't certify. I think I know a way to block his disapproval."

"Can we afford it if we have to pay?"

"It's manageable."

"Are there any alternatives?"

"I don't see any."

"Too many burned bridges?"

"That's part of it. What do your doctors think?"

"I'm sure Dr. Wakely wants me to go to Community Care, but he won't come out and say that. The doctors here don't know anything except the state system."

"How about Dr. Steiner?"

Jenny brightened. "He came to see me yesterday afternoon. He said he'd be my medical doctor again if I went to Community Care. He said he'd go out and talk to them."

"That's wonderful, Jenny. The man is extraordinary. He's like a solidly anchored rock surrounded by quicksand."

"Have you talked to Dr. Grunewald?"

"Yes. He said they've had only one severe eating disorder in their nine-year history, but they'll take you. They're not interested in your past, just your future."

"They don't have much experience with anorexia?"

"Maybe that's a good thing. They won't have a treatment bias. They certainly can't do any worse than other experts you've worked with."

"Did you like Dr. Grunewald, Dad?"

"Yes. And I liked what he said. You should talk to him."

"I will."

"What did you think of the staff you met there before?"

"I liked them."

"And their patients?"

"I only met two. But the staff says they're all young adults. I like that."

"Are you scared about making a change?"

"A little. Do you think I should go back to Glenbrook? I might be safer there."

"Was Glenbrook helping you?"

"Some of the staff were."

"So some weren't?"

"That's always the case."

"You mean mental health care workers aren't all created equally superior?"

"Dad!" Jenny scolded. "Will you be serious? I have to make a decision."

"You don't have to decide right now."

"I don't have much time. The doctors here say I'm healing fast. They want to discharge me Thursday. Do I have to visit Community Care again before I decide?"

"I don't think so."

"I don't want it to cost you more, Dad."

"Face it, Jenny. We're God's gift to the mental health care profession. We have an obligation to keep them busy and well paid so they stay off the streets and don't become more of a menace to society."

"Dad! Don't be so negative."

"I thought I was being positive."

"I still don't want you to have to pay more."

"Don't let that influence you, Jenny. Community Care's costs are less than half of Glenbrook's, and I feel really good about that even if I have to pay more."

"Will you come see me this afternoon?"

"No. Too many calls to make. I'll come tomorrow.

Dr. Wakely paced nervously in his office. His carpet revealed a wide threadbare ellipse where he habitually walked off stress from his most difficult cases. He'd done a lot of pacing the past few days—over Jennifer. Her case wasn't progressing smoothly. From a therapeutic perspective, there was no progress because there was no therapy.

What time he had to spend on her case had been consumed first by those damned meetings debriefing her suicide attempt, and now by all the phone calls involved in getting his former patient, as he already considered her, admitted to Community Care. Several long conversations with Dr. Lucas at the insurance screening service had resolved nothing. Dr. Wakely had expected questions from the reviewer but was also confident he would quickly clear Community Care as a far less expensive alternative to Glenbrook. To the contrary, Dr. Lucas balked at a transfer to Community Care.

He walked to his desk and called Jennifer's father. "Dr. Lucas won't approve Community Care. He thinks Jennifer needs to demonstrate she isn't still suicidal. He says he has to be satisfied she's in a program whose intensity matches the seriousness of her condition."

The response was a bitter, "That's gibberish. Dr. Lucas wants her locked up."

"He's quick to say it's Jennifer's decision where she goes. His involvement is only to determine insurance participation."

"More gibberish. If coverage is denied, he knows patients are forced to go where insurance will pay. He's playing God. He should review general qualifications and stay out of the question of whether Community Care is the right place for Jenny at this time. That's for Jenny and her doctors to decide."

Dr. Wakely was uncomfortable with the role of advocate for another institution. "Has Dr. Lucas spoken to Dr. Grunewald yet?"

"Yes. Just. Dr. Grunewald told me the same thing my home office told me. Dr. Lucas wants to protect himself and his company from liability. He doesn't give a damn about what's best for Jenny and will delay certification as long as he can."

"That's pretty strong condemnation."

"It was meant to be."

Dr. Wakely paused for a moment. "Will—ah—will you support Jenny financially if she goes to Community Care and coverage is denied?"

"Yes. Dr. Grunewald knows that. So does Jenny—so she won't feel trapped into making a decision based on cost. But I want to keep pressure on Dr. Lucas to do what's right."

"Can you talk to Dr. Lucas?"

"I tried. His secretary blocked me."

"Could you try again?"

"Not without getting angry and saying things I'll probably regret. I'm afraid I might make the situation worse."

"Maybe not. Your point of view might help. Think about it. We're running out of time."

Jenny lay with the foot of her hospital bed elevated to raise her legs. As her body rehydrated, her feet and ankles became painfully swollen with fluid retention. She was too uncomfortable to read or to write in her journal. Her mind raced. *All that blood to my head,* she thought. *Mustn't feed the demons.* Jenny dialed her father and Marty picked up. "I'll have him call as soon as he's free," she told Jenny.

Jenny was feeling panicky when her father called back. "They want me discharged tomorrow, and I still don't have a place to go," she said.

"Are they pressuring you to admit to the state hospital?"

"Only indirectly. They don't tell me much. I think they intend to commit me there."

"Should I drive you to Community Care today so you can get better acquainted?"

"No. I've talked to Dr. Grunewald. He says I don't have to do a visit first. I think I'd like to go there, Dad. Glenbrook doesn't want me back."

"Don't pick Community Care because Glenbrook is reluctant. We can force Glenbrook either to take you back or quit pussyfooting around the readmission issue and say no."

"I want to go to Community Care, Dad. I can't stand the thought of being tied down."

"I understand and agree. Will Community Care admit you tomorrow?"

"Yes."

"Okay, it's done. When can I pick you up?"

"In the morning, about nine. We'll have to pick up all my things at Glenbrook."

"Will it be difficult for you to see the staff at Glenbrook?"

"Yes. I don't want to talk to them again."

"I'll stop and get your things and then pick you up at ten."

"Thanks, Dad. Will Mom come?"

He paused before answering. "I . . . I don't think so."

"She's still shunning me?"

"You know?"

"It's been obvious ever since I entered Glenbrook."

"Does it upset you?"

"I think it's dumb. You can't resolve problem relationships by avoiding them."

"It's just the latest fad, recommended to families who have a member with compulsive or addictive behavior problems. Modern psychiatry's give-up approach."

"You're too cynical."

"I know."

"It's called bad attitude." Jenny laughed.

"I know. It's habitual, undisciplined, and repeatedly provoked."

"And the doctors still think you're an enabler because you do things for me?"

"Probably. When they're hung up on parent bashing and need an excuse for their own failures. Who knows . . . maybe they're right."

"Did Dr. Corbin recommend Mom shun me?"

"Yes. Jim prescribed it. To break down your codependency and protect her sanity."

"But he didn't prescribe it for you?"

"It won't work with me. I'm beyond prescription. I've been hopelessly impaired for a long time."

"Dad!" Jenny chastised. Then she laughed again. It was more like the old conversations with her father.

CHAPTER TWENTY-EIGHT

Do I Finally Get to See the Sun?

Jenny was relieved that a commitment to the state mental hospital had been averted. She was also apprehensive about moving into yet another care facility. As her father maneuvered the family station wagon into a parking space on Lee Street, she gingerly twisted her body so she could look out the window without turning her head. To stabilize her neck and compensate for its stiffness, she used her right hand as a wedge between her jaw and collarbone. She winced with pain when the car jolted slightly and halted at the curb.

"Sorry, honey," her father said. "Still sore?"

"It's my neck muscles. They hurt when my head goes unsupported for a long time."

"Are you sure you're healed enough to move?"

"I'm still weak, but the hospital said it's okay. They wanted to get rid of me, and I was ready to leave." Jenny gazed approvingly at a tidy bungalow with its neatly manicured landscaping nestled to the left of Community Care. Moving her body slightly, she inspected the care facility, smiled at its unremarkable appearance, and tried to remember her introductory visit. The suburban home sprawled casually—not really well groomed, not really unkempt, just comfortable. Then she curled her nose in disgust when she saw contrasting squalor to the right of Community Care—uncut yard with patches of bare ground and refuse heaps showing, broken steps to the porch, paint peeling from dirty frame siding. "Yard slaves on one side of me and trashers on the other," she said. "Just like a real neighborhood." Freshly planted shrubs by Community Care's entryway made her think of something. "My plants, Dad? Did you get my plants from Glenbrook?"

"I think I got them all. One isn't doing well, though . . . the big rubber plant. Most of its leaves have turned brown and lifeless. I think it's dying."

"It didn't like Glenbrook, but I think I can bring it back. Maybe it will respond here."

Holding tightly to her father's arm, Jenny walked slowly up the sidewalk. She smiled at a freshly painted blue door standing ajar. "Look . . . the door . . . it's open! It really is like a home. I didn't remember from before. It's been so long since I've slept in a real bed in a real home." She didn't see tears form in her father's eyes. "How long have I been confined in hospitals, Dad?"

"Too long, Jenny." Her father spoke softly. "Five years, I think. It's good you can think of this as a home. I'm amazed to find a psychiatric facility located right here in a residential neighborhood."

"I'm glad it's here . . . and I'm glad I can come here." Jenny reached back and squeezed her father's arm. "Thanks, Dad, thanks for helping arrange it."

"I only wish we had found Community Care sooner."

Jenny adjusted her scarf, carefully concealing an angry red welt that arced down the right side of her neck. She stepped through the open door and absorbed first impressions. Something was missing. What? She thought for a moment. No nurses. No nurses greeted her. Where were the starched uniforms, the jaded faces whose expressions screamed with fatigue and resentment, the palace guards whose waist chains jangled menacingly with keys to locked doors? Nobody greeted her, as if Community Care knew an open door greeted with a message that spoke louder than words: You are welcome here and free to come and go . . . we won't confine you. Inside Jenny heard familiar sounds of a home bustling with activity: here, close by, voices, normal voices, a man and a woman talking quietly, calmly, from a small office through the door on her left; and there, raucous noises, familiar noises, a dishwasher whooshing in its rinse cycle from the kitchen at the end of the hallway in front of her; and further off, laughter, real, unaffected laughter from a room she couldn't see off the living/dining area to her right—oh yes, now she remembered, a new sunroom addition on the south side where they had a television and an exercise bike. "Like sounds of a large family . . . like my home," Jenny said. She sighed, turned, and entered the office through another open door.

Other differences from her previous care programs made distinct impressions. A casually dressed staff of energetic, cheerful professionals who seemed genuinely eager to make her feel at home welcomed her. Bright, friendly eyes no longer deadened by sedation shone from the faces of most of the other patients she met, all young adults in their twenties. No formidable lists of dos and don'ts were presented to assault her sensibilities. Community Care had only one rule: Be considerate of others. No quiet rooms with their threat of restraints intimidated her. Were Community Care's policies and its staff/patient relationships really untainted by protectionism? "Am I emerging from a cocoon?" she asked her father. "Do I finally get to see the sun?"

"I hope so, honey. I truly hope so."

After so many years, could it be that Jenny had finally found a rational, even humane, approach to dealing with irrational minds? Community Care gave her more flexibility and responsibility within a structured program of daily activities. Its program suited Jenny. Although weakened from wounds not fully healed, she bravely faced another rehabilitation.

During her first month at Community Care, optimism she hadn't felt for a long time visited Jenny regularly. It felt good to her—to try, really try again, not just go through the motions. She even projected enthusiasm. The Community Care staff applauded her positive attitude and voted her client of the month.

Excited by her rapid progress, Jenny called her father at work. "Dad, guess what?"

"Must be something good. I can tell."

"I'm reading the newspaper again! Every day! I even understand most of it."

"That's wonderful, Jenny. Shall I test you?"

"Don't tease. Do you realize how long it's been since I could sit down and read a paper?"

"A long time. I know."

"Over five months, not since April at the nursing home."

"That's a good sign, Jenny, and animation in your voice is a better one. I haven't heard that in a long time, either."

"Dad, will you bring me a book to read?"

"Don't you have some books?"

"Yes, but they're all self-help books. I'm sick of them. I'd like to read a real book, a novel."

"Like what?"

"Like *War and Peace?* I know you have a copy, and I've always wanted to read it."

"Whew, no small steps for you! *War and Peace* is a huge book. Over one thousand pages. And not easy. Tolstoy's a plodder. Reading him can be painfully slow."

"I want to try . . . and Dad, will you bring me a new magazine . . . like *Glamour* or *Vogue?*"

"I'll bring you *War and Peace.* You're on your own for magazines."

Jenny developed a new health plan and resolved to follow it:

EMOTIONALLY—Talk at least two hours a day. Get to know my assigned staff worker, make our half-hour together really valuable. Work on hate letters to abusers: Mom, Uncle Tony, Billy, Gary, Maria, satanists, mountain men, baby-sitter. Utilize anyone who can be supportive, let them know what's inside me right now. Don't worry about being pleasant company for them. Purpose: Let me taste love so I won't give in and die. Help me to feel worthwhile outside of anorexia.

PHYSICALLY—Walk one hour at whatever pace I want each day—do it whenever I have time and with someone if I can. Stretch every day for relaxation and flexibility. Eat healthily. Go for full enough but not so full I am driven to purge. Eat balanced meals because my body needs everything right now. However, I can indulge in a large peanut butter and jelly sandwich when I wish to, or anything I want, as long as I don't get completely ritualized and unbalanced again. I need to strive for nutrition, variety, fullness but not OVERfull, self-forgiveness. Give self permission to rest. Purpose: Build muscles as I eat, prepare for running, relaxation, possible social contact. Help me deserve to eat. Keep from bingeing—go for walk instead. Survival, energy, ability to think again.

THERAPEUTICALLY—Don't demand the impossible from therapists. Spread out getting needs met. Define, clearly and concisely, what I need not only from therapy team but peers. Talk about anger, flashbacks, self-destruction, fear, loneliness, needs, grief, and self-hatred openly and honestly. Recognize anger and grief for what it really is instead of turning it inward and punishing myself. Finish Courage to Heal. Do exercises. Check out assumptions. Be honest even about most painful flashbacks. Purpose: Develop more desire to live and greater independence. Realize my goals of being a doctor and a loving person. Learn how to experience care and love from others.

INTELLECTUALLY—Read one page, at least, each day of Courage to Heal, medical text, and War and Peace. Read paper, headlines at least. Purpose: Exercise brain, notice when my concentration improves and gain awareness of things beyond my pain.

CREATIVELY—Draw, serious and funny. Look at magazines like Glamour. Paint whatever I want. Experiment with different ways of wearing my hair. Listen to music. Purpose: To experience my right brain and gain freedom from my self-abusive voices.

After a distressing binge/purge episode, Jenny presented to staff her own plan for preventing another relapse:

The half hour after every meal will be spent either with people, within a public place, walking, or exercising. If I become conscious of an urge to binge and purge, I will go to staff. (Sometimes I have no warning, BANG it just happens.) FACT: Christmas and Thanksgiving are difficult days for me and I already know I will need lots of support. Also birthday and New Year's Day. I can be VERY self-destructive and usually end up cutting on myself, bingeing and purging, and within a few days making a vicious suicide attempt. If I need to go to the bathroom and males are around, I will leave the door cracked, and if I am alone or have my privacy, the door will stay completely open. If this should ever occur again, I will throw up in the kitchen, despite the pain and humiliation, like I promised.

Jenny composed written outlines of steps to build her strength and ways *I can begin to want life more than death,* focusing on *defining myself as other than a dying, abused anorexic.* She drew up a long list of positive things she could do to combat her negative compulsions.

Rest instead of driving myself. Accept compliments instead of rejecting them. Eat when I'm hungry. Bitch when I want to and not punish myself for it; rather, work it out. Confront others and not care what they think. Quit my rituals (don't know if I can do this): have to bathe twice a day and wash in a certain way; have to be able to fit fingers around upper arm, thighs, and ankles; must have cleanliness or I am dirty also; must exercise in order to eat, or be so physically decrepit I have to eat, or die; must eat at certain times, no sooner, no later, and must eat defined food in defined amount of time; must push push push, perfectly clean kitchen, perfectly clean bathroom, clean everything; must be nice, understanding, empathetic, assertive not aggressive, in short PERFECT or I am BAD; must make bed; must not relax but always do productive and growth-involving activities; musn't rest; must brush teeth, never skip; must get out of bed, regardless of time, early enough to shower, clean kitchen, and organize myself before group; must do all assignments (this) perfectly and with as much effort as I can muster. Listen to radio and tapes I like. Watch a movie instead of producing something. Tell people when I feel like pushing them away rather than doing it. Finish this before I do work (I didn't). Not care when my stomach feels fatter today than it did yesterday. Believe emptiness and fullness, especially constipation, has nothing to do with sexual abuse. Believe I am worthy of energy.

*Not feel that I must first punish myself by overtaxing myself to deserve to
live. Believe God loves me and I am worthy of something. Nourish myself
enough so I'm not "hazy" and have enough energy, even maybe an excess,
to become what I want to become.*

*Also: Allow myself to learn about being pretty and to help fuel that by
nurturing myself so I can be pretty. Eat a peanut butter and jelly sandwich now because I want one rather than forcing myself to wait till tonight.
Like skin, flesh, color in my face as much as bones. State my opinions
and stand up for them. Allow a little chaos in my life and know I won't die.
Don't always assume responsibility (doing chores for others).*

In response to a therapy exercise, she started a letter to a staff member.

Dear Shane,

Here are the reasons why I want to be alive: 1. So I can go back
to school, pursue medicine, and make something of myself
(a psychiatrist). 2. So I don't let the abusers win. 3. Because
I think God wants me alive. The doctors say it's a miracle I
survived my suicide attempts. God is so invested in keeping me
alive, he must have a plan for me. 4. So I can experience trust
and love. 5. Because I want to know what it feels like to like
myself. 6. Because I want to be pretty again.

As with all her programs, Jenny's initial hope and determination to
get better in a healthy way fought a relentless battle with her illness, not
just its eating malfunctions but its debilitating companions: despair,
depression, compulsive overexercising, terrifying flashbacks—and a rel-
ative newcomer, persistent physical pain and exhaustion. Pain dogged
her organized recovery plans. She wrote in her journal:

*We just drove to Colorado Springs, and I am feeling guilty. I need to punish
myself for sitting so long and not doing anything but enjoying the warmth*

inside the van. It hurts to move right now. Dr. Steiner says it's okay to exercise if I can tolerate the pain, so I have continued to run my daily six. After that I'm completely drained and can't walk without extreme pain. I'm hoping if I persevere the pain will leave on its own as it has so many times in the past. I'm totally exhausted, though, and all I want to do lately is sit.

Sometimes I read War and Peace, *but mostly I just sit and do nothing. It's the only time I'm painless, but I hate myself for being inactive. If we get back in time maybe I can ride a bike this evening. That doesn't hurt so much, but right now I have no gumption to get off my duff and do anything. What's wrong with me? At least I ran and did my chores today, otherwise I would really be self-destructive.*

And a week later:

Today my legs and knees and ankles were so painful it took me about twice as long to run my route. I felt guilty about slowing down, but every time I tried to speed up, I felt I'd pass out from pain. The pain is incredible. I just took two aspirin and asked another patient to put an ice pack on my back. I stretched out, too. But God do I HURT HURT HURT.

The terrible dichotomy of her life, half hope and half despair, tormented her with daily contradictions. On November 19, Jenny sat on her bed, propped her pillow against the window, draped her quilt over her legs, and moved by dawn's half-light and feelings of optimism, wrote to her father, printing boldly.

Some of the concrete ways your love, faith, and perseverance with me is paying off now that I am at Community Care—HAPPY BIRTHDAY DAD, I'm finally getting better. I've begun to have hope and faith that I can go back to school and become a doctor even if it takes years. We have finally found some doctors who know what the hell they're doing. They believe in me, and I believe in them. I'm learning to define what I need in order to feel better and get help. I don't go crazy because my leg is hurt and I can't run lately. I'm reading 99 percent of the paper and understanding and asking questions. I'm reading books, slowly but surely. I am reaching out to people and beginning to have new friends. (Something the doctors think is a life and death issue for me.) I am starting to enjoy my art again and not feel as if I have to force myself to do it. I'm doing better at verbalizing my flashbacks. I'm not so desperately depressed. My sense of humor is returning. I absolutely adore the program and love the classes. Each day I practice being responsible, cleaning house and doing other domestic chores without hating them; in fact, doing well gives me a sense of pride. Each day I practice being honest and assertive with peers. Sometimes I let myself eat until I am no longer hungry. (FACT—eating is still a problem and might be last behavior to go.) Sometimes things seem beautiful to me—a rose, a person, a painting, whereas I never noticed pretty things before. Sometimes now I'd RATHER be alive than dead whereas before I always felt, if given the choice, I'd rather be dead.

By evening, Jenny was fighting exhaustion and despair. Seated at her desk, she labored over a journal entry, written in tiny, hesitant script.

It's so weird: I wanna die more than anything, and I wanna live more than anything—lately death wishes seem to prevail, yet when I think death is imminent (as I believe it was walking just a few blocks yesterday), I pray my heart out God won't let me die just yet. I blacked out yesterday and had a hard time breathing. I don't know where the energy to keep going came from, but it wasn't of me. I am sure it is God who keeps sustaining my decrepit body. But there is no doubt in my mind I am near death. I feel it. I am scared, but I'm equally, if not more, afraid to live. My flashbacks and the pain I felt this morning as a large number of hooded men raped me scared me to the point I actually gave in and took an Ativan. I've spent most of the day around Steve for fear the flashback will return and leave me decimated. I am scared to go to bed tonight. The flashbacks are worse on nights after I eat well. If I am empty when I go to bed, I do not experience them as severely. I'm not allowed to indulge, otherwise I punish myself with my deep dark past pain pain pain. I don't want this anymore. Please, dear God, no more. Please give me the guts to take tiny risks to get better.

Whether therapeutic or destructive, the book *Courage to Heal* shared Jenny's reading time with *War and Peace*. Her journals chronicled her occasional attempts to follow recommended essay exercises.

Coping page 54—My experience of coping with sexual abuse and physical and emotional abuse involves almost every mechanism described in the book. It was nice to know these responses have names and that other people have used them. I thought they happened just because I'm such a weird crazy person.

My main coping mechanism is my anorexia, but that's only because it's obvious. I also cope by having incredibly vivid fantasies of self-mutilation. I've acted on these and experienced the same relief I get from anorexia and being empty. Usually when I cut myself I am interested in only one thing, killing myself. Thus suicide is another way I cope. I have no self-esteem or trust of myself or my feelings. I'm adept at separating from my body when I'm in great physical or emotional pain. I can leave my body and watch the dentist do a root canal on me—actually watch! I am intimate with no one, never have been, and am terrified of the pain sex may cause me, therefore I avoid it at all costs.

As a child I escaped through horses and reading. As an adult I've mainly coped by bingeing and purging. Up to twenty or thirty times a day.

I have also coped, perhaps more healthily, by exercising. This is still my favorite form of coping. I set more limits on myself nowadays and do not exercise every moment. But I'm obsessed with being busy all the time. Even if it's meaningless, like cooking food I won't eat or staring out the window vacantly. My life is filled with overwhelming fear, and I avoid it at all costs. Sometimes I hurt and cry for hours. Avoidance and suppression have been my way of life.

The healing process page 83—I think the abuse started around three years old. Again, a vague quick flashback, someone touching me while playing with my chimes. Most of my memories are just like that, sounds and sensations and an unmistakable knowledge that what's going on is wrong, hurts, and shouldn't be. Tony forcing oral sex in front of Janis's dresser, the one with a pretty yellow and blue design. Fear, terrible fear, and ultimate disgust. Wanna throw up, get it out of my body, be empty of his poison. Too painful, too small, I swallow and forget instead. Then comes the bed my hands tied to bedpost fat bottom, round top it hurts to stretch arms that far. Ow please why do you do this, will I get a horse next week? Now the sickening plunge into my anal cavity gross throw up get it out it hurts push it out till I'm empty please take it out please I'm getting cut— focus on the bedposts, pain goes away time goes away.

YOU STINK YOU ARE GROSS WOMEN ARE GROSS YOUR BODY IS FOUL Cowering in the corner of the horse trailer filth and flies a whip snapping above me. Legs spread poking scraping. Look at the mat yucky horse shit flies, cleaner than him tobacco spit dribbles kisses between YOU GROTESQUE BODY, I WISH YOU'D GIVE UP AND DIE. Not me I will not die I think painful bloody penetration, I scream at the rug. Where is God anymore? Mom loves God, I hate Mom, I hate Billy.

Cloaks chants FEAR BEYOND CONTROL, look at chains look at wood, who are they who cares. Drawing on my body with blood naked focusing on genital area chanting white HELP look at chains look at blood too much blood whose blood? My blood. Fingers penetrating hurts too much, I am too little too many fingers. Mutilate those fingers kill these people. Where is Mommy?

Basement is cold cage is barren yummy smell of cookies upstairs none for me boredom. I am a bad girl deserve to live in cage but why me again. Why not David and Nancy. Oh ya I am FAT need to be empty need to eat less cookies. When will Mom come do I have to come tomorrow. UGLY horrible baby-sitter.

You have a beautiful round body I want it here's the bed—Remember, I came out of retirement for you Jenny. Pretty blue and white painting. Tongue in my vagina same tongue in my mouth THROW UP Damn him we were just gonna have lunch you said. LIAR I HATE YOU.

The healing process page 84 Remembering—The book says to write about my abuse experience for half an hour and only half an hour, so that's what I'm gonna do. Lately I've been having satanic flashbacks; it's as if I always knew this happened but only recently remembered it. Now I feel something's still missing, just like the satanic experience. It feels connected, but I don't know how. I guess the greatest problem is that no one understands the pain I've been feeling as I've had these flashbacks, like a little child vulnerable, needy, TOTALLY AFRAID. Another patient has experienced satanic abuse, so she knows some how I feel, and she gives me lots of hugs, but even she is unable to penetrate that shell inside me that is so lonely and frightened. Part of me is determined to die: I feel dirty and stinky with pig's grease, no matter how I wash myself in the shower I never get clean. I scrub each area of my body ten times each morning and shave my legs, wash my face and hair. If I do not do this I cannot get through the day. It's worse now. I am wondering about the anger though (I feel like throwing up right now). How do I express it other than self-destructively? I cannot feel any anger toward most of my abusers (some I can), but with the satanists I just feel fear, fear, fear and an overwhelming sadness. Yet I must be angry because I am deriving so much from being on the verge of death lately. Mostly I wonder why? But then again who cares, I am about to die, and I must make the decision to get better physically. It is sometimes scarier for me to consider living than dying and going to hell. I am afraid my life will be always that endless pit of loneliness, a burden to bear. And frankly I can't bear it anymore like that. My doctors all say life is not like that. Part of me believes, most of me doesn't. The only difference I feel about life since becoming aware of the abuse is that now there's a plausible explanation for my fear, sadness, and, when I can feel it, anger.

I need this half hour to hurry and get over. I am getting tired and having a hard time focusing my brain. My body has now begun to eat my brain in a big way. I am falling down, losing my way, forgetting everything, and ending up having to make two trips for everything. Can't focus on newspaper anymore. Totally and completely out of it. I really don't want to die today. But I think if God came down and offered me heaven right now instead of life I'd go. I'm so tired of the pain. Thank God, the half hour's up. Bye.

CHAPTER TWENTY-NINE

I'm Not Ready to Die

On Thanksgiving, Jenny was excited to have a visitor—her father's secretary. She liked Marty—so warm and cheerful, like a big sister. They talked quietly in the lounge. For once the television wasn't blaring; most residents had checked out for the day. Marty's visit helped push back the sadness Jenny felt when she had to acknowledge home was off limits to her, even on holidays. "I know it's too late to reclaim the life I've lost," she confided in Marty, "but I wonder if I'll ever see my real home again."

When Jenny became concerned about her medical condition in early December, she called Dr. Steiner. She stood beside the hall phone, leaned against a wall for support, forced herself to remain erect, and spoke haltingly, as if each word took extraordinary effort. "What's happening to me?" Jenny asked. "I'm so tired . . . too tired to do anything. I can't concentrate . . . can't think straight . . . can't focus my mind very long. All I do is sleep . . . and I'm always cold."

In his usual manner, honest, but patient and kind, Dr. Steiner explained her failing body's pathology. "Your body is rotting, Jennifer. There's no nutrition for it, so it's using tissue cells to cover nerves and muscle and to provide calcium. Your body is even destroying brain tissue to satisfy its needs."

"I . . . I know something is wrong. But I thought it was the other way . . . that my brain would dominate . . . that it would consume other parts of my body, even my heart, to survive."

"I'm sure you're now experiencing both conditions."

Jenny paused, waiting for her doctor's candor to produce a fear reaction. It didn't. "Like an internal battle for control?" she asked.

"Sort of."

"So . . . so my body destroys my sanity . . . while my brain tries to kill me by eating my heart?"

"Yes."

"Each avenging the other . . . at the same time?"

"Something like that."

"So I am dying . . . I thought so. Am I really dying this time?"

"Probably. Are you afraid?"

"No . . . not today. Does Dad know?"

"I'm sure he suspects. Should I call him?"

"Will he overreact . . . try to intervene?"

"I don't think so. He's reconciled."

"Don't call him yet." Jenny felt disembodied again. Was she really talking calmly, almost impersonally, about her own death, as if it had already happened? "Even he is uncomfortable with me now. He knows there is nothing more for him to do . . . except wait. What can I do?"

"The body's process of decay is slow to reverse. But it is reversible if you can eat more, rest, and take B vitamin supplements."

"I can still eat peanut butter."

Dr. Steiner chuckled. "That helps. But be sure you get fluids . . . enough to keep your kidneys working."

"I'll try. But the pain . . . the pain is worse now."

"That's because your body, even when you exercise, can no longer produce natural endorphins which blunt pain, just as morphine does. Is it time yet, Jennifer . . . time for morphine?"

"No. Not yet. I'm not ready to die."

The following week Jenny ate better, felt a little stronger, and participated in some of Community Care's full schedule of activities. Then her strength failed again. Worried that Community Care might release her, she called her father. "They want me to go on all the group activities," she said, feeling scared and trying not to cry. "But I'm not strong enough."

"If you participate in the mornings, will they let you rest in the afternoons?"

"I think so. But they say when I can't participate I'll have to leave. Where will I go, Dad?"

"I don't know, honey."

"Will you and Mom let me come home?" She asked hesitantly. Her father paused and cleared his throat. She knew his answer before he spoke it and could sense his struggle to be gentle but firm as he dealt with his own anguish.

He finally answered slowly, his voice husky. "No, Jenny . . . and this is the hardest thing I've ever had to say to you . . . you can never come home again."

"It's been so long."

"I know . . . but it's not safe for you at home."

"Where will I go?"

"Where do you think?"

His response brought a smile to Jenny's face. "Now you sound like a psychiatrist."

He laughed. "Why not, I've had a lot of on-the-job training."

"No mental hospital will admit me."

"We could try a hospice."

"Will they take me?"

"Maybe. If you're certified terminal."

"No doctor will do that. They're afraid to."

"I think Dr. Steiner will. I'll ask him. Maybe Dr. Weintraub will. She pronounced you terminal long ago."

"No, Dad. Please don't talk to Dr. Weintraub . . . ever. She abandoned me . . . and you and Mom. She left us without hope and with no one to talk to."

"She was just being honest . . . and frustrated."

"I don't want her involved . . . not ever again."

"I understand."

"Don't talk to Dr. Steiner yet. I don't want to leave and go somewhere else to die. I'm treated with dignity here. I haven't been suicidal the whole time, and sometimes I'm even happy."

"I know you're in a safe place . . . finally beyond torment, and I'm very grateful to Community Care. I'll do my best to keep you there. Please try to get stronger."

"I will. I was doing so well . . . back in October. I can try to recapture that."

"Can you still read?"

Jenny hesitated, as if her answer would confirm the reality she still sought to deny. "No," she spoke softly. "Not for several days now. I'm too exhausted and can't concentrate."

"How far are you into *War and Peace*?"

"About forty chapters."

"Would you like for me to come and read to you?"

"Like when I was a little girl?"

"Yes."

"I'd like that, Dad." *And it will give him something to do*, Jenny thought.

"I'll start today. I'll read while you drowse in the late-day sun, curled up like a kitten."

"I'd like that a lot."

Concerned about her ability to continue Community Care's activity schedule, Dr. Grunewald asked Jenny and her parents to meet with him on December 12. Woozy with fatigue, Jenny felt detached from the meeting and only half listened to words swirling around her as if spoken by disembodied voices. *They're talking about me like I'm not here again.* She had difficulty following who was saying what. She watched her father. He was unusually silent. She wondered why. She caught only fragments of conversation: Dr. Grunewald explaining the need for her to participate; her mother scolding her; her own voice responding in resentment.

No decisions were made at the meeting, and Jenny returned to Community Care exhausted but thankful she didn't have to face another forced move, at least not yet. Gray skies greeted her as she walked slowly up to the front door, now closed and not so hospitable as ten weeks before.

For most of the next week, Jenny languished in and out of pain, mostly in bed, only occasionally functional, without enough energy to finish wrapping her Christmas gifts. Not even brilliant sunshine and blue skies following a daylong blizzard could rouse her from lethargy.

On December 17, with shunning no longer an issue, Jenny's mother lunched with her at Community Care. No rancor marred their meeting. Jenny responded with a renewed lightness of heart and spirit she hadn't felt in weeks. They met without quarreling and without any of the under-the-surface tension that so frequently haunted their time together. They spent a relaxed hour in the Community Care lounge, a mother and a daughter still trying. Their conversation flowed easily with gentle words and pleasant recollections, as if each had finally made an unspoken peace with the other and with inevitability. *Nice lunch with Mom,* Jenny wrote on her calendar.

Over the weeks, Jenny's ability to rally had masked her general deterioration from the Community Care staff. But their concern eventually mounted. Richard, her staff psychologist, spoke with Dr. Grunewald on December 18. "She's missing our group sessions again and hasn't participated in any activities for several days."

"Any physical symptoms?"

"Not that we're aware of. Just no strength or energy. Should I call Dr. Steiner?"

"Not yet. Is she eating?"

"You know we don't monitor that. I think she's eating some, but very little. She's still drinking diet pop like crazy."

"Do you think she's failing, really failing this time?"

"Yes. What should we do?"

"Nothing. Maybe it's time all of us did nothing."

"But . . . "

"I know. We'll just have to accept the consequences."

That evening, Jenny forced herself to fix an early supper of cottage cheese and a fresh pear and ate alone. Afterward, it seemed to take forever for her to climb the stairs to her second-floor room. She had to hang on to the rail with both hands to maintain her balance and pull herself up, one agonizing step at a time. Feeling disoriented and a little dizzy, she stumbled into her room. A sudden chill shook her frail body, and she turned the dial on her portable space heater to high. Unsteadily she undressed, changed into sweats, and fell into bed. *I'm so tired tonight,* she thought . . . *too tired even to brush my teeth . . . and the pain . . . every joint feels like it's on fire.*

She pulled her down comforter around her and cradled her other comforter, a badly balding Pooh bear. "It's almost over, isn't it?" she whispered to her stuffed companion. "I think I'm ready now." Pooh smiled up at her, his faithful heart untouched.

As she lay awake, waiting for the heater's warmth to spread and blunt her pain, she looked around. *Such a spartan existence. I have so few things . . . no furniture of my own, nothing on the walls, not even a poster. In a world gone crazy for possessions, I have so few . . . my clothes, my journals, a few books and tapes, my bulletin board and pictures . . . leftovers from a life too short. Not much to show I was ever here. Look how old all my pictures are . . . as if my life ended five years ago.* Jenny looked toward the foot of her bed and smiled. The leaves of her thriving rubber plant glowed a lustrous green in the soft light from her bedside table lamp. *And I have my plants . . . coming here wasn't too late for them . . . and some things Dad brought me . . . a heater that warms my body . . . and Mom's squeaky old rocking chair that warms my heart. Dad said Mom nursed me from it every day when I was a baby. Now he sits in it and reads to me most every afternoon. It's a nice feeling to be nurtured at the end of my life like I was at the beginning.*

As she reached up to turn off her lamp, Jenny glanced at the book lying on her bedside table, picked it up, and fingered a bookmark inserted in the thick volume. *Measuring my ebbing life. Dad told me this afternoon my interest in* War and Peace *might keep me alive. "Like the autumn leaves that preserved a life in the O'Henry story," he said.*

"But what happens when you've read all the chapters?" I asked him.

He thought for a moment. "Then I will compose chapters of my own," he said.

"Like the other O'Henry character who painted a leaf on the wall when the last leaf fell?" I said, trying to smile.

Dad looked very sad. "You know the story?"

"Yes. One of my few memories from college. And I remember what happened to the other character, his sacrifice."

Then Dad said he couldn't read anymore today, and I told him he might never have to write any chapters for Tolstoy. After that, he couldn't look at me and just held his head in his hands and tried not to cry. Then I said, "Don't let them put me in the ground . . . or in a vault. I've been confined so long. Please set me free, Dad. Promise to scatter my ashes at sea, someplace where I was happy as a little girl, a place where dolphins play. Yes, I remember. In Florida where Meme and Daddad used to live . . . that long, white sand beach with all the sand dollars."

Dad took my hand then and looked into my eyes. "I promise, Jenny," he said.

Feeling warmed, Jenny replaced the book on her nightstand, extinguished the light, and slipped irretrievably into a deep sleep.

In her dream she is a child again, growing younger instead of older. Racing in the corral and dressed in faded Levi's, a ragged western shirt, and mud-encrusted boots, she rides her favorite ranch horse, Thunder, a dappled appaloosa. Synchronized in mind and movement, horse and rider form perfect loops around three barrels and streak home in a finishing cloud of dust. Spectators perched on the top fence rail shout encouragement. "Go, Jenny, go," her brothers and sisters scream. "Ride like the wind," her father calls from behind the fence. From somewhere beyond, another voice, one she doesn't recognize, urges softly, "Hurry, Jenny, hurry."

She travels further back in time. Initially the images flash too quickly to identify. Then they slow and a scene appears. At the center of the arena and holding a silver cup in her outstretched arms, she stands proudly in front of Miss Roan. She is wearing a new show outfit: powder blue cowboy hat with braided hair sticking out from under, white blouse with a frilly lace front, navy blue scarf, navy blue boots, and matching chaps over a kelly green jumpsuit. A flashbulb illuminates her face, flushed with excitement, as a photographer captures the moment. She waves her trophy and the crowd applauds. From the shadows, her mother's voice exclaims, "Great ride, Jenny." From beyond the shadows, the unknown voice calls again, this time louder, "Hurry, Jenny, hurry."

Flashing images resume, more quickly now. Once again time slows, and a beach scene appears. A freckled bundle of energy, she plays in the surf with her brothers and sisters, under watchful eyes of parents and grandparents. With Jenny in the middle, all five children race hand in hand through frothy shallows and dive into an oncoming wave. Moments later, they emerge exhausted and collapse on the sand, giggling, heads in a circle. Their bodies radiate out with arms extended and fingertips touching, forming a symmetrical pattern like the design of a giant sand dollar. They stare up into the sky and watch gulls dip and soar. Cumulus clouds drift lazily overhead. "Let this day last forever," Nancy whispers. This time the unknown voice calls from the sea. "You're ready now, Jenny."

The others remain still, but she sits up and watches a long, gray body breach and roll gracefully in a gentle swell beyond the surf. Again she hears the compelling voice. "Come play with me," it beckons. Alone, she races back to the water, plunges into the surf, and swims through the waves. The dolphin slows, raises its head, and smiles in greeting, then dips beneath her and rises again. Chattering and laughing happily with her new friend, Jenny rides easily on the dolphin's back as they frolic in a peaceful sea.

Then, in a wide arcing turn, the dolphin heads for deeper water. Jenny glances back and waves at her family standing together on shore. Their voices dance out across the waves, calling "Good-bye, Jenny." From the horizon, other voices call, muted and joined in song. Responding eagerly, she digs in her heels and urges the dolphin on. Faster and faster they race away from earth and into timelessness, beyond the distant union of sky and sea.

Final Thoughts

*R*are is the day I don't think about my daughter, how she became so sick, why she couldn't be treated, and where others can go for help.

Research into causes now focuses beyond the psychological—on neurobiological connections and on genetic/hormonal/chemical links, my own personal choice for principal culprit. In Jenny's case, the relentless search for flesh and blood culprits provided no therapeutic benefit. Childhood abuse issues were never resolved, and Jenny had to endure their devastating uncertainties. Their speculation never helped Jenny fight her illness, never accomplished anything except anguish and heartache.

Increasing relapse rates among recovered anorexics and high mortality suggest many treatment approaches are still ineffective. Until nonpsychological links are fully explored, treatment of hard-core anorexia may be only sporadically successful. Treated and untreated cases alike may have to share in an uncertain destiny.

"Not enoughs" hamper progress in improving the destiny of the eating disordered. Not enough understanding, i.e. are eating disorders an illness of choice? (Jenny's case suggests not.) Not enough money for research into cause, prevention, and treatment. Not enough integration of approaches—neurobiological, genetic, hormonal, chemical, general medical, psychological, and the most important . . . human compassion. Not enough insurance parity. Not enough support for organizations involved in the ongoing fight. But hope is a universal balm for the damaged soul, and caring people are working hard to resolve the not enoughs. I look forward to the day when their efforts will provide a future promising more joy than sorrow for all who endure a severe eating disorder.

Long a window of opportunity to a better future, the National Association of Anorexia Nervosa and Associated Disorders (ANAD) has led the battle against eating disorders for over twenty-five years. For me, ANAD was a safe harbor offering shelter from the storm of frustration that was Jenny's anorexia. At ANAD, dedicated lay and professional people sponsor programs in education, prevention, and advocacy and provide support systems to assist individuals and families. ANAD action initiatives include:

- Fighting insurance discrimination—through individual cases and urging attorneys general in all fifty states to take action
- Working for mental health parity legislation at state and federal levels
- Seeking to remove potentially dangerous advertising and websites
- National candlelight vigil

ANAD services are free and include:

- National hot line (847-831-3438) and E-mail (anad20@aol.com)
- National newsletter and website (www.anad.org)
- Referrals to therapists, health professionals, inpatient/ outpatient centers
- Support groups—hundreds throughout the nation and in eighteen foreign countries
- Presentations to schools and groups
- Comprehensive information for teachers in middle and high schools

The doors at ANAD are always open, and members invite those seeking assistance or those interested in joining to contact them directly.

G.H.
November 2002